Learn XML Tips

George M. Doss

Wordware Publishing, Inc.

Library of Congress Cataloging-in-Publication Data

Doss, George M.
    Learn XML tips / by George M. Doss.
        p.   cm.
    Includes index.
    ISBN 1-55622-757-4 (pbk.)
    1. XML (Document markup language).   I. Title.

    QA76.76.H94 D683   2000
    005.7'2--dc21   00-038180
                                                                          CIP

ISBN 1-55622-757-4
10 9 8 7 6 5 4 3 2 1
0006

Product names mentioned are used for identification purposes only and may be trademarks of their respective companies.

All inquiries for volume purchases of this book should be addressed to Wordware Publishing, Inc., at the above address. Telephone inquiries may be made by calling:

(972) 423-0090

Dedication

A.M.D.G.

Contents

Contents

Contents

Contents

Contents

Contents

Contents

Acknowledgments

One of the earliest pleasures of writing this book is working with the professional team at Wordware Publishing. In particular, I would like to thank Beth Kohler, senior editor; Kellie Henderson, editor; Martha McCuller, interior design; and Alan McCuller, cover design. In addition, Jim Hill, Wordware's publisher, has to be thanked for his special support.

I would like to thank my many neighbors who asked me each time I saw one of them, "How is the book coming?" This action enforces a certain type of discipline.

Finally, I would like to acknowledge all the members of the various committees that have worked or are working on the W3C (World Wide Web Consortium) specifications discussed in this book. Without them, there would be no need for this book.

Introduction

This book uses the frequently asked questions (FAQ) format with 785 questions that include notes and warnings. The tips are based on the set of World Wide Web Consortium (W3C) specifications on Extensible Markup Language (XML) and seven specifications on styles, links, and graphics. The seven specifications extend XML beyond being a design language for developing text or database document customized markup. The book highlights some of the ideas put forth by these specifications. In addition, there are chapters on XML initiatives, tools, and the implications of Internet Explorer 5.0 and the use of XML. There are five appendices on the terminology used in the book, important URLs, XML production rules, XML and SGML differences, and XML and HTML differences.

One of the difficulties in writing this book is that this is a very dynamic area of development. By the time this book is being read publicly, there probably will have already been new drafts to the specifications. New drafts to specifications were released during the writing of this book and chapters had to be updated. While specific examples have been given, it must be recognized that there may be new additions or changes to this information. The first principle of reading this book is to recognize the design process.

XML is foremost a design language that permits the user to design a customized markup language for a unique document, whether it is text or data. XML is not a markup language in the same sense that Hypertext Markup Language (HTML) is. HTML has predefined tags, while XML does not.

The tips (questions) range from the simple, such as "What is XML?", to the complex, such as "What is an example of a DTD for a database XML document?". Most of the chapters are primarily standalone; however, Chapters 2 through 6 should, perhaps, be read in order the first time through this book. A tip, as used in this book, means a highlight rather than an extensive answer. The focus is on the "why" rather than the specific "how" because of the very nature of XML, that is, design for unique use (customization).

Chapter 5 is on designing an XML DTD, and its related markup is an exception to the tip definition. Chapter 5 includes four different scenarios on developing a DTD and related markup. These scenarios consist of creating a memo DTD, a fiction book DTD, a technical book DTD, and a database for musical CDs DTD.

What are the essential functions of these languages and extensions?

- XML   As a design language, permits you to develop a customized markup language
- XSL   Extends the appearance or presentation of any XML document for a print or multimedia environment
- XLink   Gives you the capability to develop general links between or among XML documents
- XPointer   Gives you the capability to develop specific location links from within one XML document to within another XML document
- Namespaces   Permit you to have unique tag names among multiple documents over the Web or on an intranet
- SVG   Permits you to describe two-dimensional graphics in XML
- VML   Permits you to describe two-dimensional graphics in XML. VML also uses CSS2. VML uses path transformations to describe how lines and curves shall be connected.
- XPath   Simplifies the method of referring to XML document components or parts
- XSLT   Transforms one XML document into another according to the specifications of an XSL stylesheet

The guidelines I considered in writing this book are the following:

- The specifications are being updated frequently.
- The specifications are difficult to read. For example, XML specification is an executive summary type document and the XSL specification is over 300 pages in length and has many sections that are labeled TBD or are empty.
- The process of working with XML is design rather than just simple document markup.
- XML and its extensions require more up-front thought to use than HTML.
- XML may have been designed to have effective use on the Web, but many of the developing XML applications are for use on an intranet instead.

■ The question and answer format might be an easier method of presenting highlight information. This method is an evolution from the one used in newsgroups.

■ It is more important to know where to find information than know the details.

■ To effectively use XML, you need to know the why before the how.

This book uses the following W3C specifications:

■ XML Recommendation 1.0 (February 10, 1998) found at http://www.w3.org/TR/1998/REC-xml-19980210. The latest version is found at http://www.w3.org/TR/REC-xml.

■ Extensible Stylesheet Language (XSL) 1.0 (January 12, 2000) found at http://www.w3.org/TR/2000/WD-xsl-20000112. The latest version is found at http://www.w3.org/TR/xsl.

■ XML Linking Language (XLink) (December 20, 1999) found at http://www.w3.org/TR/1999/WD-xlink-19991220. The latest version is found at http://www.w3.org/TR/xlink.

■ XML Pointer Language (XPointer) (December 6, 1999) found at http://www.w3.org/TR/1999/WD-xptr-19991206. The latest version is found at http://www.w3.org/TR/xptr.

■ Namespaces in XML (January 14, 1999) found at http://www.w3.org/TR/1999/REC-xml-names-19990114. The latest version is found at http://www.w3.org/TR/REC-xml-names.

■ Scalable Vector Graphics (SVG) 1.0 Specification (December 3, 1999) found at http://www.w3.org/TR/1999/WD-SVG-19991203. The latest version is found at http://www.w3.org/TR/SVG.

■ Vector Markup Language (VML) (May 13, 1998) found at http://www.w3.org/TR/1998/NOTE-VML-19980513. The latest version is found at http://www.w3.org/TR/NOTE-VML.

■ XML Path Language (XPath) 1.0 (October 8, 1999) found at http://www.w3.org/TR/1999/PR-xpath-19991008. The latest version is found at http//www.w3.org/TR/xpath.

■ XSL Transformations (XSLT) 1.0 (November 16, 1999) found at http://www.w3.org/TR/1999/REC-xslt-19991116. The latest version is found at http://www.w3.org/TR/xslt.

General XML Tips

This chapter focuses on general or "open-the-door" tips using the FAQ format about the extended family of Extensible Markup Language (XML). The parent of XML is Standard Generalized Markup Language (SGML). XML's sibling is Hypertext Markup Language (HTML). Its children extend XML's features or functionality. The children include Extensible Stylesheet Language (XSL), XML Linking Language (XLink), XML Pointer Language (XPointer), XML Namespaces, Scalable Vector Graphics (SVG), and Vector Markup Language (VML). XML also has many cousins referred to as dialects. Some of the children have had children also, giving us XSL Transformations (XSLT) and XML Path Language (XPath).

 Note: A tip is a snippet of advice, a guideline, or a pointer. It is not necessarily a full explanation of a subject. It is recognized that the answers here are highly abbreviated and only high points of the topics. Syntax given may be only one of many variants, such as a = b + c could also be a = c + b or c = a − b. A definition given may only provide a level of detail comparable to defining a dog as a domestic animal. Certainly a dog can be defined in numerous other ways, but this definition does eliminate some possibilities such as the dog being a mineral.

What is a markup language?

The original purpose of a markup language was to define structure for an electronic document as a paper document. The essential markup delimiters were several levels of headers (.h1, .h2, and so forth), paragraph (.p), and lists (.ol and .ul). If this reminds you of HTML, it should. Each new markup language has been designed to handle a special need such as a text file linking over a network (HTML), a standard markup language for any document type (SGML), and a data document structure for the Internet (XML). The concepts and structure of any electronic markup language are based on paper publishing concepts because the original idea was for the electronic document to look like a paper document. However, there has been a rapid evolution away from the paper document concept, resulting in the changes in electronic markup languages.

What is XML?

XML (Extensible Markup Language) was designed to handle data over the Internet or an intranet in a manner that HTML is not capable. It was also designed to handle text over the Internet in a manner that SGML is not capable. In a very technical sense, SGML is a defining language standard of which XML is a subset. HTML is an application of SGML.

The active word is "extensible." Extensible means that an item has the capability to be extended, enhanced, or enlarged. The item does not have specified boundaries. XML is a standard that describes, captures, processes, and publishes data or text. The standard (grammar) is a document type definition (DTD). DTD design is discussed in detail in Chapter 5. You are responsible for customizing your markup. When appropriate, you have the potential to extend your tags at any given moment. You can always use other people's markup to fit your needs.

Note: This book uses Extensible Markup Language (XML) 1.0 W3C Recommendation (February 10, 1998) found at http://www.w3.org/TR/1998/REC-xml-19980210. The latest version is found at http://www.w3.org/TR/REC-xml.

XML is a meta-design language rather than a meta-markup language like HTML. HTML has a fixed set of predefined functional tags, while XML permits you to design your own set of tags. A current meaning of "meta" is "the top level" with the original Greek meaning "after." Without considering the Greek, XML is used within a computer environment to describe the data or even the metadata content used for an application.

Note: XML is discussed in detail in Chapters 2 through 6. Supplemental specifications, additions to XML to resolve issues based in the original specification, such as style, are discussed in Chapters 7 through 15.

Warning: You may not be able to do cut-and-paste operations with complex XML applications as are possible with HTML applications.

Any given XML application has its own unique syntax and language based on its DTD. One may find on a site such as Microsoft that one can get an example for a function, but changing a series of functions may be a challenge. Thus, in this book, generalized element names such as element name 1 are used where possible. Using XML is specifying a logical computing process rather than, as with HTML, developing primarily an appearance process or outcome.

What is an XML document?

An XML document consists of markup and character data. Markup is delimited by the less-than (<) and the greater-than (>) characters. XML text is that which comes between these delimiters and character data. This simplistic definition is core to the ideas and concepts put forth in Chapters 3 and 4 on an XML document's logical and physical structures. The basic components of all XML ideas are elements, attributes, and entities. Everything else is commentary.

The questions or issues on a document revolve around three areas:

- Content — Data or text
- Structure — Type and organization (element types and their attributes, sequence, location of content, and link types between content)
- Presentation — Medium and style

 Note: It is because of these three areas that nine different but related specifications have been developed thus far. These specifications are the primary emphasis of the book.

What is an XML application?

An XML application is any application used in the manipulation of a document. The document can be text or data that adheres to the production rules of the XML specification. This manipulation can occur over the Internet, on an intranet, or on a network. The document can be written completely or partially in XML.

Note: Each XML application is unique as to its syntax or grammar and its vocabulary or tags.

Is XML complicated?

Yes. Anything worth doing well is complicated. The first hurdle is to recognize XML as a set of ideas, yours being the most important. The set of XML specifications (nine are discussed in the book) define a world of productions and processor constraints. Is Microsoft Word complicated? The answer is yes, but many people use Word very effectively and efficiently without knowing every in-and-out of Word. The same is true of XML. Six chapters in the book highlight ideas, concepts, and issues based on a specification that is approximately thirty pages in length.

Is XML a typical markup language?

No. Other markup languages have a fixed set of tags. XML is a design standard or framework. It is used to describe content in the manner that is best for your needs.

Why have XML rather than proprietary markup languages?

The common denominator in the publishing world has been plain text. XML raises this denominator to layers of described information for data or text content. The XML framework acts as a lever for the development of open standards, shared tools, and homogeneous expertise foundation.

What is XML's place among other Internet technologies?

XML is a document technology that includes both publishing and database environments. It has the potential of being an important, if not the most important, technology in the world of data interchange.

What is SGML?

Standard Generalized Markup Language (SGML) is the parent of XML. XML production rules are a subset of SGML. SGML, developed between 1978 and 1986 by a team led by Charles F. Goldfarb, became an international standard (ISO 8879). It has become the interchange standard of large, complex documents. When "large" is used here, I mean like the documents required for aircraft maintenance. These documents would probably never appear on the Internet.

 Note: Some SGML and XML differences are noted in Appendix D.

What is HTML?

Hypertext Markup Language (HTML) was developed by Tim Berners-Lee beginning in 1989 to resolve the issue of hyperlinking text documents shared within CERN (French acronym for Center for Nuclear Research). He was advised to make it in the style of SGML. Out of this effort came the capability to hyperlink pages, not documents, on what is now known as the World Wide Web.

The original element types were generalized and descriptive. The importance of HTML was the capability to display text on a screen or within a graphical interface.

Because HTML did not originally have a rigid set of grammar rules (document type definition), there is a wide variation in the usage of HTML, for which the major Web browsers have compensated. XML is not a replacement of HTML, but it does put in place a discipline lacking with the HTML design mechanism. Perhaps the real issue is that the Internet is no longer a playground for HTML hackers, but rather the platform of large-scale commercial information exchange.

 Note: Some HTML and XML differences are noted in Appendix E. The Berners-Lee story, whether true or not, is certainly a part of the current Web legends and mythology.

What is XSL?

The XML Stylesheet Language (XSL) is used to convert XML from plain text into styled formats. XSL defines styles to be applied to XML documents. It requires separate software to apply an XSL stylesheet to an XML document. This is a dynamic area of growth.

 Warning: It has already been said, but XML handles document content, not document presentation. This is the fundamental reason for XSL.

Note: XSL is discussed in detail in Chapter 8. This book uses the following W3C specification: Extensible Stylesheet Language (XSL) 1.0 (January 12, 2000) found at http://www.w3.org/TR/2000/WD-xsl-20000112. The latest version is found at http://www.w3.org/TR/xsl. The specification is currently over 300 pages in length.

What is XLink?

The XML Linking Language (XLink) handles general links, as compared to XPointer, which handles links between specific locations in XML documents. XLink links or points to an XML document. XML does not have the linking capability of HTML as expressed with the <A> element. This is the fundamental reason for XLink and XPointer.

 Note: XLink is discussed in detail in Chapter 9. This book uses the following W3C specification: XML Linking Language (XLink) (December 20, 1999) found at http://www.w3.org/TR/1999/WD-xlink-19991220. The latest version is found at http://www.w3.org/TR/xlink.

What is XPointer?

The XML Pointer Language (XPointer) handles links between specific locations in XML documents as compared to XLink, which handles general links. XPointer takes XLink to a more detailed level. One can point to a specific paragraph or even a smaller location within an XML document.

 Note: XPointer is discussed in detail in Chapter 10. This book uses the following W3C specification: XML Pointer Language (XPointer) (December 6, 1999) found at http://www.w3.org/TR/1999/WD-xptr-19991206. The latest version is found at http://www.w3.org/TR/xptr.

What is an XML namespace?

XML namespaces were developed so there could be unique markup names in an Internet environment among multiple documents that might use the same element names. The basic syntax is:

```
xmlns:[prefix]="[URI of namespace]" or
<prefix:element>...</prefix:element>
```

For example, if I had a <title> </title> tag set in two different documents on two different URLs (URI), I would have:

<URL1:title>...</URL1:title>
<URL2:title>...</URL2:title>

Yes, you can have different namespaces for two documents on the same URL by using a fictitious URL.

 Note: XML namespaces are discussed in detail in Chapter 11. This book uses the following W3C specification: Namespaces in XML (January 14, 1999) found at http://www.w3.org/TR/1999/REC-xml-names-19990114. The latest version is found at http://www.w3.org/TR/REC-xml-names.

What is SVG?

The use of Scalable Vector Graphics (SVG) is the earlier of the two major efforts to specify the requirements for graphics in XML documents. It is "scalable," not "scaleable."

 Note: SVG is discussed in detail in Chapter 12. This book uses the following W3C specification: Scalable Vector Graphics (SVG) 1.0 Specification (December 3, 1999) found at http://www.w3.org/TR/1999/WD-SVG-19991203. The latest version is found at http://www.w3.org/TR/SVG.

What is VML?

Vector Markup Language (VML) is the second effort to specify the requirements for graphics in XML documents. Microsoft has been in the forefront in the implementation of VML.

 Note: VML is discussed in detail in Chapter 13. This book uses the following W3C specification: Vector Markup Language (VML) (May 13, 1998) found at http://www.w3.org/TR/1998/NOTE-VML-19980513. The latest version is found at http://www.w3.org/TR/NOTE-VML.

What is a dialect?

A dialect is a variation on the core or common language. It is a specialized usage of the common language. It can be very technical with a disciplined goal or purpose, or it can be a jargon that develops in a random manner. As used in this book, a dialect is "a language specific to an occupation or an interest group, usually with a specific technical function such as chemistry." The metalanguage is, of course, XML in all cases.

What are some of the important XML dialects?

Two of the important XML dialects are Mathematics Markup Language (MathML) and Chemical Markup Language (CML). MathML permits the rendering of mathematical notations over the Internet. CML does the same function except it handles such things as molecular structures. Both are XML applications. These two dialects were developed in parallel with the development of the XML specification. There are a number of dialect initiatives. In the broadest sense, any XML application that is to resolve a specific industrial instance is a dialect.

 Note: Some of the XML dialects are discussed in detail in Chapter 7. Chapter 17 includes brief tips on a number of developing dialects.

What is XPath?

The XML Path Language (XPath) is the latest attempt to simplify the method to link XML document components or parts.

 Note: XPath is discussed in detail in Chapter 14. This book uses the following W3C specification: XML Path Language (XPath) 1.0 (October 8, 1999) found at http://www.w3.org/TR/1999/PR-xpath-19991008. The latest version is found at http//www.w3.org/TR/xpath.

What is XSLT?

XSL Transformations (XSLT) seeks to resolve complex presentation issues for publishers and commercial interests. XSLT makes it possible to transform one XML document into another based on an XSL stylesheet. XSLT is important for the transformation of a source document into a result document without concern for appearance.

 Note: XSLT is discussed in detail in Chapter 15. This book uses the following W3C specification: XSL Transformations (XSLT) 1.0 (November 16, 1999) found at http://www.w3.org/TR/1999/REC-xslt-19991116. The latest version is found at http://www.w3.org/TR/xslt.

What international standards impact XML?

Some of the international standards that impact XML include:

- SGML (ISO 8879)
- XSL (ISO/IEC 10179 for Document Style and Semantic Specification Language (DSSSL))
- XLink and XPointer (ISO/IEC 10744 for HyTime)
- Native character set (ISO/IEC 10646 for Unicode)

Basic XML Tips

Tips on XML can be divided into at least five categories:

- General structure
- Logical structure
- Physical structure
- Document type definitions (DTD)
- Processing

This chapter considers the first category, general structure. One needs to consider the reasons, limitations, and functions of XML. An important question is, "What is basic XML jargon?" The next four chapters consider each of the categories on an individual basis. Examples are in Chapter 5.

 Note: A tip is a snippet of advice, a guideline, or a pointer. It is not a full explanation of a subject. It is recognized that the answers here are highly abbreviated and only provide high points of the topics. When syntax is given it may be only one of many variants such as x = y + z. In addition, the syntax might be x = z + y or y = x − z.

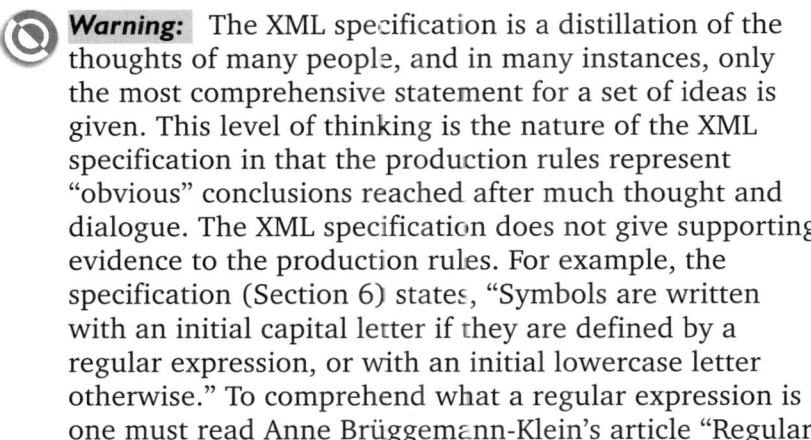 **Warning:** The XML specification is a distillation of the thoughts of many people, and in many instances, only the most comprehensive statement for a set of ideas is given. This level of thinking is the nature of the XML specification in that the production rules represent "obvious" conclusions reached after much thought and dialogue. The XML specification does not give supporting evidence to the production rules. For example, the specification (Section 6) states, "Symbols are written with an initial capital letter if they are defined by a regular expression, or with an initial lowercase letter otherwise." To comprehend what a regular expression is one must read Anne Brüggemann-Klein's article "Regular

Expressions in Finite Automata. Extended" found in
Theoretical Computer Science 120: 197-213, 1993. The
first two production rules of the specification show the
notion in use.

[1] document ::= prolog element Misc*
[2] Char ::= #x9 | #xA | #xD | [#x20-#xD7FF] |
[#xE000-#xFFFD] | [#x10000-#x10FFFF]

 Note: When production rule [n] is used within the
chapter, it is in reference to a specific production rule
within the XML specification. These rules are discussed
in more detail in Chapters 3 and 4. The full list of XML
production rules is given in Appendix C.

Without going into extensive detail, the practical implication of this is
that when there is a capital letter production such as Char, then that
production is standalone. A small letter production such as document
requires other productions such as prolog [22] and element [39]. The
asterisk (*) means "optional." The bar (|) means "or." These two pro-
ductions require the use of additional productions, which, in turn,
require other productions. XML production rules are like a complex jig-
saw puzzle that results in a powerful design metalanguage.

What is XML?

XML (Extensible Markup Language) was designed to handle data over
the Internet in a manner of which HTML is not capable. It was also
designed to handle text over the Internet in a manner of which SGML is
not capable. In a very technical sense, SGML is a defining language
standard of which XML is a subset. HTML is an application of SGML.
The latest version of the XML specification is found at http://www.w3.org/
TR/REC-xml.

 Note: XML was not designed to replace HTML. XML is
not a markup language in the same sense that HTML is.
It is a design language with a set of production rules that
permits an individual to create customized markup for a
document with unique readable syntax or grammar.

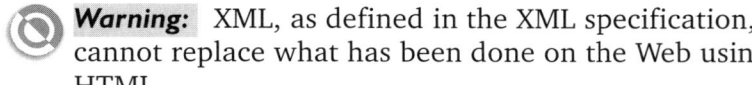 **Warning:** XML, as defined in the XML specification,
cannot replace what has been done on the Web using
HTML.

What type of language is XML?

XML is a design language that uses the document metaphor rather than the page metaphor. It handles both data and text manipulation over the Internet, an intranet, or on an individual workstation. The power of XML may be in its use in database manipulation, whether text or data, rather than as a markup language. Perhaps a better name for the Extensible Markup Language would be Extensible Manipulation Language, that is, a meta-information structural manipulator.

What are the fundamental concepts of XML?

The fundamental XML concepts come in pairs. Five such pairs are:

■ Logical structures and physical structures
■ Elements and entities
■ Well-formedness constraints and validity constraints
■ Well-formed documents and valid documents
■ Validating processors and non-validating processors

 Note: The word "style" does not appear because that is not a part of the basic nature of XML design. For more on style, see Chapter 8 on the Extensible Stylesheet Language (XSL).

What is some of the basic jargon of XML?

Because XML comes from SGML, one should expect to use the same jargon, perhaps in exactly the same manner. This is the general case.

■ Attributes
■ Case-sensitivity
■ Constructs
■ Markup
■ Production rule
■ Strings
■ Tokens
■ White space

What is an XML document?

Formally, an XML document is a data object that adheres to the well-formedness constraints as defined in the XML specification. It is important to consider that this definition says "data object," not "text object." A well-formedness constraint is a processing rule to be used to check for grammar correctness. An example of a well-formedness constraint is that when there is a start-tag, there must a paired end-tag.

An XML document consists of markup and character data. Markup is delimited by the less-than (<) and the greater-than (>) characters. XML text is that which comes between these delimiters and character data. This simplistic definition is core to the ideas and concepts put forth in Chapters 3 and 4 on an XML document's logical and physical structures.

What is a valid XML document?

An XML document is valid if it adheres to the well-formedness constraints and the validity constraints as defined in the specification. A valid document has a DTD to define its structure. A valid document can be parsed without error using a validating parser.

 Note: A validity constraint states that when an attribute is declared, the value must be of the type declared for it. For example, if the value for an attribute is defined as either "yes" or "no," you cannot choose "maybe."

What are the two basic XML document structures?

An XML document consists of logical and physical structures. These structures must nest properly.

What is the logical structure of an XML document?

An XML document has two structures, logical and physical. The cornerstone of the logical structure is the element and its attributes. However, a document is also composed logically of declarations, comments, character references, and processing instructions.

What is the physical structure of an XML document?

An XML document has two structures, logical and physical. The physical structure uses entities. They are content containers or holders of a document type. The physical structure "contains," while the logical structure "identifies."

 Note: If the document type is a database, the fields that have content might be considered physical.

What is an element?

An element is the core concept of the logical structure of an XML document. Logical structure is discussed in detail in Chapter 3. This production rule defines an element: [39] element ::= EmptyElemTag | Stag content Etag.

The rule states that an element can be either empty or non-empty, that is, the element does or does not have content. When there is content, there first must be a start-tag and after the content, there must be an end-tag. When an element has no content, it has an empty-tag. This rule makes XML different from HTML by stating in the rule that every start-tag must have an end-tag.

 Warning: This is a non-empty element because there is a space between the tags <tag> </tag>. An empty-tag is specified as <tag/>.

 Note: The XML logical structure is discussed in detail in Chapter 3.

What are XML elements?

Elements are boundaries, parameters, parts, components, and so forth of a document type. The logical structure "identifies," while the physical structure "contains."

 Note: If the document is thought of as a database, then the elements are fields.

What are the two types of elements?

The two types of elements are with content and without content (empty). If there is content, then it must be bound by a start-tag and an end-tag. If there is no content, then an empty-element tag is used. The syntax for each are <tag>content</tag> and <tag/>, respectively.

What is an attribute?

An attribute is a named value pair (name and value) that is included within an element tag.

An attribute is a characteristic of the data. An attribute of an element may be a characteristic, property, or quality. The specified attribute must have a name and a value. An attribute is defined by production rule [41].

 Warning: No attribute may appear more than once between the same start-tag and end-tag.

What is an attribute list?

An attribute list specifies the name, data type, and default value (optional) of each attribute of an element. Attribute lists are defined in production rules [52] and [53].

What are the attribute types?

The types are String, Token, and Enumerated. Attribute types are defined in production rules [54] – [56].

What are the enumerated attribute types?

The enumerated attribute types are Notation and Enumeration. Enumerated attribute types are defined in production rules [57] – [59].

What are the attribute defaults?

The attribute defaults are REQUIRED, IMPLIED, or FIXED. The attribute defaults are defined in production rule [60].

What is an entity?

An XML entity is the basic physical structure of an XML document. An entity acts as a storage unit. An entity is a container or a storage unit in that it has content. All entities have names except the document entity and the external DTD subset. The document entity is the root entity, the starting point for an XML processor, and may contain the whole document.

 Note: The XML physical structure is discussed in detail in Chapter 4.

What are the basic types of entities?

An entity can be parsed (text integral to the document) or unparsed (may or may not be text and may not even be XML). In addition, entities can be labeled as internal or external.

What is a document type definition (DTD)?

A document type definition is the user-defined set of rules that defines the grammar and structure of a document. DTD includes element names, ordering, nesting, and so forth.

 Note: The XML DTD with four scenarios is discussed in detail in Chapter 5.

What is a production rule?

A production rule has the form symbol ::= expression. There are some 90 rules that define the syntax for developing XML grammar, such as start- and end-tags. An expression can have one or more components. The form reads "a symbol consists of an expression." XML uses the Extended Backus-Naur Form (EBNF) notations.

What is an XML symbol?

Based on EBNF, an XML symbol is a production. There are about 90 XML symbols. There can be one or more parts to an expression per symbol. The most commonly used symbols or productions are probably start-tag, end-tag, empty-tag, and white space.

What is EBNF?

The Extended Backus-Naur Form (EBNF) notations establish how often components of an expression can occur or their relationship, such as either-or.

What is a construct?

A construct acts as a type of grammatical glue. The four common constructs are:

- White space
- Names
- Tokens
- Literals

What is a white space?

A white space is defined as one of the following formats:

- #x9 — horizontal tab
- #xA — line feed
- #xD — carriage return
- #x20 — space

 Note: Production rule [3] defines white space, S, within a production rule.

What is a name?

A Name [5] is a token beginning with a letter or one of a few punctuation characters, and continuing with letters, digits, hyphens, underscores, colons, or full stops, together known as name characters.

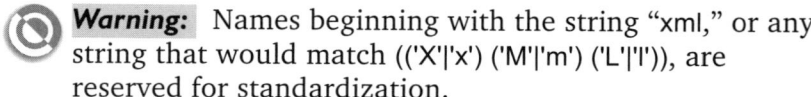 **Warning:** Names beginning with the string "xml," or any string that would match (('X'|'x') ('M'|'m') ('L'|'l')), are reserved for standardization.

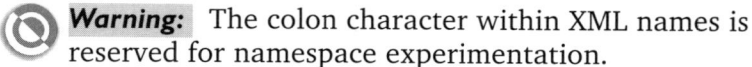 **Warning:** The colon character within XML names is reserved for namespace experimentation.

What is a token?

A token, or name token (NmToken [7]), is any mixture of name characters.

What is a literal?

A literal is a quoted expression. Production rule [17] is an example of a rule that follows the requirement for quoted literals: [17] PITarget ::= Name - (('X' | 'x') ('M' | 'm') ('L' | 'l')).

 Warning: This rule makes "XML" and "xml" reserved words in the instance of processing instructions (PI). This means that <?xml version="1.0"?> (production rule [23]) is not a PI.

What is a character?

The XML Recommendation defines character as follows: [2] Char ::= #x9 | #xA | #xD | [#x20-#xD7FF] | [#xE000-#xFFFD] | [#x10000-#x10FFFF].

 Note: This rule reads a character consisting of a horizontal tab or a line feed or a carriage return or one of three character ranges.

How is a string delimited in XML?

A literal string can be delimited with single or double quotes.

How are expressions handled in XML?

There are a number of variations for handling expressions. These variations include:
- One expression followed by another
- One expression or another expression
- Optional expression
- Required expression

These variations can be blended such as in: [1] document ::= prolog element Misc*. This means a document consists of a prolog followed by an element followed by optional miscellaneous markup. The asterisk (*) denotes optional.

What is character data?

Character data (CDATA) is anything in an XML document that is not markup.

What is XML markup?

In the XML Recommendation, markup has a specific form. There are nine forms of markup:

- Start-tags
- End-tags
- Empty-element tags
- Entity references
- Character references
- Comments
- CDATA section delimiters
- Document type declarations
- Processing instructions

 Note: The precise technical definition of markup is "an element type declaration, an attribute-list declaration, an entity declaration, or a notation declaration." It must be recognized that, in reality, a person may use "markup" in a broader sense to cover any XML usage, and also the word "code" (albeit technically incorrect) may be used because of the programming environment.

What is an XML tag?

An XML tag, the most common markup, is a unique character string that delimits the start and end of an element, or content. When there is no content, there is an empty-tag. The delimiters are the less-than (<) and the greater-than (>) characters. The empty-tag takes the form of <tag/>.

What is an entity reference?

An entity reference (EntityRef) refers to the content of a named entity. It is one of the two types of references defined in production rule [67]: Reference ::= EntityRef | CharRef.

Entity reference is governed by the following production rules: [68] EntityRef ::= '&' Name ';' and [69] PEReference ::= '%' Name ';'.

 Note: Rule [68] states that parsed general entity references use as delimiters ampersand (&) and semicolon (;). Rule [69] states that parameter-entity references use as delimiters the percent sign (%) and semicolon (;).

What is a character reference?

A character reference (CharRef) refers to a <u>specific character</u> in the ISO/IEC 10646 character set. It is <u>not</u> accessible directly from available input devices. It is one of the two types of references defined in production rule [67] Reference ::= EntityRef | CharRef.

 Note: Character reference is defined in production rule [66] CharRef ::= '&#' [0-9]+ ';'| '&#x' [0-9a-fA-F]+ ';'.

What is a comment?

A comment can appear anywhere in a document except within other markup.

[15] Comment ::= '<!--' ((Char - '-') | ('-' (Char - '-')))* '-->'

An example is: <!-- One should use comments frequently. -->.

How are CDATA sections delimited?

A CDATA section begins with a start-tag (<![CDATA[) and finishes with the end-tag (]]>).

What is a document type declaration?

A document type declaration is not a DTD, but a production rule that gives the document type a name that is the same as in production rule [5]. The basic syntax has a reserved word:

[28] doctypedecl ::= '<!DOCTYPE' S Name (S ExternalID)? S? ('[' (markupdecl | PEReference | S)* ']' S?)? '>'

What is a processing instruction?

The purpose of a processing instruction (PI, [16]) is to give an XML application or processor specific directives.

What is the importance of an XML declaration?

If a document adheres to the XML Recommendation version 1.0, it should begin with an XML declaration, which is actually a special type of processing instruction. It has the following format:
<?xml version="1.0"?>.

Is XML case-sensitive?

Yes. When the specification defines "match" it states, "Two strings or names being compared must be identical...." Simply stated, "Comic" does <u>not</u> equal "comic" or any variation of it.

What is a constraint?

There are two types of constraints, well-formedness and validity. A constraint is a requirement used by a processor to check for the correct use of a production.

What is a well-formedness constraint?

A well-formedness constraint, when ignored, can produce a fatal error for a parser while processing an XML document. A fatal error means the parser stops until you take corrective action.

What is a well-formed document?

A well-formed document is a document that does not have to be checked against a DTD, but its elements have to be properly nested. There must be a tree-like document structure of elements. Well-formed XML documents are ideal for the Internet because they require processing with simple XML tools. One of these "simple" tools is Internet Explorer (IE5).

What is a validity constraint?

A validity constraint, when ignored, can produce an unpredictable processing error that can be reported by a validating XML processor.

What is an XML parser?

The role of a validating or non-validating parser is a syntactical language checker. An important characteristic of an XML parser core is its degree of conformance to the XML Recommendation (Working Draft). Conformance means adherence to the well-formedness and the validity constraints as given in the Recommendation.

 Note: XML processing is discussed in Chapter 6.

Chapter 3

XML Logical Structure Tips

Tips on XML can be divided into at least five categories:

■ General structure

■ Logical structure

■ Physical structure

■ Document type definitions (DTD)

■ Processing

This chapter considers the second category, logical structure. The fundamental logical structure is the element. The previous chapter considers the first category. The next three chapters consider each of the categories on an individual basis. Detailed examples are given in Chapter 5.

A tip is a snippet of advice, a guideline, or a pointer. It is not a full explanation of a subject. It is recognized that the answers here are highly abbreviated and only high points of the topics. When a definition is given, it may be one of many possibilities, such as an apple is a type of fruit or a type of computer. Even the following syntax can be stated correctly in two ways: I am a human or a human I am. The second statement is strange, but syntactically correct. However, one should not use strange XML syntax.

 Note: When brackets ([]) enclose a number, it designates a related production rule for the XML specification and is not a part of the production. For example, the first general production rule is as follows: [1] document ::= prolog element Misc*.

The document production defines the global structure. The full list of XML production rules is given in Appendix C. The production rules most related to the logical structure of an XML document are from [39] to [65]. The discussion of XML production rules that relate to the physical structure of an XML document are discussed in Chapter 4.

What type of language is XML?

XML is a design language that uses the document metaphor rather than the page metaphor of HTML. It defines both data and text manipulation over the Internet, intranet, or on an individual workstation. The strength of XML over SGML over the Internet and HTML may be in its use in database manipulation, whether text or data, rather than as a markup language. XML is also much simpler to learn than SGML. Perhaps a better name for the Extensible Markup Language would be Extensible Manipulation Language, that is, a meta-information structural manipulator.

What is an XML document's logical structure?

The fundamental logical structure of an XML document, whether it is text or data, is the XML element and its attributes. A logical structure is the prescribed ordered process for parsing a set of one or more routines and subroutines when a document type definition (DTD) is used. A logical structure without a DTD is having matched start- and end-tags, and proper nesting of the tags.

 Note: The elements might be considered the routines, while the attributes are subroutines.

Logical means to be consistent or reasonable. Based on English syntax rules, a logical order according to size would be smallest, smaller, small, average, large, larger, and largest. In HTML, a logical order of tags might be <h1></h1>, <h2></h2>, <h3></h3>. Because there was originally not a rigid discipline to parsing HTML, some people designing Web pages to create a certain effect did the following: <h2><h1></h1></h2>. XML does not permit this inconsistency if the first set of tags was defined in the XML DTD as such.

What are XML elements in general?

Elements are boundaries, parameters, parts, components, and so forth of a document type. The logical structure "identifies," while the physical structure "contains." The following is a snippet from a possible XML schema that demonstrates the element types of parameters and components:

```
<ElementType name="score" content="mixed">
    <attribute type="name"/>
    <element type1="musictype"/>
    <element type2="length"/>
</ElementType>
```

 Note: If the document type is a database, the field types might be considered elements.

What is an XML element specifically?

An element is the basic logical structure of an XML document. It consists of a start-tag, content, and an end-tag. When an element has no content, it has an empty-tag.

An element is the core concept of the logical structure of an XML document. This production rule defines an element: [39] element ::= EmptyElemTag | Stag content Etag.

The rule states that an element can be either empty or non-empty, that is, the element does or does not have content. When there is content, there first must be a start-tag, and after the content, there must be an end-tag. When an element has no content, it has an empty-tag.

 Note: In the example in the previous question, both types of tags were used. The empty tag is used for length in particular because I may not know the length without some research, but I still can develop my music listing with a "place setting" to be entered later.

 *Warning:* Every start-tag <u>must</u> have an end-tag.

 Warning: This is a non-empty element because there is a space between the tags: <tag> </tag>. An empty-tag is declared as <tag/>.

What is an XML attribute?

An attribute is a named value pair (name and value) that is included within an element tag. In addition, it is a characteristic of the data. An attribute of an element may be a characteristic, property, or quality. An attribute is defined as follows: [41] Attribute ::= Name Eq AttValue.

Note: The allowable values that are used in AttValue are given in the attribute-list declaration [52] in the DTD. See the answer to the next question for the handling of production rule [52].

Warning: The attribute value cannot be delimited by either single or double quotation marks. In addition, the less-than (<) and ampersand (&) characters are not allowable as the delimiter.

Warning: No attribute may appear more than once between the same start-tag and end-tag or empty-element tag.

Warning: The specified attribute must have a name and a value.

What is an attribute list?

An attribute list specifies the name, data type, and default value (optional) of each attribute of an element. Attribute lists are defined in the following production rules:

[52] AttlistDecl ::= '<!ATTLIST' S Name AttDef* S? '>'
[53] AttDef ::= S Name S AttType S DefaultDecl

 Note: The attribute-list declaration [52] in the DTD is used to declare the allowable values that are used in the AttValue declaration [10]. For <element type1="musictype"/>, I might specify the following in its attribute-list declaration:

<!ATTLIST element type1
    musictype (Classical | Jazz | Soundtracks | Other) #REQUIRED>

What are the attribute types?

Attribute types are String, Token, and Enumerated. Attribute types are defined in this production rule: [54] AttType ::= StringType | TokenizedType | EnumeratedType.

What is a string attribute type?

A string attribute type is character data (CDATA). CDATA is anything in an XML document that is not markup: [55] StringType ::= 'CDATA'.

 Note: Markup is start-tags, end-tags, empty-element tags, entity references, character references, comments, CDATA section delimiters, document type declarations, and processing instructions.

What is a token attribute type?

A token attribute can be one of six values of which three are the plurals of the other three. There are a number of constraints in the use of these values. These basic constraints are stated as warnings below since not following the production rule will not produce a parsing fatal error, but a validity parsing error: [56] TokenizedType ::= 'ID' | 'IDREF' | 'IDREFS' | 'ENTITY' | 'ENTITIES' | 'NMTOKEN' | 'NMTOKENS'.

Warning 1: ID attribute must equal Name production [5], and it must be unique to the XML document.

Warning 2: Only one ID attribute per element type.

Warning 3: An ID attribute must have a default of either #IMPLIED or #REQUIRED. You cannot use #FIXED.

Warning 4: IDREF attribute must equal Name production [5].

Warning 5: IDREFS attribute must equal Names production [6].

Warning 6: ENTITY attribute must equal Name production [5].

Warning 7: ENTITIES attribute must equal Names production [6].

Warning 8: NMTOKEN attribute must equal Nmtoken production [7].

Warning 9: NMTOKENS attribute must equal Nmtokens production [8].

What are the enumerated attribute types?

The enumerated attribute types are Notation and Enumeration. Enumerated attribute types are defined in the following production rules:

[57] EnumeratedType ::= NotationType | Enumeration
[58] NotationType ::= 'NOTATION' S '(' S? Name (S? '|' S? Name)* S? ')'
[59] Enumeration ::= '(' S? Nmtoken (S? '|' S? Nmtoken)* S? ')'

What is an enumeration? The example used in a prior question has an enumeration: musictype (Classical | Jazz | Soundtracks | Other) #REQUIRED.

Warning 1: Notation Name must equal Name production [5].

Warning 2: There can only be one notation per element type [45].

Warning 3: Enumeration Nmtoken must equal Nmtoken production [7].

What are the attribute defaults?

The attribute defaults are REQUIRED, IMPLIED, or FIXED. The attribute defaults are defined in production rule [60] DefaultDecl ::= '#REQUIRED' | '#IMPLIED' | (('#FIXED' S)? AttValue).

What is an attribute default example? The example used in the previous chapter showed an attribute default: musictype (Classical | Jazz | Soundtracks | Other) #REQUIRED.

Warning 1: If #REQUIRED is declared, then the attribute must be specified.

Warning 2: If #IMPLIED (the default) is declared, the default declared must meet the lexical constraints of the declared attribute type.

Warning 3: If #FIXED is declared, then any instance of that attribute must match the default value.

Warning 4: No value may contain the less-than (<) character directly or indirectly.

What is a document type definition (DTD)?

A document type definition is the set of rules that governs the grammar of a document. In XML, it is user-defined, while in HTML it is fixed. Do not confuse DTD with document type declaration, which is production rule [28].

 Note: The XML DTD is discussed in detail in Chapter 5.

What is the most important design consideration for an XML document?

The most important consideration for an XML document is for you to design XML elements (markup) that best describe and can be read by other people familiar with the content type. If your element design is well thought out, a search of an occurrence could be closer to what you expected than with HTML. Element and tag can be used interchangeably.

What is an XML tag for an element?

An XML tag is a unique character string that delimits the start and end of an element, or content. When there is no content, there is an empty-tag. The standard is "<"and">".

 Warning: A space between tags is considered content such as <tag> </tag>. An empty-tag is declared as <tag/>.

What is XML markup?

In the XML specification, markup has a specific form. There are nine forms of markup:

- Start-tags
- End-tags
- Empty-element tags
- Entity references
- Character references
- Comments
- CDATA section delimiters
- Document type declarations
- Processing instructions

 Note: This is the precise technical definition of markup: "A markup declaration is an element type declaration, an attribute-list declaration, an entity declaration, or a notation declaration." It must be recognized that, in reality, a person may use "markup" in a broader sense to cover any XML usage, and also the word "code" (albeit technically incorrect) may be used because of the programming environment.

What production rules govern XML markup?

The two production rules that define the document type declaration syntax and the constituent markup are the following:

[28] doctypedecl ::= '<!DOCTYPE' S Name (S ExternalID)? S? ('[' (markupdecl | PEReference | S)* ']' S?)? '>'
[29] markupdecl ::= elementdecl | AttlistDecl | EntityDecl | NotationDecl | PI | Comment

The document type declaration appears after the XML declaration [23] and before any markup. It essentially is the internal identifier and has the syntax of:

<!DOCTYPE *string* [
<!- - markup - ->
]>

A possible string based on the music example would be MusicDB. It is a unique identifier.

 Note: These two rules are stated in normal language in the Note for the previous question.

What is the fundamental difference between XML and HTML tags?

The fundamental difference between XML and HTML is that you can define the tags in your XML document so they can be readable and interpretable. The HTML tags are predefined.

What are the basic criteria any XML document should meet?

An XML document must meet two criteria: it has to be well-formed and valid. This means the XML document adheres to the production rules so no parsing errors are found. The parser that you use when checking the document has in its design a checking process for well-formedness and validity constraints. Many of the warnings in the book reflect these constraints.

What is an XML constraint?

A constraint is supplemental limitaticn to a production rule for clarifying parser design. The two types of constraints are well-formedness and validity. The first type produces fatal errors (terminating) during parser processing and the second type can produce a random type of error during parser processing.

What is a well-formed XML document?

An XML document is valid if it adheres to the well-formedness constraints as defined in the specification. An XML document is well formed when it also follows these rules:

- The document starts with an XML declaration [23] <?xml version="1.0"?> if the entire markup adheres to the XML specification.
- There is a root element (document entity [28]) in which all other elements are contained.
- There are paired name tags (start- and end-tags) [39].
- All elements are properly nested as defined by your DTD.

What is a valid XML document?

An XML document is valid if it adheres to the well-formedness constraints and the validity constraints as defined in the specification. In other words, an XML document is valid if it has an associated document type declaration (DTD) and if the document complies with the constraints expressed within it.

What is the most important design consideration for XML tags?

Perhaps the most important design consideration for XML tags is that they can be designed to be readable by humans. This means instead of having ... one could have <bold>...</bold> or <book>...</book>.

What are the basic parsing checks specified on the DTD?

The basic checks include:
- Matching start- and end-tags with content

- Matching empty tags with no content
- Content is parsed character data
- Elements are ordered according to the DTD
- Nesting is according to the DTD
- An attribute is given only once within an element

What is the first line of XML markup?

The first line of markup is usually [23] <?xml version="1.0"?>.

This is an XML declaration. It should begin any XML coding if the markup conforms to the XML specification version 1.0. The following discussion shows how an apparent production may have a series of complex implications. Considering production rules [23] — [26], you get the syntax for the basic XML declaration, which is stated between the quotation marks in the rules: <?xml version="..."?>.

The only possible valid XML declaration at this time is <?xml version="1.0"?> because there is only the first release of the XML specification. Considering production rules [80] and [81], you can have the following example: <?xml version="1,0" encoding="UTF-8"?>.

The encoding schema supported by XML are:
- UTF-8
- UTF-16
- EUC-JP
- ISO-2022-JP
- ISO-8859-1 to -9
- ISO-10646-UCS-2
- ISO-10646-UCS-4
- Shift_JIS

Considering production rule [81], you could have the following: <?xml version="1.0" standalone="yes"?>.

The value "yes" indicates there are no markup declarations external to the document entity that affect the information passed from the XML processor to the application. The value "no" indicates there are or may be such external markup declarations.

By combining all of these rules, you could have this example: <?xml version="1.0" encoding="UTF-8" standalone="yes"?>.

You may also write it in the following manner because the production rules permit either single or double quotation marks: <?xml version='1.0' encoding='UTF-8' standalone='yes'?>.

Also, since each production rule has the either-or syntax, you can use any variation such as: <?xml version='1.0' encoding="UTF-8" standalone="yes"?>.

However, all values must be within quotation marks, so you cannot have this example: <?xml version=1.0?>.

There are eight possible combinations of double (D) and single (S) quotation marks for this production:

```
D   D   D
D   S   D
D   D   S
D   S   S
S   S   S
S   D   S
S   S   D
S   D   D
```

Is XML spoken language specific?

No. For example, the following is a complete, well-formed XML document, but not valid:

```
<?xml version="1.0"?>
<Encabezamiento>Declaración de XML</Encabezamiento>
```

and so is this: <Encabezamiento>Déclamtión de XML</Encabezamiento>

This XML document is readable and meaningful if you read Spanish. The point here is that XML tags are not necessarily language specific. For those who do not read Spanish, here is the equivalent using English language tags:

```
<?xml version="1.0"?>
<heading><XML Declaration</heading>
```

What is the prolog?

The prolog is one of the three expressions of which the document consists that is [1] document ::= prolog element Misc*.

The document production defines the global structure. The rule for prolog is: [22] prolog ::= XMLDecl? Misc* (doctypedecl Misc*)?.

The prolog production includes:

- An optional XML declaration
- Zero or more miscellaneous markup comments
- An optional document type declaration that can be followed by zero or more miscellaneous markup comments

What is an XML declaration (XMLDecl)?

The XML declaration (XMLDecl) is only required when the XML document conforms to the XML specification. The XMLDecl production rule is: [23] XMLDecl ::= '<?xml' VersionInfo EncodingDecl? SDDecl? S? '?>'.

The only possible valid XML declaration at this time is <?xml version="1.0"?> or <?xml version='1.0'?>.

This is because there is only the first release of the XML specification as a W3C working draft.

What are the miscellaneous markup components (Misc)?

The three miscellaneous markup components are the following:

- Comments
- Processing instructions (PI)
- White space (S)

This is based on the following production rule: [27] Misc ::= Comment | PI | S.

 Note: A space can be defined as one of the following formats:

- #x9 — horizontal tab
- #xA — line feed
- #xD — carriage return
- #x20 — space

What is a document type declaration (doctypedecl)?

A simple definition of a document type declaration is that it includes the root element name and the reserved word DOCTYPE. A more complex definition is that it contains the markup declarations to define the logical structure's constraints for an XML document or a document class. In addition, it supports predefined storage units. The production rule that governs the document type declaration is: [28] doctypedecl ::= '<!DOCTYPE' S Name (S ExternalID)? S? ('[' (markupdecl | PEReference | S)* ']' S?)? '>'.

 Warning: The document type declaration must appear before the first element in the document. It must be the second line of code after the XML declaration when used.

 Note: This is a reminder that the book contains tips, not a complete explanation of XML. In fact, a full bookshelf of books on XML will not give you a full explanation of the power of XML. A full discussion would include comprehensive information on system identifiers and parameter-entity references. Also see the question, "What production rules govern XML markup?" for more information on the document type declaration.

How does XML specify encoding schema?

XML specifies an encoding schema using the following production rule: [80] EncodingDecl ::= S 'encoding' Eq (' " ' EncName ' " ' | " ' " EncName " ' ").

An example using production rule [23] (XML declaration (XMLDecl)) is: <?xml version="1.0" encoding="UTF-8"?>.

What encoding schema are supported by XML?

The encoding schema supported by XML are the following:
- UTF-8
- UTF-16
- EUC-JP
- ISO-2022-JP
- ISO-8859-1 to -9
- ISO-10646-UCS-2
- ISO-10646-UCS-4
- Shift_JIS

What is a standalone XML document?

A standalone XML document can be processed without reference to any external markup declarations. A standalone document is very useful in a distributed environment, since you do not have to do extra downloading during application processing.

How is a standalone XML document declared?

To create a standalone document you would use the following production rule: [32] SDDecl ::= S 'standalone' Eq ((""" ('yes' | 'no') """) | ("'" ('yes' | 'no') "'")).

 Warning: This declaration can only be used within an XML declaration.

An example of a standalone declaration is: <?xml version="1.0" standalone="yes"?>.

 Note: The value "no" indicates there are or may be external markup declarations.

How do I declare an encoding schema and a standalone document?

You could declare an encoding schema and a standalone document by combining production rules [1], [80], and [32] as given in the following example: <?xml version="1.0" encoding="UTF-16" standalone="yes"?>

You could also write it this way because the production rules permit either single or double quotation marks: <?xml version='1.0' encoding='UTF-16' standalone='yes'?>

Also, since each production rule has the either-or syntax, you can use any variation such as: <?xml version='1.0' encoding="UTF-16" standalone="yes"?>

However, all values must be within quotation marks, so you cannot have this example: <?xml version=1.0 encoding=UTF-16 standalone=yes?>

 Note: While you can code many XML declarations in a variety of ways, it is recommended you be consistent with such things as quotation marks.

When must a standalone="no" document declaration be used?

The standalone document declaration must have the value "no" if any external markup declaration contains:

- Attributes with default values, if elements to which these attributes apply appear in the document without specifications of values for these attributes
- Entities (other than amp, lt, gt, apos, quot), if references to those entities appear in the document
- Attributes with values subject to normalization, where the attribute appears in the document with a value that will change as a result of normalization
- Element types with element content, if white space occurs directly within any instance of those types

What is a generic identifier (GI)?

Each element has a type, identified by name, sometimes called its generic identifier (GI).

Are there any semantic constraints for XML?

The only semantic constraint beyond syntax of the XML specification is that names of the element types and attributes cannot begin with a match of (('X'|'x')('M'|'m')('L'|'l')). See production rule [17]. This means you cannot use any of the following element names:

- XML
- XMl
- XmL
- Xml
- xml
- xMl
- xML
- xmL

What is a valid start-tag name for an element?

A valid start-tag is the element name or generic identifier. The required end-tag must case match. You can have <tag>content</tag>, but you cannot have <tag>content </Tag> because of the capital T in the end-tag. See production rule [40].

What is a valid end-tag name for an element?

A valid end-tag must match the element type in the start-tag. See the answer for the above question and production rule [42].

When is an element valid?

In the DTD an element [39] is valid if there is a declaration matching elementdecl [45] where the Name [5] matches the element type [28], and one of the following holds:

■ The declaration matches EMPTY [46], and the element has no content.

■ The declaration matches children [46] and the sequence of child elements belongs to the language generated by the regular expression in the content model, with optional white space (characters matching the nonterminal S) between each pair of child elements.

■ The declaration matches Mixed [46], and the content consists of character data and child elements whose types match names in the content model.

■ The declaration matches ANY [46], and the types of any child elements have been declared.

 Note: This answer should prove that one could not acquire comprehensive knowledge of XML in 24 minutes or 24 hours.

How case-sensitive is XML?

XML is absolutely case-sensitive. You cannot have the following: <comic> ... </Comic> (not an exact match because of "c" and "C").

Can I have different start-tag and end-tag names?

You cannot have different start-tag and end-tag names: <comic> ... </funnies> (different names).

 Note: If you think this is an unnecessary question, read some of the questions asked in XML newsgroups.

What is meant by improper nesting?

An example of improper nesting is the following: <comic><funnies>...</comic>...</funnies>.

How do I declare an empty element?

The following example uses the break concept from HTML: <!ELEMENT br EMPTY>.

The br (break) element has no content and uses an empty-element tag. This means that when this element is used it must be declared as the following: <br/>.

 Note: In an HTML document, this element would have to also be declared the same to be XML compliant.

How would document versions be handled with XML?

The following element might be used to do document version control: <!ELEMENT Revision ANY>.

What are the production rules for the start-tag?

The production rules for the start-tag are:

```
[40] Stag ::= '<' Name (S Attribute)* S? '>'
[41] Attribute ::= Name Eq AttValue
```

These production rules read that the first Name [5] in the start- and end-tags gives the element's type. A Name-AttValue pair refers to the attribute specifications of the element. The second Name [5] in a pair refers to the attribute name and the content of the AttValue, text between the ' or " delimiters, as the attribute value.

What are the constraints or limitations on an element?

The five constraints on an element are the following:
- An attribute name may appear only once within an element.
- The attribute must have been declared.
- The attribute value must have been declared.
- An attribute value cannot contain any references to external entities.
- The replacement text in an attribute value, other than "<" must not contain a <.

What is the production rule for an end-tag?

The production rule for the end-tag is: [42] Etag ::= '</' Name S? '>'.

The end of every element that begins with a start-tag must be marked by an end-tag containing a name that matches the element's type as given in the start-tag.

What is content?

The text between the start-tag and end-tag is called the element's content. A white space is considered content. This means <tag> </tag> is an element because there is a single white space between the tags.

What is the production rule for content?

The production rule for the content is: [43] content ::= (element | CharData | Reference | CDSect | PI | Comment)*.

The expressive power of XML is based on the expansion for element [39], which allows content [43] to be recursive. This allows for elements within elements.

 Note: The productions impacted by the content production are [39], [14], [67], [18], [17], and [15].

What is an empty element?

If an element is empty, it must be represented either by a start-tag immediately followed by an end-tag or by an empty-element tag.

Warning: A white space is content, thus one can have <tag></tag>, but not <tag> </tag>. You should use <tag/> for an empty-tag.

What is the production rule of an empty-element tag?

The production rule for an empty-element tag is: [44] EmptyElemTag ::= '<' Name (S Attribute)* S? '/>'.

 Warning: The empty-element tag must be used, and can only be used, for elements that are declared EMPTY.

What is the importance of an element type declaration?

An element type declaration [44] would be of interest to people writing a parser or developing XML authoring software. The software developer might want to enforce such things as not letting a user insert a chapter element inside a paragraph element.

What production rules govern element type declarations?

The production rules for the element type declaration are:

[45] elementdecl ::= '<!ELEMENT' S Name S contentspec S? '>'
[46] contentspec ::= 'EMPTY' | 'ANY' | Mixed | children

Two examples of production rule [46] are:

<!ELEMENT br EMPTY>
<!ELEMENT revision ANY>

What is an important constraint for element type declarations?

An important constraint is that, within a DTD, no element type may be declared more than once. However, you could do the following because XML is case-sensitive:

<!ELEMENT br EMPTY>
<!ELEMENT BR EMPTY>

As far as XML is concerned, br and BR are two different elements.

What is a content model?

A content model provides a pattern or grammar for what may appear inside (content) of elements of a given element type. The grammar of a content model is built on content particles (cps).

What are content particles?

The content particles (cps) are the names of the allowable child element within content.

- Production rule [48] reads that a content particle consists of a name, choice lists of content particles, or sequence lists of content particles, where each Name [5] is the type of an element which may appear as a child.
- Production rule [49] reads that any content particle in a choice list may appear in the element content at the location where the choice list appears in the grammar.
- Production rule [50] reads that content particles occurring in a sequence list must each appear in the element content in the order given in the list.

What is mixed content?

An element type has mixed content when elements contain character data, optionally interspersed with child elements. A simple translation of the specification is that mixed content is anywhere you can put character data [14].

What is the production rule for a mixed content declaration?

The production rule for a mixed content declaration is: [51] Mixed ::= '(' S? '#PCDATA' (S? '|' S? Name)* S? ')*' | '(' S? '#PCDATA' S? ')'.

 Warning: Two basic points of this rule are that a white space is not allowed in the sequence ')*' and the keyword #PCDATA must be uppercase.

What are the important constraints for handling mixed content?

The two important constraints for handling mixed content are the following:

- Parameter-entity replacement text must be properly nested with parenthetical groups.
- The same name must not appear more than once in a single mixed-content declaration.

What is an attribute-list declaration?

An attribute-list declaration found in the DTD may be used:

- To define the set of attributes pertaining to a given element type
- To establish type constraints for these attributes
- To provide default values for attributes

 Note: The above list means that an attribute-list declaration can specify the name (attribute), data type (such as #CDATA), and default value (if any) for an element type.

What are the attribute value types and their labels?

Attribute value types and their labels are as follows:

- Plain text   #CDATA
- Unique ID   ID
- Nontext entity   ENTITY
- Predefined   (value | ... | value)

What are the attribute types and their labels?

Attribute types and their labels are as follows:

- Fixed   #FIXED
- Implied   #IMPLIED
- Required   #REQUIRED

What are some important actions in handling attribute-list declarations?

One must consider three actions in handling attribute-list declarations. One should provide:

■ At most, one attribute-list declaration for a given element type

■ At most, one attribute definition for a given attribute name in an attribute-list declaration

■ At least one attribute definition in each attribute-list declaration

What are the three XML attribute types?

There are three XML attribute types:

■ String type [55] (any literal string as a value)

■ Set of tokenized types [56] (varying lexical and semantic constraints)

■ Enumerated types [57]

What is the basis of the tokenized attribute types?

The tokenized types list was taken originally from SGML. The reality is that you may only infrequently use ID, IDREF, and ENTITY.

What is an enumerated attribute type?

An enumerated attribute can take one of a list of values provided in the declaration. There are two kinds of enumerated types: Notation and Enumeration.

What is the purpose of a notation for an attribute type?

The purpose of a notation is to identify the format either of an element's content to which it is attached or of an external unparsed entity that has been specified by an ENTITY-valued attribute for the element.

How is a notation identified?

The reserved word NOTATION is used. The notation must be declared in the DTD with associated system and/or public identifiers, to be used in interpreting the element to which the attribute is attached.

What is the purpose of an enumeration for an attribute type?

The purpose of an enumeration is to name all the possible values for a given attribute.

What is an attribute default?

An attribute declaration can declare one of three default types that provides information on whether the attribute's presence is required, and if not, how an XML processor should react if a declared attribute is absent in a document. The three default types are the following:

- #REQUIRED
- #IMPLIED
- #FIXED

 Warning: This declaration affects all validating processors. An attribute default should be used with care because a non-validating parser may ignore it for several reasons.

What is the production rule for attribute types?

The production rule for the attribute defaults is: [60] DefaultDecl ::= '#REQUIRED' | '#IMPLIED' | (('#FIXED' S)? AttValue).

These three defaults mean the following:

- #REQUIRED means that the attribute must always be provided.
- #IMPLIED means that no default value is provided.
- #FIXED means that the attribute must always have a default value.

What is a conditional section?

A conditional section is a document type declaration's external subset that is included in, or excluded from, the logical structure of the DTD based on the keyword, either INCLUDE or IGNORE, that governs it. A conditional section may contain one or more complete declarations, comments, processing instructions, or nested conditional sections, intermingled with white space.

What does the reserved word INCLUDE mean?

INCLUDE means the contents of the conditional section are logically part of the DTD.

 Warning: If INCLUDE occurs within a larger conditional section with a keyword of IGNORE, both the outer and the inner conditional sections are ignored.

What does the reserved word IGNORE mean?

IGNORE means the contents of the conditional section are not logically part of the DTD.

Chapter 4

XML Physical Structure Tips

Tips on XML can be divided into at least five categories:

- General structure
- Logical structure
- Physical structure
- Document type definitions (DTD)
- Processing

This chapter considers the physical structure, with the basic structure being the entity. The first category was considered in Chapter 2, the second in Chapter 3, and the last two categories will be discussed in Chapters 5 and 6. Detailed examples are given in Chapter 5.

 Note: A tip is a snippet of advice, a guideline, or a pointer. It is not a full explanation of a subject. It is recognized that the answers here are highly abbreviated and only high points of the topics. When syntax is given, it may be only one of many variants.

What is the physical structure of an XML document?

A physical structure is the container of external text or data. The physical structure points to external sources that are local server files or Uniform Resource Identifiers (URIs) or Uniform Resource Locators (URLs) or even data in memory.

What is the foundation of the physical structure?

The entity is the foundation of the physical structure of an XML document, whether it is text or data.

What is an entity?

An entity is a storage unit in an XML document with one exception: the root element is the document entity. It is defined in the DTD. An entity is identified by name except for the document entity and the external document type definition (DTD) subset.

What are the production rules that govern entities?

The basic production rules that govern entities are the following:

[70] EntityDecl ::= GEDecl | PEDecl
[71] GEDecl ::= '<!ENTITY' S Name S EntityDef S? '>'
[72] PEDecl ::= '<!ENTITY' S '%' S Name S PEDef S? '>'
[73] EntityDef ::= EntityValue | (ExternalID NDataDecl?)
[74] PEDef ::= EntityValue | ExternalID

 Note: These rules are basic because, as you tree through the rules, you have other rules such as External ID [75] that uses [3] and [11], and NDataDecl [76] that uses [3] and [5]. There are very few standalone XML productions, if any. One could say that the basic production rules are [70] to [83] for the XML physical structure.

What are the various types of entities?

The six basic types of entities are the following:
- Document
- General
    - External
    - Internal
- Parameter
- Parsed
- Unparsed
- Character

What is the purpose of the document entity?

The document entity serves as the starting point for the XML processor and may contain the whole document. Your logical structure is contained within the document entity or root element.

 Note: When there is a single file for an XML document, the container is the document entity (that is, <?xml version"1.0" standalone="yes" ?> or <?xml version="1.0" ?>). If there is more than one XML document entity, the document entity is the main part (that is, <?xml version"1.0" standalone="no" ?>).

What is an example of a document entity?

This is an example of the simplest document entity:

```
<!DOCTYPE Comics-DB [
...
]>
```

What are the types of general entities?

A general entity can be either internal or external. When external, an external identifier (SYSTEM or PUBLIC) is required. When internal, the content is given. A general entity [71] is an entity used within the document content.

What is an example of an external general entity?

An external general entity could be declared as follows: <!ENTITY FMiller SYSTEM "text.xml">.

What is the production rule for an external entity declaration?

The production rule for an external entity is as follows: [75] ExternalID ::= 'SYSTEM' S SystemLiteral | 'PUBLIC' S PubidLiteral S SystemLiteral.

What is an example of an internal general entity?

An internal general entity could be declared as follows: <!ENTITY FMiller "One of the greatest comic artists.">.

What is an internal entity?

An internal entity is a quoted string. The entity is a literal value and neither the SYSTEM keyword nor the PUBLIC keyword is used in the declaration. In addition, it is a parsed entity.

What is a parameter entity?

A parameter entity [72] is either an internal or an external parsed entity for use within the DTD.

How is a parameter entity delimited?

A percentage sign (%) is used at the beginning of a parameter entity and is closed by a semicolon (;). It can only be used with a DTD.

What is an example of a parameter entity?

Here is an example of a parameter entity (second line):

```
<!ENTITY % Comics SYSTEM "Comics1.dtd">
%Comics;
```

What is a parsed entity?

A parsed entity is an included external entity. Its content is replacement text and is an integral part of an XML document. A parsed entity is invoked by name using entity references.

What are the characteristics of an unparsed entity?

The five characteristics of an unparsed entity are the following:

- May or may not be text; it could be a binary.
- Text does not have to be XML.

■ It has an associated notation, identified by a name that is used to assist in processing by an application.

■ It is invoked by name using the value given in an ENTITY or ENTITIES attribute.

■ It is passed on to an application without any consideration of content by the processor.

How are parsed and unparsed entities differentiated syntactically?

If NDataDecl is present, the entity is a general unparsed entity. The reverse is that if you have a parsed entity, NDataDecl is not present.

 Note: This supporting production rule is: [76] NDataDecl ::= S 'NDATA' S Name

What are the characteristics of unparsed entity declarations?

An unparsed entity declaration has one of the following characteristics:

■ Has an associated NOTATION in its declaration, using NDATA as its keyword

■ Never included in an XML document, only referenced in an attribute value

What is an example of an unparsed entity with NDATA?

An example of the use of NDATA is as follows:

```
<!ENTITY FMiller SYSTEM "SinCity1001.jpg" NDATA JPEG>
<!ENTITY text SYSTEM "SinCity01.xml">
```

 Note: This example requires several assumptions. The JPEG notation has been declared and FMiller (Frank Miller (writer and artist in this instance) is a declared unparsed entity and text (text on the comic *Sin City* number 1) is a declared parsed entity.

What is an example of an unparsed entity in an attribute value?

An example of an unparsed entity in an attribute value is as follows:

```
<!ELEMENT graphic (#PCDATA)>
<!ATTLIST Graphic Image ENTITY #REQUIRED>
...
<Graphic Image="SinCity001">&text;</Graphic>
```

Can a general entity and a parameter have the same name?

Yes. A general entity and a parameter occupy different namespaces. You can have a parameter entity and a general entity with the same name because they are considered distinct entities.

 Note: Namespace, as used here, should not be confused with XML namespaces. As used here, it makes a distinction between the entities of parameter and general.

What is a character reference?

A character reference refers to a specific character in the ISO/IEC 10646 character set, that is, a character not directly accessible from an accessible input device. This means that when a character is not accessible from your keyboard, you use a Unicode character.

What are the production rules for a character reference?

The production rules for a character reference are:

```
[66] CharRef ::= '&#' [0-9]+ ';' | '&#x' [0-9a-fA-F]+ ';'
[67] Reference ::= EntityRef | CharRef
```

Do not confuse a character reference with an entity reference just because they look similar. The first is &#; or &#x;, while the second is %;.

 Warning: It is not recommended to use a character reference to escape markup. If an XML parser is not being used, there could be unexpected consequences.

What is an entity reference?

An entity reference refers to a named entity's content.

 Note: This means the document entity cannot have an entity reference.

What are the production rules for an entity reference?

The production rules for an entity reference are:

[67] Reference ::= EntityRef | CharRef
[68] EntityRef ::= '&' Name ';'
[69] PEReference ::= '%' Name ';'

What are the predefined entities?

The five predefined entities are the following:
- amp
- lt
- gt
- apos
- quot

What is important about these predefined entities?

A document with no DTD can only use the five predefined general entities list.

What is a major constraint on the use of general entities?

A general entity can appear only as an attribute list's default value.

How does a standalone="yes" declaration restrict entity usage?

When a standalone="yes" declaration is used in a well-formed document, entities not defined in the internal DTD cannot be used.

What is a major restriction on the parsed entities?

A parsed entity must not contain a recursive reference to itself, either directly or indirectly.

This means you cannot have:

```
<!ENTITY CAT "CAT then &TAC;">
<!ENTITY TAC "TAC then &CAT;">
```

This is a loop.

What is an important constraint on the use of parameter-entity references?

Parameter-entity references may only appear in the DTD. The reasons for this constraint are the following:

- A parameter-entity reference is replacement text for a general entity.
- Expansion happens when the general entity declaration is parsed.

What is an example of a character reference?

An example of a character reference: Type <key>greater-than</key> (>) to delete options.

This also could have been written: Type <key>greater-than</key> (>) to delete options.

What is an example of an entity reference?

An example of an entity reference is as follows:

This novel was prepared on &docdate; and is categorized as &status;.

What is an example of a parameter-entity reference?

An example of a parameter-entity reference:

```
<!-- declare the parameter entity "MyComics"... -->
<!ENTITY % MyComics SYSTEM
"http://www.MySite.com/standards/MyComics-xml.entities" >
<!-- ... now reference it. -->
%MyComics;
```

What is an example of an entity declaration?

This example declares the general entity artist whose replacement text is Frank Miller: <!ENTITY artist "Frank Miller">.

 Note: The related production rules are EntityDecl [70], GEDecl [71], EntityDef [73], and EntityValue [9]. You use &artist in the XML document and "Frank Miller" is substituted.

What is an example of an external parameter entity?

The following example declares an external parameter entity:

```
<!ENTITY % ArtistList SYSTEM "artists.dtd">
%ArtistList;
```

 Note: The related production rules are EntityDecl [70], GEDecl [71], EntityDef [73], and EntityValue [9].

 Warning: The space after the % must be present for a PEDecl (first line). If it is omitted, it is a parameter entity reference.

What is the SystemLiteral?

The SystemLiteral is called the entity's system identifier. It is a Uniform Resource Identifier (URI), which may be used to retrieve the entity.

 Warning: The hash mark (#) and fragment identifier frequently used with URIs are not, formally, part of the URI itself; an XML processor may signal an error if a fragment identifier is given as part of a system identifier.

What are examples of the external entity declarations?

Examples of external entity declarations:

```
<!ENTITY ComicDB SYSTEM
"http://www.MySite.com/ComicsDB/Comics.xml">
<!ENTITY ComicDB PUBLIC "-//MySite//TEXT Basic descriptive data.//EN"
"http://www.MySite.com/ComicsDB/Comics.xml">
<!ENTITY pictures SYSTEM "../graphics/Sandman1001.jpg" NDATA JPG >
```

Note: When PUBLIC is used, SYSTEM must be omitted even if a system identifier is given.

What is a text declaration?

The optional text declaration must be provided literally and must appear at the beginning of an external parsed entity. The production rule of text declaration is: [77] TextDecl ::= '<?xml' VersionInfo? EncodingDecl S? '?>'

 Note: It is good to compare this declaration against the XML declaration: [23] XMLDecl ::= '<?xml' VersionInfo EncodingDecl? SDDecl? S? '?>'. The difference is that the XML declaration includes a standalone document declaration [32].

What are the guidelines to ensure well-formed parsed entities?

Well-formed parsed entities are determined by how they match certain productions. The guidelines are as follows:

- Document entity matches document production [1]
- Internal general parsed entity matches the content production [43]
- External general parsed entity matches the extParsedEnt production [78]
- External parameter entity matches the extPE production [79]

How is character encoding handled in entities?

Each external parsed entity in an XML document may use a different encoding for its characters.

 Warning: All XML processors must be able to read entities in either UTF-8 or UTF-16.

What encoding schema are supported by XML?

The encoding schema supported by XML are:

- UTF-8
- UTF-16

- EUC-JP
- ISO-2022-JP
- ISO-8859-1 to -9
- ISO-10646-UCS-2
- ISO-10646-UCS-4
- Shift_JIS

What are the forms for an entity value?

There are two forms of the entity's value:
- The literal entity value is the quoted string present in the entity declaration. It corresponds to the non-terminal EntityValue [9].
- The replacement text is entity content, after replacement of character references and parameter-entity references.

What are the numeric character references for the predefined entities?

The numeric character references of the predefined entities are as follows:
- lt   &#60;
- gt   >
- amp   &#38;
- apos '
- quot "

What does a notation declaration identify?

A notation (the reserved word NOTATION) identifies, by name, the format of an unparsed entity.

What are the production rules for a notation declaration?

The production rules for a notation declaration are:

[82] NotationDecl ::= '<!NOTATION' S Name S (ExternalID | PublicID) S? '>'
[83] PublicID ::= 'PUBLIC' S PubidLiteral

XML DTD Tips

Questions on XML can be divided into at least five categories:

- General structure
- Logical structure
- Physical structure
- Document type definitions (DTD)
- Processing

This chapter considers the place of the document type definition (DTD) in XML design and development. The DTD defines the rules of an XML document's grammar. The first three categories were considered in Chapters 2 through 4, while the last category will be discussed in Chapter 6.

This chapter highlights the process for developing DTDs for four different types of XML documents:

- Memo
- Fiction book
- Technical book
- Database

The discussion is constrained by the format of the book and tips, and not detailed discussions. Many of the tips in the chapter are lengthy and perhaps seem repetitive because of the nature of DTD design. To get a clear view of DTD design you need to see the DTD enhancements in stages. The chapter also focuses on "pure" XML design rather than being inclusive with styles, links, and graphics. If you have not read the earlier chapters, doing so may allow for better use of this chapter. The emphasis is on design development rather than completeness. The power of XML is for each user to develop a unique and readable XML grammar to resolve an issue in an effective and efficient manner.

 Note: A tip is a snippet of advice, a guideline, or a pointer. It is not a full explanation of a subject. It is recognized that the answers here are highly abbreviated and only high points of the topics. When syntax is given, it may be only one of many variants.

What is a document type definition (DTD)?

A document type definition is the set of rules that governs the grammar of a document. In XML, it is user defined, while in HTML, it is fixed. Do not confuse DTD with a document type declaration (doctypedecl [28]). A DTD is the content of a document type declaration. This content defines allowable grammar using four types of markup declarations for usable elements and attributes, and defines entities that are the reusable components of an XML document.

What are the four markup declarations used in a DTD?

The four types of markup declarations used in a DTD are:
- Element type declarations
- Attribute-list declarations
- Entity declarations
- Notation declarations

Is a DTD easy to create from scratch?

Yes, if you do the following:
- Use only an internal subset, also known as the internal document type declaration subset or internal DTD subset.
- Work only with a logical structure.
- Comprehend the logical structure of the text document or database that is to be manipulated.
- Use only XML; not XSL, XLink, XPointer, or XPath.

 Note: From this positive position one can write very small XML DTD easily; however, can a programmer be called a programmer after writing one program of 100 lines? I have seen some very functional XML applications that adhere to the above points. The rule for XML is to learn the basics before trying to be bold. Remember, you are working with text or data manipulation and not with visual appearance, as you would be with HTML. This means checking for expected results can be difficult. I am not trying to speak down to anyone. I am aware that in most Web development budgets an average of twenty percent is used to handle the differences in HTML processing implementation between the two major browsers so there is an apparent consistency in appearance.

You can test a DTD in a number of ways. Two examples are:

- ■ Write a document using an ASCII editor that conforms to a DTD, then parse the document using a validating parser.
- ■ Write a document using an XML editor that reads a DTD.

Is a DTD easy to create?

This question is not the same as the question above in one very significant way, the phrase "from scratch." Just as there are tools to create Web pages without knowing the basic reasons for using an HTML tag set, one can use tools to create XML applications. This subject is discussed in Chapter 17, "XML Applications and Initiatives Tips."

What is the basic process for developing a complete XML DTD?

The basic process or design path includes the following components:

- ■ Markup
- ■ DTD (document type definition or your own personal XML grammar rules)
- ■ Entities (external data sources)
- ■ Presentation (stylesheets)
- ■ Links to other documents (XLink)
- ■ Links to specific location within documents (XPointer)
- ■ Use of multiple XML documents (namespaces)

It is similar to building a house. At each step, the DTD has to be enhanced to reflect the design changes to the grammar.

 Note: This chapter only looks at the first three bulleted items. Chapters 8 through 11 look at the other items.

What are the fundamental problems in doing an XML DTD?

The fundamental problem is how to quickly design, develop, and implement various document types that primarily handle text rather than data, the perceived bits of information or values.

What is the basic design consideration for a DTD?

Even with a simple document type, one should go through a basic design process of "house building." One should not try to have everything on the first design, but should decide that the basic goals of the document are to name the components and organize the logical structure of the components. You start with an outline of elements, as discussed later in the chapter.

 Note: The emphasis should be on the logical structure of the XML document rather than the physical structure. You should design, when possible, an internal document subset.

What are the formal design steps for developing a DTD?

The formal steps for a DTD and an XML document are as follows:

- Determine your design goals.
- Design a markup content model.
- Design a content model with a DTD.
- Design the inclusion of a physical structure.
- Add styles, links, pointers, namespaces, and vector graphic definitions.

 Note: The last step is discussed, where appropriate, in Chapters 8 through 13.

What is the result of determining your design goals?

The design goals determine the basic components of the XML document. It is nothing more than a simple list of components.

What is a markup content model?

The markup content model is doing a "tag" model, that is, a logical ordering of the components for processing.

Why are parsing considerations important to design?

As a part of the design, each element's attribute and subelements should be added. This is designing the XML document's logical structure. A part of this activity is considering the consequences of adherence to the well-formedness and validity constraints, that is, the prescribed order for parsing and the occurrence states.

 Note: The key to the use of all the capabilities of XML is to have a DTD. The document type definition is the grammar, the markup rules, of your document. It is used to determine that your markup document is valid by the parser.

When should I include the physical structure for the XML DTD?

The inclusion of a physical structure comes after you have a clear definition of the logical structure's grammar. A physical structure is the container of external text or data. The physical structure points to external sources that are local server files or URIs (URLs) or even data in memory. You need to comprehend when there should be the inclusion or even the exclusion of data after the logical structure is designed because you also have the logical parsing process.

What is the final step in design of the DTD?

The final step is the extending of XML, that is, the use of XSL, XLink, XPointer, XML namespaces, and the addition of vector graphics. You may not even use this step or you may only use one of these extensions. Probably the most used extension is XSL. It may be more useful to ensure that all prior design actions are viable before trying to include this step.

Can comments be included in a DTD?

Yes, comments can be included as in the rest of an XML document. There is one obvious exception: you cannot include a comment within a declaration. The processor ignores comments.

Why would I want to comment a DTD?

There are a number of reasons one might want to comment a DTD. Two important ones are to explain abbreviations and to explain why some element was used or omitted. For example, one might say that the customer decided on a certain date that a certain element or attribute was to be added to the DTD.

 Note: Mathematics Markup Language (MathML), developed by a committee, is an excellent example of an XML dialect that has a fully documented DTD. Chemical Markup Language (CML), developed by an individual, has a DTD, but is lacking in documentation. Microsoft Channel Definition Format (CDF) does not have a DTD currently available and the documentation is informal at its best. You can decide for yourself where there is a commitment to an open standard in this area. You can also reflect on the importance of having good DTD documentation if one desires to achieve the excellence of the ISO 9000 standards.

Why would I want to use abbreviated tags in a DTD?

In lengthy markup, for example 500K or larger, the size of the markup might be reduced significantly.

What other significant action might I consider in designing a DTD?

One should probably consider whether the DTD is going to be used in sharing common data. In an accounting group in a corporation, there are many departments, but they share common data. All should use the same element or attribute name for a given piece of data.

What is a conditional section in a DTD?

A conditional section permits you to comment out parts of the DTD not yet developed, but included in the general design effort. The syntax is as follows:

```
<![ IGNORE
... declarations not processed ...
]]>
```

You also can comment parts of the DTD in by changing IGNORE to INCLUDE.

What must I do first in developing any DTD?

The first activity is to identify the root element using the doctypedecl [28] production. The !DOCTYPE declaration for a memo would be as follows:

```
<!DOCTYPE memo [
...
]>
```

What are the important rules for declaring an element?

There are at least five important rules for declaring an element:

- All element type declarations [45] must begin with <!ELEMENT (case sensitive) and end with >.
- Any element used in the markup must be declared in the DTD.
- The type of data for the element must be declared such as #PCDATA.
- Elements need to be sequenced in the DTD as you expect them to be processed.
- Review Chapter 3 on the production rules for logical structure.

How do I handle a DTD for multiple documents?

If you have multiple documents and want to use one DTD, you specify a URL in the document type declaration. The syntax would be similar to the following: <!DOCTYPE memo SYSTEM "http://MySite.com/xml/dtds/memo.ctd">.

Note: The SYSTEM keyword is for private DTDs used by an individual or a group. For general use, the keyword is PUBLIC. See production rule [75] in Appendix C for syntax. The general syntax is as follows: <!DOCTYPE root_name PUBLIC "DTD_name" "DTD_URL">.

What are the two important rules of DTD validation?

The two important rules of a valid DTD are as follows:

■ A valid document must adhere to the DTD specified constraints.

■ The root element must be the one specified in the document type declaration [28] production.

 Note: A valid document does not permit arbitrary tags, while a well-formed document does.

How do I design a memo DTD?

This lengthy tip goes through the design goals. The results are for both a paper and an electronic version of a memo.

Memo Design Step One

In the first step of the design, you list the basic components. The order is not important, but identifying the components is. When one thinks about how to design a memo, one only has to think of the format used in e-mail. The basic components of a memo usually are:

■ Body

■ Carbon copy (cc)

■ Date

■ From

■ Subject

■ To

One could add to this list in a number of ways. In an electronic environment, an intranet or the Internet, one could have components that are perhaps uniquely different from a paper environment.

Memo Design Step Two

In the second design step, you have to consider a formal ordering of the components. One can look at examples of memos or even e-mail and then determine the order that is required for your location. A "standard" memo template has been in use for some time so one should use the expected. You would not put the body component prior to the subject component. Using a markup content model one might do the following:

```
<memo>
<date>...</date>
<to>...</to>
<from>...</from>
<subject>...</subject>
<cc>...</cc>
<body>...</body>
</memo>
```

 Note: At this point, you have seven named elements, one root element and six child elements. The root element is the document type, memo. In addition, you have a logical order defined for a simple memo.

Memo Design Step Three

Next, you add to the order by including the occurrence states and create a content model using the DTD format. The punctuation marks that signify the occurrence status of each element are based on the Extended Backus-Naur Form (EBNF). They are

- None   The element is *required* to be present.
- * (asterisk)   The element is *optional*; if it is present, it occurs as frequently as required.
- + (plus sign)   The element is *required*; it occurs as frequently as required.
- ? (question mark)   The element is *optional*; if it is present, it may occur once.

Based on the punctuation marks you can create a draft DTD with state occurrences. Let us create a draft DTD based on the basic markup, then with the state occurrences.

```
<!DOCTYPE memo [
  <!ELEMENT date>
  <!ELEMENT to>
  <!ELEMENT from>
  <!ELEMENT subject>
  <!ELEMENT cc>
```

```
    <!ELEMENT body>
]>
```

This markup is straightforward—a doctypedecl declaration [28] and six child element declarations [39].

The first reflection on the elements gives that at least date, to, subject, and from elements should be required and only appear once. One might declare the subject as an optional element because some e-mail applications permit an omission of the subject; however, it is not recommended. If you want an optional subject, you would probably use the question mark (?). Thus, no punctuation mark is needed for the four elements.

The cc element needs to be an optional element, but it can have more than one occurrence. The asterisk (*) would be used. When the body element is declared, it should be required that it only appears once. What if a para element had been used instead of body element? With a para element one would define it as required, but with multiple occurrences. This element would use the plus sign (+).

No attributes or other child elements such as "first" or "last" for the name element have been included in the design. With these design points, one might create a DTD, that is, a content model that includes a defined processing order and the occurrence states.

```
<!DOCTYPE memo [
  <!ELEMENT date>
  <!ELEMENT to>
  <!ELEMENT from>
  <!ELEMENT subject?>
  <!ELEMENT cc*>
  <!ELEMENT para+>
]>
```

Here is a fully declared DTD with a logical structure for a document type of memo that uses the above examples:

```
<!DOCTYPE memo [
<!ELEMENT memo (date, to, from, subject?, cc*, para+)>
<!ELEMENT date      (#PCDATA)>
<!ELEMENT to        (#PCDATA)>
<!ELEMENT from      (#PCDATA)>
<!ELEMENT subject   (#PCDATA)>
<!ELEMENT cc        (#PCDATA)>
<!ELEMENT para      (#PCDATA)>
]>
```

The second line declares the document type, the memo's elements, and the order in which they will be parsed. The question mark (?) denotes the subject element is optional and can occur only once. The asterisk (*) says that the cc element is optional, but can only have one occurrence when used. The plus sign (+) denotes there can be one or more para elements. Lines 3-6 declare the elements as ordered in the second line. #PCDATA is XML's notation for plain text. This means that no element's content can include an ampersand (&), a less-than symbol (<), or a greater-than symbol (>). This is because the parser is looking for markup and entities.

The following listing shows the type of comments one might include within the markup:

```
<!- - markup based on memo DTD - ->
<!- - 1. XML declaration. - ->
<!- - Use only if markup conforms to Specification. - ->
<?xml version="1.0"?>
<!- - Must be xml not XML. - ->
<!- - memo is the root element - ->
<!- - Start-tag for memo - ->
<!- - for each start-tag there must be an end-tag - ->
<!- - 2. Date element declaration - ->
<memo><date>3 January 2000</date>
<!- - other option January 1 or 1/01/2001 - ->
<to>Programmers</to>
<!- - could be addressed to each programmer - ->
<!- - 3. From element declaration - ->
<from>John Watson</from>
<!- - 4. Subject element declaration - ->
<subject>Y2K Bug</subject>
<!- - could be omitted because of ? in DTD - ->
<!- - 5. Text element declaration - ->
<para>It went well.</para>
<para>I am glad.<para>
<para>No bonuses.</para>
<para>Prepare for February 29.</para>
<para>Regards</para>
<!- - could have additional text because of + - ->
<!- - end-tag for memo - ->
</memo>
```

Note: The following is a further clarification of the five numbered commented lines:

- Comment-1 is an XML declaration that says this markup is compliant with the XML specification.
- Comment-2 is a date element declaration. Since a specific date type was not defined as an attribute, any type of date is valid. It was defined in the DTD that the date element's content would be #PCDATA, any plain text. A memo database might be developed with a series of <memo>... </memo>.
- Comment-3 is a from element declaration. Any plain text is also valid here. Until you define child elements for this element, such as firstname and lastname, any plain text is valid as this element's content.
- In Comment-4 the subject content could have been omitted because of the question mark (?) used with this element.
- Comment-5, <para> </para>, could be used here in a similar manner to HTML's <p> </p>. The reason for the capability to have multiple para elements is inclusion of the plus sign (+) used in the DTD for this element.

Memo Design Step Four

In step four, you might consider the inclusion of a physical structure. The foundation of the XML physical structure is the entity. There are various entity types, so it is best to use a qualifying adjective such as the following:

- Document
- External
- General
- Parsed
- Unparsed

These entity types are discussed in detail in Chapter 4.

As one considers the various entity types, one quickly concludes that one can use an external entity, declaration [75]. Examples of external entity declarations are as follows:

```
<!ENTITY Memodatabase SYSTEM
"http://www.MySite.com/MemoTemplate/Memo-Template.xml">
<!ENTITY Memodatabase PUBLIC "-//MySite//TEXT Basic descriptive
data.//EN"
<!ENTITY pictures SYSTEM "../graphics/Fired.jpg" NDATA JPG >
```

These types of declarations could be included in the memo DTD, not these examples per se.

How do I design a DTD for a fiction book?

As with the memo DTD you need to go through the design steps to develop markup and DTD content models. This answer looks at the fiction book using novel as the document type. The final output is to the paper format rather than the electronic book or the e-book. XML is being used in the development of some e-book implementations.

The book is, of course, being drafted on a computer rather than being drafted on paper. Why should you even be concerned with XML since you can use any good word processor to create and format a book? You may desire to set up a Web site that includes a link to a section of your book.

Fiction Book Design Step One

First, you should brainstorm a list of the basic components for a novel. Order is not important at this time. Pick up any fiction book and check its components. The basic components of a fiction book might be defined at a minimum as:

- Author
- Book title
- Chapter number
- Paragraph

One can add rapidly to this list. If one looks in more detail at the fiction book one might include:

- Chapter name
- Copyright
- Cover designer
- ISBN
- LC number
- Price
- Publisher information
- Publication date
- Section name
- Section number

You probably can find more fiction book components beyond those in these two lists. At first, one should not expect necessarily to define all the components, but identify the components that require frequent use. Most of the components in the second list are only used once in the creation of a novel. As the author of the book, you probably would not necessarily need many of the components given in the second list.

Fiction Book Design Step Two

The next step is the formal logical ordering of novel components. The parser uses this order as a part of the validation of the document against the grammar defined by the DTD. You should first be concerned with components that as an author you use frequently rather than the "publishing" components such as ISBN. However, as is shown with a database DTD, all the listed components are perhaps on an equal playing field. A first draft of the markup might simply look like the following:

```
<novel>
  <chapter>
    <number>...</number>
    <chaptername>...</chaptername>
    <para>...</para>
    <linebreak/>
  </chapter>
</novel>
```

It appears that the basic logical components of a fiction book may be even less than those of a memo. There is one important difference between the fiction book and the memo as designed here in that there is an empty component. This is not the same as an optional element. The linebreak element is required and has multiple occurrences. One could read linebreak as br.

It was said in an earlier paragraph that the markup "might look as follows." Below is markup that could be used as a template for developing any text document. This markup would not be used in and of itself because it is not meaningful, thus breaking one of the basic design goals of XML:

```
<element0>
  <element1>
    <element2>...</element2>
    <element3>...</element3>
    <element4>...</element4>
    <element5/>
  </element1>
</element0>
```

This markup is in exactly the same form and logical order as the previous markup. There is one root element, four elements, and one empty-element.

The markup has the following:

- Five elements, one root element, and five child elements
- The root element, the document type, is novel or element0
- Defined logical order
- An empty-element

Fiction Book Design Step Three

Next are the inclusion of occurrence states and the creation of a content model in the DTD format. The punctuation marks used to define the occurrence states are discussed earlier in the chapter.

The markup shows a novel DTD without state occurrences and content type declarations:

```
<!DOCTYPE novel [
<!ELEMENT novel (chapter)>
<!ELEMENT chapter (number, chaptername, para, linebreak)>
]>
```

This DTD reads that novel is the document type and there is one element with four child elements. All elements are required, and they appear once. This DTD does not fulfill the requirements for any novel.

Let us consider the necessary occurrence states for this markup.

- Novel is the document type so none is required.
- Chapter is required and has multiple occurrences.
- Number appears once, but can be optional, under a chapter element.
- Chaptername appears once, but can be optional, under a chapter element.
- The para element is required and has multiple appearances under chapter.
- The linebreak element is required and has multiple appearances under chapter.

 Note: One might want a line after the number and chaptername elements. In this case, the linebreak element needs to be declared a child of the novel element rather than a child of the chapter element. To simplify the discussion, the first option is selected rather than the second.

Using the above points, a more meaningful novel DTD could be designed than the one given in the earlier markup. Here are the novel elements with state occurrences:

```
<!DOCTYPE novel [
<!ELEMENT novel (chapter)+>
<!ELEMENT chapter (number, chaptername?, para+, linebreak+)>
]>
```

This DTD says that the novel document type has required multiple chapter elements. A chapter element has one required number element that can appear once and one optional chaptername element that can only appear once. The para and linebreak elements are required and can have multiple occurrences.

However, this DTD is not yet complete. There is at least one more requirement. The content type has to be declared. It appears that the novel only needs parsed character data so #PCDATA is used. The resulting DTD looks as follows:

```
<!DOCTYPE novel [
<!ELEMENT novel (chapter)+>
<!ELEMENT chapter (number, chaptername?, para+, linebreak+)>
<!ELEMENT chapter        (#PCDATA)>
<!ELEMENT number         (#PCDATA)>
<!ELEMENT chaptername    (#PCDATA)>
<!ELEMENT para           (#PCDATA)>
<!ELEMENT linebreak       EMPTY>
]>
```

 Note: The major markup points for this simple DTD are:

- Line 1 declares the document type.
- Line 2 declares the novel will have multiple occurrences of the chapter element.
- Line 3 gives the child elements of the chapter element and the logical order in which they shall be parsed. The question mark (?) denotes the subject element is optional and can occur only once. The plus sign (+) denotes there can be one or more para and linebreak elements.
- Lines 4-8 declare the elements as ordered in line 3.
- Line 9 ends the markup for the novel document type.

- #PCDATA is XML's notation for plain text. This means that no element's content can include an ampersand (&), a less-than symbol (<), or a greater-than symbol (>).
- The linebreak element is declared EMPTY, an empty element. This means in the markup that the linebreak element appears as <linebreak/>.

A brief example of the markup for the above is as follows:

```
<?xml version="1.0"?>
<novel>
<chapter>
<number>1</number>
<chaptername>Nightlife on Mongo</chaptername>
<para>Paragraph 1</para>
<linebreak/>
<para>Paragraph 2</para>
<linebreak/>
...
<para>Last paragraph</para>
</chapter>
<chapter>
<number>2</number>
<chaptername>Flash Hunted on Mongo</chaptername>
<para>Paragraph 1</para>
<linebreak/>
<para>Paragraph 2</para>
<linebreak/>
...
<para>Last paragraph</para>
</chapter>
</novel>
```

You might now create a commented DTD for future references. You might also want to share this DTD with other authors. The commented DTD should be done during the design and development phases so you can determine if there need to be changes or additions.

```
<!- - A DTD for a novel - ->
<!- - Logical structure only - ->
<!- - All capitals for DOCTYPE - ->
<!DOCTYPE novel [
<!- - Need multiple occurrences of chapter - ->
<!ELEMENT novel (chapter)+>
<!- - Other element children of chapter - ->
<!- - number is required once - ->
<!- - chaptername is optional, but can only appear once - ->
```

```
<!- - para is required and has multiple occurrences - ->
<!- - linebreak is required and has multiple occurrences - ->
<!ELEMENT chapter (number, chaptername?, para+, linebreak+)>
<!- - PCDATA for all content - ->
<!ELEMENT chapter      (#PCDATA)>
<!ELEMENT number       (#PCDATA)>
<!ELEMENT chaptername  (#PCDATA)>
<!ELEMENT para         (#PCDATA)>
<!- - linebreak is an empty element to be a break - ->
<!- - between para elements - ->
<!ELEMENT linebreak      EMPTY>
<!- - End of document type declaration - ->
]>
```

The logical components of a completed fiction book have been considered. What about a fiction book that is in draft? Additional things that might be considered are the version levels of each chapter and writing status, that is, draft, edit, and final. These are not components; they are attributes of the chapter element. Let us first look at a possible attribute-list declaration and then the markup:

```
<!DOCTYPE novel [
<!ELEMENT novel (chapter)+>
<!- - Chapter has child elements. - ->
<!ELEMENT chapter (number, chaptername?, para+, linebreak+)>
<!ELEMENT chapter        (#PCDATA)>
<!- - Chapter has attributes. - ->
<!ATTLIST chapter
      version CDATA #REQUIRED
      level (draft | edit | final)>
<!ELEMENT number       (#PCDATA)>
<!ELEMENT chaptername  (#PCDATA)>
<!ELEMENT para         (#PCDATA)>
<!ELEMENT linebreak      EMPTY>
]>
```

The markup for the above DTD might look similar to the following:

```
<?xml version="1.0"?>
<novel>
<chapter>
<!- - Attribute markup - ->
<chapter version="2" level="edit">
<number>1</number>
<chaptername>Nightlife on Mongo</chaptername>
<para>Paragraph 1</para>
<linebreak/>
```

```
<para>Paragraph 2</para>
<linebreak/>
...
<para>Last paragraph</para>
</chapter>
<chapter>
<number>2</number>
<chaptername>Flash Hunted on Mongo</chaptername>
<!- - Attribute markup - ->
<chapter version "1" level="draft">
<para>Paragraph 1</para>
<linebreak/>
<para>Paragraph 2</para>
<linebreak/>
...
<para>Last paragraph</para>
</chapter>
</novel>
```

Fiction Book Design Step Four

You might consider the inclusion of a physical structure. The foundation
of the XML physical structure is the entity. There are various entity
types so it is best to use a qualifying adjective such as one of the
following:

- Document
- External
- General
- Parsed
- Unparsed

 Note: These entity types are discussed in more detail in
Chapter 4 on the XML physical structure.

I know in my book that I have a hero, Flash; a bad guy, the malcontent
and malignant Emperor; and a battle location, the planet Mongo. (If my
book sounds like another book or two, it is.) If you did not want to
write "Flash," "malcontent and malignant Emperor," or "Mongo" every
time they appear in the book, you would want some shortcuts. An XML
shortcut is an entity declaration. For these three shortcuts, you could
have the following:

```
<!ENTITY MME "malcontent and malignant Emperor">
<!ENTITY F "Flash">
<!ENTITY M "Mongo">
```

Within the markup, you would use these declarations as follows:

```
<?xml version="1.0"?>
<novel>
<chapter>
<number>1</number>
<chaptername>Nightlife on &M;</chaptername>
<para>The &MME; contemplated the death of &F;. And more thoughts
....</para>
<linebreak/>
<para>&F; was not ready to die;. So &F; decided to ....</para>
<linebreak/>

...
<para>&F; did flee. He did....</para>
</chapter>
<chapter>
<number>2</number>
<chaptername>&F; Hunted on &M;</chaptername>
<para>&F; thought it would be a good idea to leave &M;, so he ....</para>
<linebreak/>
<para>However the &MME; knew that &F; had fled to ....</para>
<linebreak/>

...
<para>&F; was more clever than the &MME;. He ....</para>
</chapter>
</novel>
```

The markup is the expanded version of the above listing:

```
<?xml version="1.0"?>
<novel>
<chapter>
<number>1</number>
<chaptername>Nightlife on Mongo</chaptername>
<para>The malcontent and malignant Emperor contemplated the death of
Flash. And more thoughts ....</para>
<linebreak/>
<para>Flash was not ready to die;. So Flash decided to ....</para>
<linebreak/>

...
<para>Flash did flee. He did....</para>
</chapter>
<chapter>
<number>2</number>
<chaptername>Flash Hunted on Mongo</chaptername>
<para>Flash thought it would be a good idea to leave Mongo, so he
....</para>
<linebreak/>
```

```
<para>However the malcontent and malignant Emperor knew that Flash had
fled to ....</para>
<linebreak/>
...
<para>Flash was more clever than the malcontent and malignant Emperor. He
....</para>
</chapter>
</novel>
```

There is another advantage to using this type of entity declaration. If you had decided you really wanted to say "malignant and malcontent Emperor," you would have to change every instance of this phrase if you had not used the entity declaration. However, since you did use the entity declaration, you only make one change to <!ENTITY MME " malignant and malcontent Emperor">.

 Note: One of the options in Microsoft Word is to view a document as a master. You emulate this option with XML by doing an entity declaration such as the following: <!ENTITY ch1 SYSTEM '../MyNovel/chapter1.xml">.

By doing a series of this type of entity declaration, one could "call" all the chapters in one DTD.

How do I create a technical book DTD?

As with the memo and fiction book scenarios you need to go through the design steps to develop markup and DTD content models. Each scenario requires a different level of design focus. The memo DTD looked at the XML logical structure. The fiction book showed highlights of the XML logical structure and the XML physical structure. This answer focuses on the differences between a fiction book and a technical book up to the point of adding styles, which may be the major difference in the DTD and markup.

Neither XML extensions nor graphics handling are discussed in this answer because each publishing house has its own rules for governing graphics. There are exciting potentials for using the concepts as outlined by the SVG and VML specifications. These specifications are discussed in Chapters 12 and 13.

When using XML a major difference between creating a fiction book and creating a technical book is a more active use of styles. One can go beyond just bold and italic. There are font sizes for headers. There are multiple types of listings. Thus, this concept is covered in Chapter 8 in a question about the potentials of XSL.

The result for this design is for a paper technical book to be in a printed form. However, as is true with the fiction book DTD and markup, the book is developed in an electronic environment, the computer.

Technical Book Design Step One

Step one of the design is to brainstorm a list of the basic components for a technical book. Order is not important at this time. Get a technical book off your bookshelf. The basic components of a technical book may be defined as:

■ Title
■ Author
■ Chapter (number and name)
■ Paragraph
■ Figure information (number, and caption)
■ Table information (number, column name, item)
■ Header (1 to 5 levels)
■ List (ordered, unordered, and numbered)
■ Box information (note, caution, warning, and tip)
■ Markup (one line or multiple lines)

 Note: This list is based on a publisher's template for this type of book. The list is not comprehensive even to the template.

The list below is similar to the one for the fiction book. Most of these components are only used once. A couple of these components might be included in your book content model.

■ Publication date
■ Footnote
■ Copyright
■ Introduction
■ Dedication
■ Part number
■ Part name
■ ISBN
■ Publisher information
■ Cover designer

- Price
- LC number

Even with these two lists, one can find more technical book components. The point is at first that one should not expect to define all the components, but identify the components required frequently for authoring.

Technical Book Design Step Two

This step is the formal logical ordering of the technical book components. The parser uses this order as a part of the validation of the document against the grammar defined by the DTD. In this DTD, we want to consider both the "publishing" attributes, such as book title, and the components used frequently in developing the draft, such as a paragraph element. A first draft of the markup might simply look like the following:

```
<book>
<front>
<title>...</title>
<author>...</author>
<date>...</date>
<publisherinfo>
<name>...</name>
<location>...</location>
</publisherinfo>
<dedication>...</dedication>
</acknowledgment>...</acknowledgment>
<misc>
<copyright>...</copyright>
<editor>...</editor>
<ISBN>...</ISBN>
<LCNumber>...</LCNumber>
<price>...</price>
<coverdesigner>...</coverdesigner>
</misc>
<summary>...</summary>
</front>
<chapter>
<number>...</number>
<chaptername>...</chaptername>
<header1>...</header1>
<header2>...</header2>
<header3>...</header3>
<figure>
```

```
<figno>...</figno>
<figcap>...</figcap>
</figure>
<list>...</list>
<box>
<note>...</note>
<caution>...</caution>
<warning>...</warning>
<tip>...</tip>
</box>
<table>
<tablenumber>...</tablenumber>
<columnname>...</columnname>
<item>...</item>
</table>
<markup>
<c1>...</c1>
<c2>...</c2>
</markup>
<para>...</para>
<linebreak/>
</chapter>
</book>
```

This markup is divided into two major elements, front and chapter. The front element could be used easily in association with a Web page. For example, a publishing house or an author with many books could create a common template for book information. The chapter element is the logical structure to be used as the author. The front element, of course, will be given an optional occurrence that can only appear once.

There is clearly one empty element. This not an optional element. In fact, this element has multiple occurrences. It is the linebreak element. You can read it as the <br> tag of HTML.

This markup is significantly more complex than the fiction book markup. However, there is still only one root element, book. The book element has two child elements, front and chapter. Some of the child elements of the front and chapter elements also have child elements. This scenario markup does show an important difference between XML and HTML; in XML one can create nests, rather than being limited as in HTML.

Technical Book Design Step Three

The inclusion of occurrence states and the creation of a content model in the DTD format are the next design steps. The punctuation marks used to define the occurrence states were discussed earlier in this chapter.

The following DTD is without state occurrences and content type declarations:

```
<!DOCTYPE book [
<!ELEMENT book (front, chapter)>
<!ELEMENT front (title, author, date, pub isherinfo, dedication,
acknowledgment, misc, summary)>
<!ELEMENT chapter (number, chaptername, header1, header2, header3,
figure, list, box, table, markup, para, linebreak)>
<!ELEMENT front>
<!ELEMENT title>
<!ELEMENT author>
<!ELEMENT date>
<!ELEMENT publisherinfo (name, location)>
<!ELEMENT publisherinfo>
<!ELEMENT name>
<!ELEMENT location>
<!ELEMENT dedication>
<!ELEMENT acknowledgment>
<!ELEMENT misc (copyright, editor, ISBN, LCNumber, price, coverdesigner)>
<!ELEMENT misc>
<!ELEMENT copyright>
<!ELEMENT editor>
<!ELEMENT ISBN>
<!ELEMENT LCNumber>
<!ELEMENT price>
<!ELEMENT coverdesigner>
<!ELEMENT summary>
<!ELEMENT chapter>
<!ELEMENT number>
<!ELEMENT chaptername>
<!ELEMENT header1>
<!ELEMENT header2>
<!ELEMENT header3>
<!ELEMENT figure (figno, figcap)>
<!ELEMENT figure>
<!ELEMENT figno>
<!ELEMENT figcap>
<!ELEMENT list>
<!ELEMENT box (note, caution, warning, tip)>
<!ELEMENT box>
```

```
<!ELEMENT note>
<!ELEMENT caution>
<!ELEMENT warning>
<!ELEMENT tip>
<!ELEMENT table (tablenumber, columnname, item)>
<!ELEMENT table>
<!ELEMENT tablenumber>
<!ELEMENT columnname>
<!ELEMENT item>
<!ELEMENT markup (c1, c2)>
<!ELEMENT markup>
<!ELEMENT c1>
<!ELEMENT c2>
<!ELEMENT para>
<!ELEMENT linebreak>
]>
```

 Note: This DTD reads that:

- Book is the document type or root element.
- There are two first-level elements, front and chapter.
- The front element has eight child elements.
- The chapter element has 12 child elements.
- The publisherinfo element has two child elements.
- The misc element has six child elements.
- The figure element has two child elements.
- The box element has four child elements.
- The table element has three child elements.
- The markup element has two child elements.
- There are 42 elements in this basic book DTD.
- All the elements are required.

The list is the basic design for the book document type and does not include attributes, entities, or any XML extension declarations. While this DTD seems to be comprehensive, one can probably easily add more elements.

The occurrence states for the markup have to be considered also. Here is the reasoning for the selection of occurrence states for this DTD:

- Book is the document type so none is required.
- The front element is optional and only can appear once.
- The chapter element is required and should have multiple occurrences.

- All the child elements of the front element are required and can occur only once.
- All third-level child elements of the front element are optional and can only occur once.
- The number and chaptername elements are optional, but can only occur once if used.
- The header1, header2, and header3 elements are optional and can occur as frequently as needed.
- The figure element is optional and can occur as frequently as needed. However, when the figure element appears, the figno and figcap elements are required and can only appear once.
- The list element is optional and can occur as frequently as needed.
- The box element is optional and can occur as frequently as needed. Any child element can occur only once within a box element.
- The table element is optional and can occur as frequently as needed. However, when the table element appears, the tablenumber element is required and can only appear once. However, the columnname and item elements are required and can occur as frequently as required.
- The markup element is optional with multiple occurrences and either of its child elements can occur once within a markup element.
- The para element is required and can have multiple occurrences.
- The linebreak element is an empty element, is required, and can have multiple occurrences.

With the above occurrence definitions, one might develop a content model within a DTD format. The occurrence state punctuation marks were discussed earlier in this chapter.

```
<!DOCTYPE book [
<!ELEMENT book (front?, chapter+)>
<!ELEMENT front (title, author, date, publisherinfo, dedication,
acknowledgment, misc, summary)>
<!ELEMENT chapter (number?, chaptername?, header1*, header2*,
header3*, figure*, list*, box*, table*, markup*, para+, linebreak+)>
<!ELEMENT front>
<!ELEMENT title>
<!ELEMENT author>
<!ELEMENT date>
<!ELEMENT publisherinfo (name, location)?>
<!ELEMENT publisherinfo>
<!ELEMENT name>
<!ELEMENT location>
<!ELEMENT dedication>
<!ELEMENT acknowledgment>
```

```
<!ELEMENT misc (copyright, editor, ISBN, LCNumber, price,
coverdesigner)?>
<!ELEMENT misc>
<!ELEMENT copyright>
<!ELEMENT editor>
<!ELEMENT ISBN>
<!ELEMENT LCNumber>
<!ELEMENT price>
<!ELEMENT coverdesigner>
<!ELEMENT summary>
<!ELEMENT chapter>
<!ELEMENT number>
<!ELEMENT chaptername>
<!ELEMENT header1>
<!ELEMENT header2>
<!ELEMENT header3>
<!ELEMENT figure (figno, figcap)>
<!ELEMENT figure>
<!ELEMENT figno>
<!ELEMENT figcap>
<!ELEMENT list>
<!ELEMENT box (note | caution | warning | tip)>
<!ELEMENT box>
<!ELEMENT note>
<!ELEMENT caution>
<!ELEMENT warning>
<!ELEMENT tip>
<!ELEMENT table (tablenumber, columnname+, item+)>
<!ELEMENT table>
<!ELEMENT tablenumber>
<!ELEMENT columnname>
<!ELEMENT item>
<!ELEMENT markup (c1 | c2)>
<!ELEMENT markup>
<!ELEMENT c1>
<!ELEMENT c2>
<!ELEMENT para>
<!ELEMENT linebreak>
]>
```

This DTD requires one more step to be a completed content model, content type definition. It seems that a book document type needs only #PCDATA, parsed character data. The one exception is the linebreak element that has to be declared an empty element.

```
<!- - Line 1 - ->
<!DOCTYPE book [
<!- - Line 2 - ->
<!ELEMENT book (front?, chapter+)>
<!- - Line 3 - ->
<!ELEMENT front (title, author, date, publisherinfo, dedication,
acknowledgment, misc, summary)>
<!- - Line 4 - ->
<!ELEMENT chapter (number?, chaptername?, header1*, header2*,
header3*, figure*, list*, box*, table*, markup*, para+, linebreak+)>
<!- -Line 5 - ->
<!ELEMENT front              (#PCDATA)>
<!ELEMENT title              (#PCDATA)>
<!ELEMENT author             (#PCDATA)>
<!ELEMENT date               (#PCDATA)>
<!ELEMENT publisherinfo (name, location)?>
<!ELEMENT publisherinfo      (#PCDATA)>
<!ELEMENT name               (#PCDATA)>
<!ELEMENT location           (#PCDATA)>
<!ELEMENT dedication         (#PCDATA)>
<!ELEMENT acknowledgment     (#PCDATA)>
<!ELEMENT misc (copyright, editor, ISBN, LCNumber, price,
coverdesigner)?>
<!ELEMENT misc               (#PCDATA)>
<!ELEMENT copyright          (#PCDATA)>
<!ELEMENT editor             (#PCDATA)>
<!ELEMENT ISBN               (#PCDATA)>
<!ELEMENT LCNumber           (#PCDATA)>
<!ELEMENT price              (#PCDATA)>
<!ELEMENT coverdesigner      (#PCDATA)>
<!ELEMENT summary            (#PCDATA)>
<!- - Line 24 - ->
<!ELEMENT chapter            (#PCDATA)>
<!ELEMENT number             (#PCDATA)>
<!ELEMENT chaptername        (#PCDATA)>
<!ELEMENT header1            (#PCDATA)>
<!ELEMENT header2            (#PCDATA)>
<!ELEMENT header3            (#PCDATA)>
<!ELEMENT figure (figno, figcap)>
<!ELEMENT figure             (#PCDATA)>
<!ELEMENT figno              (#PCDATA)>
<!ELEMENT figcap             (#PCDATA)>
<!ELEMENT list               (#PCDATA)>
<!ELEMENT box (note | caution | warning | tip)>
<!ELEMENT box                (#PCDATA)>
<!ELEMENT note               (#PCDATA)>
<!ELEMENT caution            (#PCDATA)>
```

```
<!ELEMENT warning          (#PCDATA)>
<!ELEMENT tip              (#PCDATA)>
<!ELEMENT table (tablenumber, columnname+, item+)>
<!ELEMENT table            (#PCDATA)>
<!ELEMENT tablenumber      (#PCDATA)>
<!ELEMENT columnname       (#PCDATA)>
<!ELEMENT item             (#PCDATA)>
<!ELEMENT markup (c1 | c2)>
<!ELEMENT markup           (#PCDATA)>
<!ELEMENT c1               (#PCDATA)>
<!ELEMENT c2               (#PCDATA)>
<!ELEMENT para             (#PCDATA)>
<!ELEMENT linebreak          EMPTY>
]>
```

 Note: The extended clarifications of the numbered lines in the DTD are as follows:

- Line 1 declares the root element or document type to be the book element.
- Line 2 declares that the book element has two child elements, front and chapter.
- Line 3 declares the logical structure of the front element.
- Line 4 does the same for the chapter element.
- Lines 5-23 declare the content types for the front elements.
- Lines 24 through the end do the same for the chapter elements.
- All the elements in this particular DTD, except the linebreak element, are declared to have the content type #PCDATA. #PCDATA is XML notation for plain text. This means that no element's content can include an ampersand (&), a less-than symbol (<), or a greater-than symbol (>).
- The linebreak element is declared EMPTY, an empty element. This means in the markup that the linebreak element appears as <linebreak/>.

An example using some of the markup for the above is as follows:

```
<?xml version="1.0"?>
<book>
<front>
<title>Learn XML Tips</title>
<author>George M. Doss</author>
<date>2000</date>
<publisherinfo>
```

```
<name>Wordware</name>
<location>Plano, TX</location>
</publisherinfo>
<dedication>My best friend</dedication>
</acknowledgment>...</acknowledgment>
<misc>
<copyright>...</copyright>
<editor>...</editor>
<ISBN>1-123-12345-1</ISBN>
<LCNumber>...</LCNumber>
<price>...</price>
<coverdesigner>...</coverdesigner>
</misc>
<summary>Markup-intensive reference</summary>
</front>
<chapter>
<number>1</number>
<chaptername>Opening Thoughts</chaptername>
<header1>Thought 1</header1>
<para>Opening paragraph</para>
<linebreak/>
<para>Middle paragraph</para>
<linebreak/>
<para>Closing paragraph</para>
<header1>Thought 2</header1>
<para>Paragraph 1</para>
<linebreak/>
<para>Paragraph 2</para>
<linebreak/>
<header2>Thought 2A</header2>
<para>Only paragraph</para>
<header3>Thought 2B</header3>
<para>Paragraph A</para>
<linebreak/>
<figure>
<figno>1.1</figno>
<figcap>Visual of Thought 2B</figcap>
</figure>
<para>Paragraph B</para>
<linebreak/>
<box>
<note>This is an example note</note>
</box>
<para>Paragraph 3</para>
</chapter>
</book>
```

Note: It is recommended that you comment your DTD for future reference. The commented DTD should be done during the design and development phases so you can determine if any area needs to be enhanced.

The following is one way the above DTD might be commented:

```
<!- - A DTD for a technical book - ->
<!- - Logical structure only - ->
<!DOCTYPE book [
<!- - Has two child elements, optional front matter - ->
<!- - Chapter is required with multiple occurrences. - ->
<!ELEMENT book (front?, chapter+)>
<!- - Child elements for the front element - ->
<!ELEMENT front (title, author, date, publisherinfo, dedication,
acknowledgment, misc, summary)>
<!- - Child elements for the chapter element- ->
<!- - number and chaptername optional, one occurrence - ->
<!- - header elements optional, multiple occurrences - ->
<!- - figure, element optional, multiple occurrences - ->
<!- - list, element optional, multiple occurrences - ->
<!- - box, element optional, multiple occurrences - ->
<!- - box element has multiple choice elements - ->
<!- - table element optional, multiple occurrences - ->
<!- - markup, element optional, multiple occurrences - ->
<!- - para, element required, multiple occurrences - ->
<!- - linebreak, element empty, required, multiple occurrences - ->
<!ELEMENT chapter (number?, chaptername?, header1*, header2*,
header3*, figure*, list*, box*, table*, markup*, para+, linebreak+)>
<!- -Content type declarations for front elements- ->
<!ELEMENT front            (#PCDATA)>
<!ELEMENT title            (#PCDATA)>
<!ELEMENT author           (#PCDATA)>
<!ELEMENT date             (#PCDATA)>
<!ELEMENT publisherinfo (name, location)?>
<!ELEMENT publisherinfo    (#PCDATA)>
<!ELEMENT name             (#PCDATA)>
<!ELEMENT location         (#PCDATA)>
<!ELEMENT dedication       (#PCDATA)>
<!ELEMENT acknowledgment   (#PCDATA)>
<!ELEMENT misc (copyright, editor, ISBN, LCNumber, price,
coverdesigner)?>
<!ELEMENT misc             (#PCDATA)>
<!ELEMENT copyright        (#PCDATA)>
<!ELEMENT editor           (#PCDATA)>
<!ELEMENT ISBN             (#PCDATA)>
<!ELEMENT LCNumber         (#PCDATA)>
```

```
<!ELEMENT price              (#PCDATA)>
<!ELEMENT coverdesigner      (#PCDATA)>
<!ELEMENT summary            (#PCDATA)>
<!- - Content type declarations for chapter elements - ->
<!ELEMENT chapter            (#PCDATA)>
<!ELEMENT number             (#PCDATA)>
<!ELEMENT chaptername        (#PCDATA)>
<!ELEMENT header1            (#PCDATA)>
<!ELEMENT header2            (#PCDATA)>
<!ELEMENT header3            (#PCDATA)>
<!ELEMENT figure (figno, figcap)>
<!ELEMENT figure             (#PCDATA)>
<!ELEMENT figno              (#PCDATA)>
<!ELEMENT figcap             (#PCDATA)>
<!ELEMENT list               (#PCDATA)>
<!- - Optional elements for box - ->
<!ELEMENT box (note | caution | warning | tip)>
<!ELEMENT box                (#PCDATA)>
<!ELEMENT note               (#PCDATA)>
<!ELEMENT caution            (#PCDATA)>
<!ELEMENT warning            (#PCDATA)>
<!ELEMENT tip                (#PCDATA)>
<!ELEMENT table (tablenumber, columnname+, item+)>
<!ELEMENT table              (#PCDATA)>
<!ELEMENT tablenumber        (#PCDATA)>
<!ELEMENT columnname         (#PCDATA)>
<!ELEMENT item               (#PCDATA)>
<!ELEMENT markup (c1 | c2)>
<!ELEMENT markup             (#PCDATA)>
<!ELEMENT c1                 (#PCDATA)>
<!ELEMENT c2                 (#PCDATA)>
<!ELEMENT para               (#PCDATA)>
<!- - Linebreak element is like break, must be empty - ->
<!ELEMENT linebreak      EMPTY>
<!- - End of document type declaration
]>
```

The logical components of a completed book have been considered. What about a book that is in draft? There are additional things that might be considered in this case, such as the version levels of each chapter and writing status, that is, draft, edit, and final. These are not components; they are attributes of the chapter element.

The next two steps look at a possible attribute-list declaration and then the markup. This is a highly abbreviated version of the book DTD and markup presented up to this point.

```
<!DOCTYPE book [
<!ELEMENT book (chapter)+>
<!- - Chapter has child elements. - ->
<!ELEMENT chapter (number, chaptername?, para+, linebreak+)>
<!ELEMENT chapter          (#PCDATA)>
<!- - Chapter has attributes. - ->
<!ATTLIST chapter
        version CDATA #REQUIRED
        level (draft | edit | final)>
<!ELEMENT number          (#PCDATA)>
<!ELEMENT chaptername     (#PCDATA)>
<!ELEMENT para            (#PCDATA)>
<!ELEMENT linebreak          EMPTY>
]>

<?xml version="1.0"?>
<book>
<chapter>
<!- - Attribute markup - ->
<chapter version="2" level="edit">
<number>1</number>
<chaptername>Opening Thoughts</chaptername>
<para>Paragraph 1</para>
<linebreak/>
<para>Paragraph 2</para>
<linebreak/>
...
<para>Last paragraph</para>
</chapter>
<chapter>
<number>2</number>
<chaptername>Secondary Thoughts</chaptername>
<!- - Attribute markup - ->
<chapter version "1" level="draft">
<para>Paragraph 1</para>
<linebreak/>
<para>Paragraph 2</para>
<linebreak/>
...
<para>Last paragraph</para>
</chapter>
</book>
```

Technical Book Design Step Four

At this point, you might consider the inclusion of a physical structure. The foundation of the XML physical structure is the entity. There are various entity types, so it is best to use a qualifying adjective such as the following:

- Document
- External
- General
- Parsed
- Unparsed

These entity types are discussed in more detail in Chapter 4 on the XML physical structure.

In this technical book, you know that you are going to use a number of words or phrases frequently. You'll want some shortcuts for these words. An XML shortcut is an entity declaration. The following are example shortcuts:

```
<!ENTITY D "declaration">
<!ENTITY PS "physical structure">
<!ENTITY LS "logical structure">
```

The following two markups show the use of the entities within markup and what the markup would look like if expanded.

This is an example of entities with markup:

```
<?xml version="1.0"?>
<book>
<chapter>
<number>1</number>
<chaptername>&LS;</chaptername>
<para>The essential concept of XML &LS; is an element. This is ....<para>
<linebreak/>
<para>One can do an XML document with only a &LS;.</para>
<linebreak/>
...
<para> The &LS; has a number of &D;s. </para>
</chapter>
<chapter>
<number>2</number>
<chaptername>&PS;</chaptername>
<para>The &PS; can be thought of as containers or entities.</para>
<linebreak/>
<para>A document with only &D;s from the &PS; would be a pointer to
...</para>
<linebreak/>
...
<para The &PS; also has a number of &D;s.</para>
```

```
</chapter>
</book>
```

This is the expanded version of the above markup:

```
<?xml version="1.0"?>
<book>
<chapter>
<number>1</number>
<chaptername>logical structure</chaptername>
<para>The essential concept of XML logical structure is an element. This is
....<para>
<linebreak/>
<para>One can do an XML document with only a logical structure.</para>
<linebreak/>
...
<para> The logical structure has a number of declarations. </para>
</chapter>
<chapter>
<number>2</number>
<chaptername>physical structure</chaptername>
<para>The physical structure can be thought of as containers or
entities.</para>
<linebreak/>
<para>A document with only declarations from the physical structure would be
a pointer to ...</para>
<linebreak/>
...
<para The physical structure also has a number of declarations.</para>
</chapter>
</book>
```

 Note: There are two significant results of this type of markup. First, both of the entities &LS; and &PS; produce lowercase words so that would have to be changed in both of the chaptername elements. This situation might happen frequently. You could have &LS; for Logical Structure and &ls; for logical structure, etc. Second, you are able to have a plural declaration by stating &D;s without a space.

There is another advantage to using this type of entity declaration. If you really want to use a production rule rather than a declaration, you would have to change every location if you had not used the entity declaration. However, since you did use the entity declaration you only just make one change to <!ENTITY D " production rule">.

Note: One of the options in Microsoft Word is to view a document as a master. You emulate this option with XML by doing entity declaration such as the following: <!ENTITY ch1 SYSTEM "../MyBook/chapter1.xml">.

By doing a series of this type of entity declaration, one could "call" all the chapters in one DTD.

How do I design a DTD for a database?

This very lengthy answer looks at building an XML application for a large music collection. The basic process or design path is first markup, then the DTD (document type definition or your own personal XML grammar rules) and entities (external data sources). Presentation (stylesheets), links to other documents (XLink), links to specific locations within documents (XPointer), and the use of multiple XML documents (namespaces) are considered in Chapters 8 through 11. This task is similar to building a house room by room. At each stage, the DTD has to be enhanced to reflect the design changes to the grammar.

The difference between this answer and the answers given in prior questions above is that you have to think of an XML document as a database with records and fields rather than as documentation-type components. In addition, you have to think of a container as a file or set of files in a folder.

The problem is how to quickly design, develop, and implement a collection of more than 2,200 musical CDs that cover various areas such as:

- Classical
- Folk
- Soundtracks
- New Age
- Other

Also, there are many recording companies, but at least 15 major ones need to be identified including:

- BIS
- Chandos
- DG
- London
- Naxos
- Windham

The minimum fields of data of interest are:

- Record CD ID
- Composer data
- Title (CD and pieces on CD)
- Opus
- Conductor data
- Orchestra
- Artists
- Recording company
- Catalog number
- Year of performance
- Date of acquisition
- Price
- Musical category
- Time (CD and tracks)
- Live or studio

As this DTD and markup are developed, you should expect that there will be additional fields and attributes. It seems one can gather plenty of information about a single musical CD.

The essential components of the application might include:

- Logical structure (elements and attributes)
- Physical structure (entities)
- Presentation (stylesheets)
- Ability to get from one document to another (XLink)
- Ability to get within a specific location of a document (XPointer)
- Ability to manipulate multiple documents without conflict of element and attribute names (Namespaces)
- Ability to add vector graphics, such as background, on a Web page (VML and SVG)

The above lists assist in the first step in the development of an XML application. You need to make a note of the fundamental data structure and the basic functions of the application.

 Note: Only the first two bulleted items are discussed in this answer. The other bulleted items are discussed in Chapters 8 through 13.

Database Design Step One – Content Model

This is the precise technical definition from the XML specification of markup, "A markup declaration is an element type declaration, an attribute-list declaration, an entity declaration, or a notation declaration." These are production rules [39], [52], [70], and [82] and their associated productions. See Appendix C for the syntax of these productions.

It must be recognized that, in reality, a person may use markup in a broader sense to cover any XML usage. At this point, you should only be concerned with the element type and the fields in the database, CD-Library. We are also concerned with the record, CD, which contains these fields.

Before developing a content model that describes the structure of a valid document, you first need to indicate if your markup is XML specification 1.0 compliant. You do this with the XML declaration [23] <?xml version="1.0"?>.

This declaration will be discussed again for two reasons: for an encoding declaration [30] and for a standalone document declaration [32]. At this point, you want to stay with the fundamentals.

Next, you need to declare a document (database) type declaration [28]. The simplest document type declaration is Name is CD-Library:

```
<!DOCTYPE CD-Library [
...
]>
```

There will be more information that needs to be added to this declaration as you progress. CD-Library is declared the root element, that is, everything must come in between its declaration and its close. Next, you want to establish the content that goes in between the beginning and ending of this declaration. The next step is to declare the "record," CD. You use an element declaration [39]:

```
<CD>
...
</CD>
```

 Note: In between the CD element start- and end-tags go the fields that are just other XML elements. They are children of the CD element.

The content model below is a template for establishing a potential logical order (structure) for processing your markup with a parser. It does not show nesting, whether an element is mandatory or optional, occurrence status of an element (remember the plus sign (+) and the question mark (?), or that some of the elements may be included another element. It does give a "feel" and sense for the fundamentals of the structure. It is similar to a house line drawing. A more detailed content model is established in the DTD. Taking the list given above, here is a first effort at a CD-Library database (XML document):

```
<CD-Library>
<CDID></CDID>
<Composer></Composer>
<Title></Title>
<Opus></Opus>
<Conductor></Conductor>
<Orchestra></Orchestra>
<Artist></Artist>
<Label></Label>
<CatalogNumber></CatalogNumber>
<PFYear></PFYear>
<AcquisitionDate></AcquisitionDate>
<Price></Price>
<Category></Category>
<Time></Time>
<Audience></Audience>
</CD-Library>
```

Next, merge the four efforts into one and you have a well-formed CD-Library XML document (database structure), but with no content. The following is the CD-Library XML document:

```
<?xml version="1.0"?>
< CD-Library >
<CD>
<CDID></CDID>
<Composer></Composer>
<Title></Title>
<Opus></Opus>
<Conductor></Conductor>
<Orchestra></Orchestra>
<Artist></Artist>
<Label></Label>
<CatalogNumber></CatalogNumber>
<PFYear></PFYear>
<AcquisitionDate></AcquisitionDate>
<Price></Price>
```

```
<Category></Category>
<Time></Time>
<Audience></Audience>
</CD>
</CD-Library
]>
```

You can now put some content in this document:

```
<?xml version="1.0"?>
<CD-Library >
<CD>
<CDID>2000A</CDID>
<Composer>Zoltán Kodály</Composer>
<Title>Dances of Galánta</Title>
<Opus></Opus>
<Conductor>Gabriel Koncer</Conductor>
<Orchestra>Czecho-Slovak Radio Symp.></Orchestra>
<Artist></Artist>
<Label>Naxos</Label>
<CatalogNumber>8.550520</CatalogNumber>
<PFYear>1987</PFYear>
<AcquisitionDate>99-12-30</AcquisitionDate>
<Price>6.48</Price>
<Category>Classical</Category>
<Time>56:07</Time>
<Audience>Studio</Audience>
</CD>
</CD-Library>
```

This is a very basic XML document. This is the goal of XML: design a document quickly with meaningful markup. Most of this markup is human-legible (PFYear is performance year), but perhaps it can be interpreted in various ways. However, in the context of the example you probably would enter approximately the same content. Notice my use of the word "approximately" instead of "exactly." The ultimate objective is to get to a point that has mutual agreement on the content. This is the reason for a commented DTD.

For example, you would wonder about what the AcquisitionDate element is if you had not read the earlier list. One might wonder what content goes in the markup such as the Audience element. You might put "yes" or "no" as content. Is there an easy way to clear up confusion without going to the next step of creating a DTD? There is an obvious solution: add comments. Let us look at some possible comments that could be used to assist in entering content:

```
<!- - markup complies with XML specification 1.0 - ->
<?xml version="1.0"?>
<!- - start of document - ->
<CD-Library >
<!- - start of record  - ->
<CD>
<!- - ID in the form of nnnnL    - ->
<!- - Letter A represents multiple - ->
<!- - compositions rather than tracks - ->
<CDID>2000A</CDID>
<!- - first name and last name - ->
<!- - if unknown use anonymous - ->
<!- - if multiple use various - ->
<Composer>Zoltán Kodály</Composer>
<!- -  CD Title or first composition - ->
<Title>Dances of Galánta</Title>
<!- - optional - ->
<!— use recognized forms - ->
<Opus></Opus>
<!- - first name and last name - ->
<Conductor>Gabriel Koncer</Conductor>
<!- -  orchestra name, group name  - ->
<Orchestra>Czecho-Slovak Radio Symp.></Orchestra>
<!- - prime Artist - ->
<Artist></Artist>
<!- - recording company, not distributor - ->
<Label>Naxos</Label>
<!- - prime Label number - ->
<CatalogNumber>8.550520</CatalogNumber>
<!- - yyyy  - ->
<PFYear>1987</PFYear>
<!- - yy-mm-dd - ->
<AcquisitionDate>99-12-30</AcquisitionDate>
<!- -  dd.cc - ->
<Price>6.48</Price>
<!- - folk, new age, classical, other - ->
<Category>Other</Category>
<!- - mm:ss - ->
<Time>56:07</Time>
<!- - either studio or live - ->
<Audience>Studio</Audience>
<!- - end of record - ->
</CD>
<!- - end of document - ->
</CD-Library>
```

Note: With comments similar to those in this markup, you should be able to enter almost the same content. It is recognized, for example, that only I know the exact acquisition date and the price I paid. The form of the date might be different for you. The date format used in this case is for ease of sorting. However, that is not the issue. You can use this straightforward template to create your own XML musical CD database that will produce well-formed documents. If you only have a jazz collection you would omit the Opus element and perhaps add a major instrument element.

Database Design Step Two – Valid Document

In addition to having a well-formed document, you want a valid document. To have a valid document you need an implied or explicit DTD. An explicit DTD is needed here so a validating parser can verify this document is valid.

The first content model did not show nesting. It did show whether an element is mandatory or optional and the occurrence status of an element (remember the plus sign (+) and the question mark (?)). It also did not show that some of the elements, children of the CD element, might include other elements. The content model below (second stage) is a template for establishing the logical order (structure) for processing your XML with a parser. Logical order means here that the CDID element cannot appear after the Composer element. It does give the basic grammar for developing the CD-Library document type.

A dictionary definition of grammar is "the rules implicit in a language." There are the production rules of the XML specification that are used to declare the grammar for your XML document, usually referred to as the syntax (only a branch of grammar). There is also the DTD that establishes the grammar for a given document. In this case, the grammar for the document type, CD-Library, is being established.

It is like adding sizing to your desired house line drawing. This DTD gives detail to the content model. Using the content model given above, here is a second effort at the CD-Library database (XML document) using only one element declaration:

```
<!DOCUMENT TYPE CD-Library [
<!ELEMENT CD (CDID, Composer+, Title, Opus*, Conductor+, Orchestra+,
Artist*, Label, CatalogNumber, PFYear+, AcquisitionDate, Price?, Category+,
```

```
  Time, Audience)>
]>
```

Since line breaks and spacing are not significant in parsing, perhaps this model can be laid out where it is even more readable:

```
<!DOCUMENT TYPE CD-Library [
<!ELEMENT CD
(CDID,
Composer+,
Title,
Opus*,
Conductor+,
Orchestra+,
Artist*,
Label,
CatalogNumber,
PFYear+,
AcquisitionDate,
Price?,
Category+,
Time,
Audience)>
<!ELEMENT CDID              (#PCDATA)>
<!ELEMENT Composer         (#PCDATA)>
<!ELEMENT Title            (#PCDATA)>
<!ELEMENT Opus             (#PCDATA)>
<!ELEMENT Conductor        (#PCDATA)>
<!ELEMENT Orchestra        (#PCDATA)>
<!ELEMENT Artist           (#PCDATA)>
<!ELEMENT Label            (#PCDATA)>
<!ELEMENT CatalogNumber    (#PCDATA)>
<!ELEMENT PFYear           (#PCDATA)>
<!ELEMENT AcquisitionDate  (#PCDATA)>
<!ELEMENT Price            (#PCDATA)>
<!ELEMENT Category         (#PCDATA)>
<!ELEMENT Time             (#PCDATA)>
<!ELEMENT Audience         (#PCDATA)>
]>
```

This DTD states that there is a record, CD. It contains a series of fields or other elements. Some punctuation marks that signify the occurrence status of each element have been included. They are the following:

- None   The element is required to be present.
- * (asterisk)   The element is optional; if it is present, it occurs as frequently as required.

- **+ (plus sign)**   The element is required; it occurs as frequently as required.
- **? (question mark)**   The element is optional; if it is present, it may occur once.

Based on these criteria the required elements are:

- **CDID**   This is a unique identifier because of its numeric location in the collection. There is a second unique identifier, the catalog number, CatalogNumber.
- **Title**   As declared, you only have the CD title or a prime identifying title. However, a plus sign could have been used so that all or some of the compositions on the CD could be listed.
- **Label**   The recording company name needs to be given, but only once.
- **CatalogNumber**   The catalog number is a unique identifier as compared to all other CDs. With a box collection, the box catalog number needs to be used rather than the separate CD catalog numbers.
- **AcquisitionDate**   The acquisition date needs to be present.
- **Time**   As defined, this represents the total CD time. If you use Time+, you could use it for timing each track.
- **Audience**   Here use either "live" or "studio."

Based on these criteria the elements that are optional and can occur more than once are:

- **Opus**   Because there may be several compositions on the same CD, there can be an Opus element for each, if known.
- **Artist**   There are a number of singers that might need to be listed for an opera, or if there is a musical group you might desire to list all or some of the group.

The elements that are required and may appear more than once are:

- **Composer**   Many CDs have more than one composer.
- **Conductor**   There are CDs that may have one or more conductors.
- **Orchestra**   A CD may contain a series of compositions that were done over time by various orchestras or groups.
- **PFYear**   Multiple performance years on a CD are uncommon.

■ Category   On a CD, there can be different styles of music. For example, *Dances of Galánta* mentioned earlier in this chapter contains both symphonic and dance music.

Only one element was made optional and could be used only once. It is the Price element. This was done only to show the use of the question mark. In an actual database this element should be required.

Based on the production rules, you might want a contentspec production to consist of "Mixed," and the Mixed production to consist of "#PCDATA." You might need an element type declaration for each of the children of the CD element.

Database Design Step Three - Searching

One of the goals of any database design is to have the functionality of searching. A part of the overall XML design and development effort is the development of an XML query language. A proposal has been put forth to the W3C entitled "XML-QL: A Query Language for XML" (August 19, 1998). This proposal is found at http://www.w3.org/TR/NOTE-xml-ql.

In this context, you need to look at present XML grammar and determine if perhaps some of the elements could or should have subelements, just as the CD element. The composer and conductor elements seem to require a first and last name. Why is the word "seem" used? Is the first name required in all searches? In addition, you might forget if you spell Rachmaninov's first name Sergei or Sergey. The conclusion is to have an optional first name, but it should be included for advanced searches. For example, if you have an employee database how many Smiths are in it?

Look at the new elements FirstName and LastName. You might use them in both the composer and conductor elements, if you desire, because FirstName and LastName are different in these two situations.

```
<composer>
<FirstName> Sergey</FirstName>
<LastName>Rachmaninov</LastName>
</composer>
```

or

```
<conductor>
<FirstName> Sergey</FirstName>
```

```
<LastName>Rachmaninov</LastName>
</conductor>
```

However, you may feel uncomfortable with this. There may be a search conflict that has not been taken into consideration or you may need namespaces if this database interacts with other databases. Perhaps the first idea is to use FirstName1 and FirstName2, but is this meaningful? The next idea is to use CoFirstName for composer, but conductor also has the same first two letters. You could use ComposerFirstName, but that is probably a longer field than most of the content names. You might try CmpFName and CndFName. These element names in this context are probably meaningful to anyone using this database. You would now have:

```
<composer>
<CmpFName> Sergey</CmpFName>
<CmpLName>Rachmaninov</CmpLName>
</composer>
```

and

```
<conductor>
<CndFName> Sergey</CndFName>
<CndLName>Rachmaninov</CndLName>
</conductor>
```

Now that you have useful markup, it is necessary to define it in the DTD. Here is how you would enhance or change the DTD to reflect these two new subelement sets (enhancements 1 and 2):

```
<!DOCUMENT TYPE CD-Library [
<!ELEMENT CD
(CDID,
Composer+
Title,
Opus*,
Conductor+,
Orchestra+,
Artist*,
Label,
CatalogNumber,
PFYear+,
AcquisitionDate,
Price?,
Category+,
Time,
Audience)>
```

```
<!ELEMENT CDID                 (#PCDATA)>
<!- - Enhancement 1  A - ->
<!ELEMENT Composer (CmpFName*, CmpLName+)>
<!- - Enhancement 1 B - ->
<!ELEMENT CmpFName             (#PCDATA)>
<!ELEMENT CmpLName             (#PCDATA)>
<!ELEMENT Title                (#PCDATA)>
<!ELEMENT Opus                 (#PCDATA)>
<!- - Enhancement 2 A - ->
<!ELEMENT Conductor (CndFName*, CndLName+)>
<!- - Enhancement 2 B - ->
<!ELEMENT CndFName             (#PCDATA)>
<!ELEMENT CdnLName             (#PCDATA)>
<!ELEMENT Orchestra            (#PCDATA)>
<!ELEMENT Artist               (#PCDATA)>
<!ELEMENT Label                (#PCDATA)>
<!ELEMENT CatalogNumber        (#PCDATA)>
<!ELEMENT PFYear               (#PCDATA)>
<!ELEMENT AcquisitionDate      (#PCDATA)>
<!ELEMENT Price                (#PCDATA)>
<!ELEMENT Category             (#PCDATA)>
<!ELEMENT Time                 (#PCDATA)>
<!ELEMENT Audience             (#PCDATA)>
]>
```

Are there any other elements that have to be changed or enhanced? The way the Title element has been declared, you only have the CD title or a prime identifying title. However, a plus sign could be used with the result that all or some of the compositions on the CD could be listed. There are times when you might desire to distinguish between the CD title and a track title such as in this example, *By Request...*. You may want to add a track element that is optional, but can occur as often as needed. The markup would look like this example:

```
<Title>By Request...
<track>March from Superman</track>
</Title>
```

After doing this, immediately you will have this question: what is the track number? You really want to have:

```
<Title>By Request...
<trackno> 7
<track>March from Superman</track>
</trackno>
</Title>
```

It is now once again time to enhance the DTD (enhancement 3):

```
<!DOCUMENT TYPE CD-Library [
<!ELEMENT CD
(CDID,
Composer+
Title,
Opus*,
Conductor+,
Orchestra+,
Artist*,
Label,
CatalogNumber,
PFYear+,
AcquisitionDate,
Price?,
Category+,
Time,
Audience)>
<!ELEMENT CDID            (#PCDATA)>
<!- - Enhancement 1  A - ->
<!ELEMENT Composer (CmpFName*, CmpLName+)>
<!- - Enhancement 1 B - ->
<!ELEMENT CmpFName        (#PCDATA)>
<!ELEMENT CmpLName        (#PCDATA)>
<!- - Enhancement 3 A - ->
<!ELEMENT Title (trackno, track)*>
<!- - Enhancement 3 B - ->
<!ELEMENT trackno         (#PCDATA)>
<!ELEMENT track           (#PCDATA)>
<!ELEMENT Opus            (#PCDATA)>
<!- - Enhancement 2 A - ->
<!ELEMENT Conductor (CndFName*, CndLName+)>
<!- - Enhancement 2 B - ->
<!ELEMENT CndFName        (#PCDATA)>
<!ELEMENT CdnLName        (#PCDATA)>
<!ELEMENT Orchestra       (#PCDATA)>
<!ELEMENT Artist          (#PCDATA)>
<!ELEMENT Label           (#PCDATA)>
<!ELEMENT CatalogNumber   (#PCDATA)>
<!ELEMENT PFYear          (#PCDATA)>
<!ELEMENT AcquisitionDate (#PCDATA)>
<!ELEMENT Price           (#PCDATA)>
<!ELEMENT Category        (#PCDATA)>
<!ELEMENT Time            (#PCDATA)>
<!ELEMENT Audience        (#PCDATA)>
]>
```

As you look over the list, you have to consider the Artist element because it can be treated like the Composer and Conductor elements. However, at this time you might rarely search for artists, so you could leave it for future considerations.

In addition, right now you do not need to track time. Tracking time would be excellent if this application is used for a radio station.

 Note: In enhancements 1 and 2, an asterisk (*) was used after the CmpFName and CndFName elements to specify them as optional, but you could use them as necessary. Likewise, the plus sign (+) was used after the CmpLName and CndLName elements to specify them as required, but you could have multiple occurrences. In enhancement 3 the asterisk was put outside the parentheses to designate that these elements have a common occurrence status. Title (trackno*, track*) could have been used. Like the other elements, the data content types for these elements had to be declared.

Database Design Step Four - Attributes

The final enhancement that must be considered for this application's logical structure is attributes, the specific values required. Attributes are used to refine a given element. An attribute is not content. The general format is <element-name attribute-name="value">...</element-name>.

It appears, based on the earliest content model, that there are three elements that need attributes. They are the Label, Category, and Audience elements. Why these three elements? First, at least 15 major recording companies need to be identified specifically. Two types of music with subcategories need to be identified. Finally, the Audience element's values need to be specified as "Live," "Studio," or "Both."

The production rules for attributes are [52] — [60]. Based on the design requirements and these production rules you would require the following attribute list declarations:

```
<!ELEMENT Label EMPTY>
<!ATTLIST Label
    RecCo  (Archiv | BIS | Chandos | DG |
            EMI | Gimell | Hyperion | London |
            Narada | Naxos | RCA | Sony |
            Telarc | Virgin | Windham | Other) #REQUIRED>
<!ELEMENT Category (#PCDATA)>
<!ATTLIST Category
```

```
Type     (Chamber | Concerto | Opera | Symphony |
          Chant | Folk | New Age | Sndtrk) #REQUIRED
Century  (14 | 15| 16 | 17 | 18 | 19 | 20) #IMPLIED>
<!ELEMENT Audience EMPTY>
<!ATTLIST Audience
   LSB    (Live | Studio | Both) "Studio">
```

Here is what the above says:

- The Label element has one attribute with 16 values, thus you require the attribute RecCo. The Label element is also declared an empty element.

- The Category element has two attributes, Type and Century. The use of the first attribute is required, while the second is optional.

- The Audience element has one attribute with three values with "Studio" the default value. This is an empty element.

Let us now look at markup examples for the three attribute list declarations using the musical CD *Dances of Galánta*:

```
<Label RecCo="Naxos"/>
<Category Other="Dances"> Czech dances.</Category>
<Audience/>
```

How does one read these three markup examples? They show three possible variations.

- The Label element has been declared EMPTY and REQUIRED. You have an empty-element tag with a value.

- Since the Type attribute is required for the Category element, you must enter it. Since it is known that Zoltán Kodály is a twentieth century composer and the century is optional, it is not entered in this markup.

- The Audience is "Studio" because the value was declared the default and Audience is an empty element.

It is time to do another enhancement on the DTD (enhancement 4):

```
<!DOCUMENT TYPE CD-Library [
<!ELEMENT CD
(CDID,
Composer+
Title,
Opus*,
Conductor+,
Orchestra+,
Artist*,
Label,
```

```
                    CatalogNumber,
                    PFYear+,
                    AcquisitionDate,
                    Price?,
                    Category+,
                    Time,
                    Audience)>
<!ELEMENT CDID            (#PCDATA)>
<!- - Enhancement 1  A - ->
<!ELEMENT Composer (CmpFName*, CmpLName+)>
<!- - Enhancement 1 B - ->
<!ELEMENT CmpFName        (#PCDATA)>
<!ELEMENT CmpLName        (#PCDATA)>
<!- - Enhancement 3 A - ->
<!ELEMENT Title (trackno, track)*>
<!- - Enhancement 3 B - ->
<!ELEMENT trackno         (#PCDATA)>
<!ELEMENT track           (#PCDATA)>
<!ELEMENT Opus            (#PCDATA)>
<!- - Enhancement 2 A - ->
<!ELEMENT Conductor (CndFName*, CndLName+)>
<!- - Enhancement 2 B - ->
<!ELEMENT CndFName        (#PCDATA)>
<!ELEMENT CdnLName        (#PCDATA)>
<!ELEMENT Orchestra       (#PCDATA)>
<!ELEMENT Artist          (#PCDATA)>
<!ELEMENT Label EMPTY>
<!- - Enhancement 4 - ->
<!ATTLIST Label
   RecCo   (Archiv | BIS | Chandos | DG |
            EMI | Gimell | Hyperion | London |
            Narada | Naxos | RCA | Sony |
            Telarc | Virgin | Windham | Other) #REQUIRED>
<!ELEMENT CatalogNumber   (#PCDATA)>
<!ELEMENT PFYear          (#PCDATA)>
<!ELEMENT AcquisitionDate (#PCDATA)>
<!ELEMENT Price           (#PCDATA)>
<!ELEMENT Category        (#PCDATA)>
<!- - Enhancement 4 - ->
<!ATTLIST Category
   Type  (Chamber | Concerto | Opera | Symphony |
          Chant | Folk | New Age | Sndtrk) #REQUIRED
   Century  (14 | 15| 16 | 17 | 18 | 19 | 20) #IMPLIED>
<!ELEMENT Time            (#PCDATA)>
<!ELEMENT Audience EMPTY>
<!- - Enhancement 4 - ->
<!ATTLIST Audience
```

```
LSB   (Live | Studio | Both) "Studio">
]>
```

Database Design Step Five A - Entities

An entity is a storage unit in an XML document, with one exception: the root element is the document type entity. The document type entity serves as the starting point for the XML processor and may contain the whole document. An entity contains content and is identified by name, except for the document entity and the external DTD subset. The basic document type entity as declared by production [28] for the above application is:

```
<!DOCTYPE CD-Library [
...
]>
```

The general syntax for production rule [28] is: <!DOCTYPE Name externalDTDpointer internalDTDsubset>

Briefly the three components of the expression for the doctype production [28] are:

- The Name is generally the label for the document type or the root element. It is the place where the parser starts parsing.
- The externalDTDPointer is the declaration for the location of the grammar to which the document must adhere. The basic syntax includes SYSTEM and the URI. Together these are the system ID.
- The internalDTDPointer can be used instead of or as a supplementary DTD for the external DTD. If both the internal and external DTDs declare the same tag, the internal tag carries precedence.

If you wanted to, you could keep your DTD in a separate location. You could have a document type declaration with a system ID as follows:
<!DOCTYPE CD-Library SYSTEM http:///www.MySite.com/music/CDLibrary.dtd>

If you wanted to use any element that is not declared in the CDLibrary DTD, you could do the following:

```
<!DOCTYPE CD-Library SYSTEM
http:///www.MySite.com/music/CDLibrary.dtd [!ELEMENT Remarks ANY]
]>
```

The enclosing brackets [] are a part of the required syntax since markup is being declared.

It is time again to enhance the DTD (enhancement 5):

```
<!- - Enhancement 5 - ->
<!DOCTYPE CD-Library SYSTEM
http:///www.MySite.com/music/CDLibrary.dtd [!ELEMENT Remarks ANY] [
<!ELEMENT CD
(CDID,
Composer+
Title,
Opus*,
Conductor+,
Orchestra+,
Artist*,
Label,
CatalogNumber,
PFYear+,
AcquisitionDate,
Price?,
Category+,
Time,
Audience)>
<!ELEMENT CDID          (#PCDATA)>
<!- - Enhancement 1  A - ->
<!ELEMENT Composer (CmpFName*, CmpLName+)>
<!- - Enhancement 1 B - ->
<!ELEMENT CmpFName  (#PCDATA)>
<!ELEMENT CmpLName  (#PCDATA)>
<!- - Enhancement 3 A - ->
<!ELEMENT Title (trackno, track)*>
<!- - Enhancement 3 B - ->
<!ELEMENT trackno       (#PCDATA)>
<!ELEMENT track         (#PCDATA)>
<!ELEMENT Opus          (#PCDATA)>
<!- - Enhancement 2 A - ->
<!ELEMENT Conductor (CndFName*, CndLName+)>
<!- - Enhancement 2 B - ->
<!ELEMENT CndFName  (#PCDATA)>
<!ELEMENT CdnLName  (#PCDATA)>
<!ELEMENT Orchestra     (#PCDATA)>
<!ELEMENT Artist        (#PCDATA)>
<!ELEMENT Label EMPTY>
<!- - Enhancement 4 - ->
<!ATTLIST Label
   RecCo   (Archiv | BIS | Chandos | DG |
            EMI | Gimell | Hyperion | London |
            Narada | Naxos | RCA | Sony |
            Telarc | Virgin | Windham | Other) #REQUIRED>
```

```
<!ELEMENT CatalogNumber    (#PCDATA)>
<!ELEMENT PFYear           (#PCDATA)>
<!ELEMENT AcquisitionDate  (#PCDATA)>
<!ELEMENT Price            (#PCDATA)>
<!ELEMENT Category         (#PCDATA)>
<!- - Enhancement 4 - ->
<!ATTLIST Category
   Type    (Chamber | Concerto | Opera | Symphony |
            Chant | Folk | New Age | Sndtrk) #REQUIRED
   Century (14 | 15| 16 | 17 | 18 | 19 | 20) #IMPLIED>
<!ELEMENT Time             (#PCDATA)>
<!ELEMENT Audience EMPTY>
<!- - Enhancement 4 - ->
<!ATTLIST Audience
   LSB     (Live | Studio | Both) "Studio">
]>
```

When you do enhancement 5 all you will need is:

```
<!- - Enhancement 5 - ->
<!DOCTYPE CD-Library SYSTEM
http:///www.MySite.com/music/CDLibrary.dtd [!ELEMENT Remarks ANY] [
]>
```

The rest of the lines would be found in CDLibrary.dtd. All of these lines are kept together so you might see the total thinking process.

Database Design Step Five B – Unparsed Entities

An unparsed entity differs from a parsed entity in two ways:

■ It has an associated NOTATION in its declaration, using NDATA as its keyword.

■ It is never included in an XML document, only referenced in an attribute value.

An example of the first item in the above list is:

```
<!ENTITY LvBeethoven SYSTEM "Beethoven.jpg" NDATA JPEG>
<!ENTITY text SYSTEM "Beethoven.xml">
```

This example requires several assumptions. The JPEG notation has been declared, LvBeethoven is a declared unparsed entity, and text is a declared parsed entity. You might use these declarations if you were interested in doing a "report" that included graphics. You might have graphics for any of the composers or conductors in the database. You might also include recording company logos.

You might desire to use some of the data for a training course on music. In addition, you might want to use Microsoft PowerPoint as the presentation medium. This would be a case where it would be appropriate to include a graphic on the same slide with text.

In addition, you may have separate XML files for each composer rather than having one big database with all the data in it. This technique might be easier to manage and is certainly safer than a single huge database.

An example of the second difference is:

```
<!ELEMENT graphic (#PCDATA)>
<!ATTLIST Graphic Image ENITY #REQUIRED>
...
<Graphic Image="Beethoven">&text;</Graphic>
```

A general entity can be either internal or external. When external an external identifier (SYSTEM or PUBLIC) is required. The PUBLIC option is a carryover from SGML. The specification says nothing about its syntax. In a document type declaration, it may only be used for very specific local or group-oriented applications. When internal, the content is given.

An external general entity could be declared as follows: <!ENTITY Beethoven SYSTEM "Beethoven.xml">.

An internal general entity could be declared as follows: <!ENTITY Beethoven "One of the greatest composers.">.

A percentage sign (%) is used at the beginning of a parameter entity and is closed by a semicolon (;). It can only be used with a DTD. Here is an example:

```
<!ENTITY % ClassicalCDs SYSTEM "Classical.dtd">
%ClassicalCDs;
```

Why might you want to have many different DTDs? You might want to use specific XSL declarations that are different from the ones in another type of music. In addition, you do need the Opus element for classical music but not for any other musical type or category.

You could have a general DTD to handle any type of musical CD and you could have specialized external DTDs for any or all musical categories.

Database Design Step Five C – General Entities

A general entity is declared by using this production rule: [71] GEDecl ::= '<!ENTITY' S Name S EntityDef S? '>'.

This declaration permits you to define a shortcut for a long phrase or name. For example, you could do the following: <!ENTITY LvB "Ludwig van Beethoven">.

You could then use it in the application as &LvB; and have "Ludwig van Beethoven" appear when the XML is expanded. How can you use this in this application? Here are two possibilities of general entities that can be used: recording company names and musical categories or types. Here are the declarations:

```
<!ENTITY A "Archiv">
<!ENTITY B "BIS">
<!ENTITY C "Chandos">
<!ENTITY D "DG">
<!ENTITY E "EMI">
<!ENTITY G "Gimell">
<!ENTITY H "Hyperion">
<!ENTITY L "London">
<!ENTITY N "Narada">
<!ENTITY P "Naxos">
<!ENTITY R "RCA">
<!ENTITY S "Sony">
<!ENTITY T "Telarc">
<!ENTITY V "Virgin">
<!ENTITY W "Windham">
<!ENTITY O "Other">
```

Would you normally use all of the above entities? You would probably not use &D; for DG. However, you could change "DG" to "Deutsche Grammophon." Nevertheless, what is the value-added reason for doing this? What if someone said, "I do not want DG or Deutsche Grammophon, but PolyGram Record Operations, the distributor of DG?" You only need to make one simple change: <!ENTITY D "PolyGram Record Operations">.

The second use of the general entities is for the musical categories:

```
<!ENTITY Ch "Chamber">
<!ENTITY Co "Concerto">
<!ENTITY Op "Opera">
<!ENTITY Sy "Symphony">
<!ENTITY Ca "Chant">
<!ENTITY Fo "Folk">
```

```
<!ENTITY Na "New Age">
<!ENTITY Mo "Sndtrk">
<!ENTITY Ot "Other">
```

Why were two characters used instead of one as in the recording list? You cannot define two general entities as "O." The parser could not determine whether it is "other" or "opera." Notice that instead of using "Sn" for "soundtrack," "Mo" for "movie" was used.

Earlier it was suggested that you might like to have recording logos that could be used in training presentations. To do this you would need to add an NDATA declaration:

```
[73] EntityDef ::= EntityValue | (ExternalID NDataDecl?)
[76] NDataDecl ::= S 'NDATA' S Name
```

As you work your way through the productions, the general format becomes <!ENTITY shortcut-name SYSTEM "URI" NDATA graphic-type>.

Since you may be interested in logos for recording companies, an example is <!ENTITY LDG SYSTEM "graphics/DGlogo.gif" NDATA gif>.

The graphic entities for the DTD would be as follows:

```
<!ENTITY LA SYSTEM "graphics/Archiv.gif" NDATA gif>
<!ENTITY LB SYSTEM "graphics/BIS.gif" NDATA gif>
<!ENTITY LC SYSTEM "graphics/Chandos.gif" NDATA gif>
<!ENTITY LD SYSTEM "graphics/DG.gif" NDATA gif>
<!ENTITY LE SYSTEM "graphics/EMI.gif" NDATA gif>
<!ENTITY LG SYSTEM "graphics/Gimell.gif" NDATA gif>
<!ENTITY LH SYSTEM "graphics/Hyperion.gif" NDATA gif>
<!ENTITY LL SYSTEM "graphics/London.gif" NDATA gif>
<!ENTITY LN SYSTEM "graphics/Narada.gif" NDATA gif>
<!ENTITY LP SYSTEM "graphics/Naxos.gif" NDATA gif>
<!ENTITY LR SYSTEM "graphics/RCA.gif" NDATA gif>
<!ENTITY LS SYSTEM "graphics/Sony.gif" NDATA gif>
<!ENTITY LT SYSTEM "graphics/Telarc.gif" NDATA gif>
<!ENTITY LV SYSTEM "graphics/Virgin.gif" NDATA gif>
<!ENTITY LW SYSTEM "graphics/Windham.gif" NDATA gif>
```

The three sets of general entity declarations can now be included in the DTD as enhancement 6:

```
<!- - Enhancement 5 - ->
<!DOCTYPE CD-Library SYSTEM
http:///www.MySite.com/music/CDLibrary.dtd [!ELEMENT Remarks ANY] [
<!ELEMENT CD
(CDID,
Composer+
```

```
Title,
Opus*,
Conductor+,
Orchestra+,
Artist*,
Label,
CatalogNumber,
PFYear+,
AcquisitionDate,
Price?,
Category+,
Time,
Audience)>
<!- - Enhancement 6 - ->
<!ENTITY A "Archiv">
<!ENTITY B "BIS">
<!ENTITY C "Chandos">
<!ENTITY D "DG">
<!ENTITY E "EMI">
<!ENTITY G "Gimell">
<!ENTITY H "Hyperion">
<!ENTITY L "London">
<!ENTITY N "Narada">
<!ENTITY P "Naxos">
<!ENTITY R "RCA">
<!ENTITY S "Sony">
<!ENTITY T "Telarc">
<!ENTITY V "Virgin">
<!ENTITY W "Windham">
<!ENTITY O "Other">
<!ENTITY Ch "Chamber">
<!ENTITY Co "Concerto">
<!ENTITY Op "Opera">
<!ENTITY Sy "Symphony">
<!ENTITY Ca "Chant">
<!ENTITY Fo "Folk">
<!ENTITY Na "New Age">
<!ENTITY Mo "Sndtrk">
<!ENTITY Ot "Other">
<!ENTITY LA SYSTEM "graphics/Archiv.gif" NDATA gif>
<!ENTITY LB SYSTEM "graphics/BIS.gif" NDATA gif>
<!ENTITY LC SYSTEM "graphics/Chandos.gif" NDATA gif>
<!ENTITY LD SYSTEM "graphics/DG.gif" NDATA gif>
<!ENTITY LE SYSTEM "graphics/EMI.gif" NDATA gif>
<!ENTITY LG SYSTEM "graphics/Gimell.gif" NDATA gif>
<!ENTITY LH SYSTEM "graphics/Hyperion.gif" NDATA gif>
<!ENTITY LL SYSTEM "graphics/London.gif" NDATA gif>
```

```
<!ENTITY LN SYSTEM "graphics/Narada.gif" NDATA gif>
<!ENTITY LP SYSTEM "graphics/Naxos.gif" NDATA gif>
<!ENTITY LR SYSTEM "graphics/RCA.gif" NDATA gif>
<!ENTITY LS SYSTEM "graphics/Sony.gif" NDATA gif>
<!ENTITY LT SYSTEM "graphics/Telarc.gif" NDATA gif>
<!ENTITY LV SYSTEM "graphics/Virgin.gif" NDATA gif>
<!ENTITY LW SYSTEM "graphics/Windham.gif" NDATA gif>
<!ELEMENT CDID            (#PCDATA)>
<!- - Enhancement 1  A - ->
<!ELEMENT Composer (CmpFName*, CmpLName+)>
<!- - Enhancement 1 B - ->
<!ELEMENT CmpFName        (#PCDATA)>
<!ELEMENT CmpLName        (#PCDATA)>
<!- - Enhancement 3 A - ->
<!ELEMENT Title (trackno, track)*>
<!- - Enhancement 3 B - ->
<!ELEMENT trackno         (#PCDATA)>
<!ELEMENT track           (#PCDATA)>
<!ELEMENT Opus            (#PCDATA)>
<!- - Enhancement 2 A - ->
<!ELEMENT Conductor (CndFName*, CndLName+)>
<!- - Enhancement 2 B - ->
<!ELEMENT CndFName        (#PCDATA)>
<!ELEMENT CdnLName        (#PCDATA)>
<!ELEMENT Orchestra       (#PCDATA)>
<!ELEMENT Artist          (#PCDATA)>
<!ELEMENT Label EMPTY>
<!- - Enhancement 4 - ->
<!ATTLIST Label
  ReCo    (Archiv | BIS | Chandos | DG |
           EMI | Gimell | Hyperion | London |
           Narada | Naxos | RCA | Sony |
           Telarc | Virgin | Windham | Other) #REQUIRED>
<!ELEMENT CatalogNumber   (#PCDATA)>
<!ELEMENT PFYear          (#PCDATA)>
<!ELEMENT AcquisitionDate (#PCDATA)>
<!ELEMENT Price           (#PCDATA)>
<!ELEMENT Category        (#PCDATA)>
<!- - Enhancement 4 - ->
<!ATTLIST Category
  Type    (Chamber | Concerto | Opera | Symphony |
           Chant | Folk | New Age | Sndtrk) #REQUIRED
  Century  (14 | 15| 16 | 17 | 18 | 19 | 20) #IMPLIED>
<!ELEMENT Time (#PCDATA)>
<!ELEMENT Audience EMPTY>
<!- - Enhancement 4 - ->
<!ATTLIST Audience
```

```
    LSB      (Live | Studio | Both) "Studio">
]>
```

Database Design Step Six - Notations

If you want to use multimedia in the application, then you need to have notation declarations in the DTD. A notation is a statement that there is a need to use an external application to process your document. A notation is declared using this production rule: [82] NotationDecl ::= '<!NOTATION' S Name S (ExternalID | PublicID) S? '>'.

The two related production rules are:

[75] ExternalID ::= 'SYSTEM' S SystemLiteral | 'PUBLIC' S PubidLiteral S SystemLiteral
[83] PublicID ::= 'PUBLIC' S PubidLiteral

To translate these rules the basic notation format is <!NOTATION notation-name SYSTEM "programURI">.

This means you have the medium type, SYSTEM, and the location of the program to handle the medium. Before looking at an example, you have probably said "but" more than once. Yes, you have to consider the following:

■ Can the program run on the user's machine?

■ How do you know the location of the program?

■ Where will the image appear in the document?

The conclusion is that work is required in a browser to handle this situation.

With all of these questions considered, here is an example: <!NOTATION jpeg SYSTEM file://C:\Utilities\myviewer.exe>.

You can now consider a set of notations for the DTD:

```
<!NOTATION gif      SYSTEM "music/hijaak.exe">
<!NOTATION jpg      SYSTEM "music/hijaak.exe">
<!NOTATION jpeg     SYSTEM "music/hijaak.exe">
<!NOTATION pcx      SYSTEM "music/hijaak.exe
<!NOTATION png      SYSTEM "music/hijaak.exe">
<!NOTATION au       SYSTEM "music/mplayer.exe">
<!NOTATION mid      SYSTEM "music/mplayer.exe">
<!NOTATION mov      SYSTEM "music/mplayer.exe">
<!NOTATION mpg      SYSTEM "music/mplayer.exe">
<!NOTATION mpeg     SYSTEM "music/mplayer.exe">
<!NOTATION qtw      SYSTEM "music/mplayer.exe">
```

Enhancement 7 for the DTD is the inclusion of these notations:

```
<!- - Enhancement 5 - ->
<!DOCTYPE CD-Library SYSTEM
http:///www.MySite.com/music/CDLibrary.dtd [!ELEMENT Remarks ANY] [
<!ELEMENT CD
(CDID,
Composer+
Title,
Opus*,
Conductor+,
Orchestra+,
Artist*,
Label,
CatalogNumber,
PFYear+,
AcquisitionDate,
Price?,
Category+,
Time,
Audience)>
<!- - Enhancement 6 - ->
<!ENTITY A "Archiv">
<!ENTITY B "BIS">
<!ENTITY C "Chandos">
<!ENTITY D "DG">
<!ENTITY E "EMI">
<!ENTITY G "Gimell">
<!ENTITY H "Hyperion">
<!ENTITY L "London">
<!ENTITY N "Narada">
<!ENTITY P "Naxos">
<!ENTITY R "RCA">
<!ENTITY S "Sony">
<!ENTITY T "Telarc">
<!ENTITY V "Virgin">
<!ENTITY W "Windham">
<!ENTITY O "Other">
<!ENTITY Ch "Chamber">
<!ENTITY Co "Concerto">
<!ENTITY Op "Opera">
<!ENTITY Sy "Symphony">
<!ENTITY Ca "Chant">
<!ENTITY Fo "Folk">
<!ENTITY Na "New Age">
<!ENTITY Mo "Sndtrk">
<!ENTITY Ot "Other">
```

```
<!ENTITY LA SYSTEM "graphics/Archiv.gif" NDATA gif>
<!ENTITY LB SYSTEM "graphics/BIS.gif" NDATA gif>
<!ENTITY LC SYSTEM "graphics/Chandos.gif" NDATA gif>
<!ENTITY LD SYSTEM "graphics/DG.gif" NDATA gif>
<!ENTITY LE SYSTEM "graphics/EMI.gif" NDATA gif>
<!ENTITY LG SYSTEM "graphics/Gimell.gif" NDATA gif>
<!ENTITY LH SYSTEM "graphics/Hyperion.gif" NDATA gif>
<!ENTITY LL SYSTEM "graphics/London.gif" NDATA gif>
<!ENTITY LN SYSTEM "graphics/Narada.gif" NDATA gif>
<!ENTITY LP SYSTEM "graphics/Naxos.gif" NDATA gif>
<!ENTITY LR SYSTEM "graphics/RCA.gif" NDATA gif>
<!ENTITY LS SYSTEM "graphics/Sony.gif" NDATA gif>
<!ENTITY LT SYSTEM "graphics/Telarc.gif" NDATA gif>
<!ENTITY LV SYSTEM "graphics/Virgin.gif" NDATA gif>
<!ENTITY LW SYSTEM "graphics/Windham.gif" NDATA gif>
<!- - Enhancement 7 - ->
<!NOTATION gif   SYSTEM "music/hijaak.exe">
<!NOTATION jpg   SYSTEM "music/hijaak.exe">
<!NOTATION jpeg   SYSTEM "music/hijaak.exe">
<!NOTATION pcx   SYSTEM "music/hijaak.exe">
<!NOTATION png   SYSTEM "music/hijaak.exe">
<!NOTATION au   SYSTEM "music/mplayer.exe">
<!NOTATION mid   SYSTEM "music/mplayer.exe">
<!NOTATION mov   SYSTEM "music/mplayer.exe">
<!NOTATION mpg   SYSTEM "music/mplayer.exe">
<!NOTATION mpeg   SYSTEM "music/mplayer.exe">
<!NOTATION qtw   SYSTEM "music/mplayer.exe">
<!ELEMENT CDID          (#PCDATA)>
<!- - Enhancement 1  A - ->
<!ELEMENT Composer (CmpFName*, CmpLName+)>
<!- - Enhancement 1 B - ->
<!ELEMENT CmpFName      (#PCDATA)>
<!ELEMENT CmpLName      (#PCDATA)>
<!- - Enhancement 3 A - ->
<!ELEMENT Title (trackno, track)*>
<!- - Enhancement 3 B - ->
<!ELEMENT trackno       (#PCDATA)>
<!ELEMENT track         (#PCDATA)>
<!ELEMENT Opus          (#PCDATA)>
<!- - Enhancement 2 A - ->
<!ELEMENT Conductor (CndFName*, CndLName+)>
<!- - Enhancement 2 B - ->
<!ELEMENT CndFName      (#PCDATA)>
<!ELEMENT CdnLName      (#PCDATA)>
<!ELEMENT Orchestra     (#PCDATA)>
<!ELEMENT Artist        (#PCDATA)>
<!ELEMENT Label EMPTY>
```

```
<!- - Enhancement 4 - ->
<!ATTLIST Label
  ReCo    (Archiv | BIS | Chandos | DG |
           EMI | Gimell | Hyperion | London |
           Narada | Naxos | RCA | Sony |
           Telarc | Virgin | Windham | Other) #REQUIRED>
<!ELEMENT CatalogNumber    (#PCDATA)>
<!ELEMENT PFYear           (#PCDATA)>
<!ELEMENT AcquisitionDate  (#PCDATA)>
<!ELEMENT Price            (#PCDATA)>
<!ELEMENT Category         (#PCDATA)>
<!- - Enhancement 4 - ->
<!ATTLIST Category
  Type   (Chamber | Concerto | Opera | Symphony |
          Chant | Folk | New Age | Sndtrk) #REQUIRED
  Century  (14 | 15| 16 | 17 | 18 | 19 | 20) #IMPLIED>
<!ELEMENT Time             (#PCDATA)>
<!ELEMENT Audience EMPTY>
<!- - Enhancement 4 - ->
<!ATTLIST Audience
  LSB   (Live | Studio | Both) "Studio">
]>
```

Database Design Step Seven – Conditional Sections

A conditional section is a document type declaration's external subset that is included in, or excluded from, the logical structure of the DTD based on the keyword, either INCLUDE or IGNORE, that governs it.

The production rules of a conditional section are:

[61] conditionalSect ::= includeSect | ignoreSect
[62] includeSect ::= '<![' S? 'INCLUDE' S? '[' extSubsetDecl ']]>'
[63] ignoreSect ::= '<![' S? 'IGNORE' S? '[' ignoreSectContents* ']]>'
[64] ignoreSectContents ::= Ignore ('<![' ignoreSectContents ']]>' Ignore)*
[65] Ignore ::= Char* - (Char* ('<![' | ']]>') Char*)

A conditional section may contain one or more complete declarations, comments, processing instructions, or nested conditional sections intermingled with white space.

There are two conditional section types and they have the syntax <![INCLUDE | IGNORE] ...]]>.

INCLUDE means the contents of the conditional section are logically part of the DTD.

IGNORE means the contents of the conditional section are not logically part of the DTD.

 Note: For reliable parsing, even the contents of ignored conditional sections must be read in order to detect nested conditional sections and ensure that the end of the outermost (ignored) conditional section is properly detected.

If INCLUDE occurs within a larger conditional section with a keyword of IGNORE, both the outer and the inner conditional sections are ignored.

If the keyword of the conditional section is a parameter-entity reference, the parameter entity must be replaced by its content before the processor decides whether to include or ignore the conditional section.

An example:

```
<!ENTITY % report1 'INCLUDE' >
<!ENTITY % report2 'IGNORE' >
<![%report1;[
<!ELEMENT composition (CD+, title+)>
]]>
<![%report2;[
<!ELEMENT composition (CD+, title+, Label*, LabelNo?)>
]]>
```

Using this code you can have two reports and only have to reverse report1 and report2.

XML Processing Tips

Tips on XML can be divided into at least five categories:

- General structure
- Logical structure
- Physical structure
- Document type definitions (DTD)
- Processing

This chapter considers the last category. This chapter discusses the special requirements for processing an XML document for a parser. The first categories were considered in Chapters 2 through 5.

 Note: A tip is a snippet of advice, a guideline, or a pointer. It is not a full explanation of a subject. It is recognized that the answers here are highly abbreviated and only high points of the topics. When syntax is given, it may be only one of many variants such as 7 = 3 + 4. In addition, the syntax could be 7 = 4 + 3 or 3 = 7 − 4.

In particular, this chapter gives tips on the XML features that enhance the core markup for processing. These features are not your normal day-to-day features. The four "advanced" features discussed here are:

- Conditional sections
- Character references
- Processing instructions
- Language identification

There is one "special" processing instruction that is actually the XML declaration [23] that is of great importance and that is, of course: <?xml version="1.0"?>.

Why are conditional sections important to you as an XML document designer?

Conditional sections can be used with a design XML DTD or document during development to exclude parts of either from being processed so you do not get parsing errors, especially fatal ones.

What are conditional sections?

Technically, conditional sections (rules [61] – [65]) are portions of the DTD external subset which are included in or excluded from the DTD's logical structure based on the keyword, which governs them. In English, you can use either the keyword "INCLUDE" or "IGNORE" to declare (rules [62] and [63]) how a document portion is to be processed.

What are the components of a conditional section?

A conditional section is like either an internal or an external DTD subset. It may contain one or more of the following components intermingled with white space:

■ Declarations
■ Comments
■ Processing instructions
■ Nested conditional sections

How do I handle conditional sections?

Here are the five related production rules:

[61] conditionalSect ::= includeSect | ignoreSect

This rule specifies the two types of conditional sections, include and ignore. The usual antonym for include is exclude, but the valid keyword is "IGNORE."

[62] includeSect ::= '<![' S? 'INCLUDE' S? '[' extSubsetDecl ']]>'

When this rule is used, the content of the conditional section is included in the DTD. This rule references: [31] ExtSubsetDecl ::= (markupdecl | condtionalSect | PEReference | S)*

It is important to note that in an external subset, parameter-entity references (PEReference) are permitted within markup declarations.

[63] ignoreSect ::= '<![' S? 'IGNORE' S? '[' ignoreSectContents ']]>'

When this rule is used, the content of the conditional section is not included in the DTD. If "IGNORE" is used with a nested "INCLUDE," they are <u>both</u> ignored.

[64] ignoreSectContents ::= Ignore ('<![' ignoreSectContents ']]>' Ignore)*
[65] Ignore ::= Char* - (Char* ('<!' | ']]>') Char*)

Here is an example of basic conditional sections:

```
<![INCLUDE[
<!ELEMENT book (query*, title, chapter+, appendix?)>
]]>
<![IGNORE[
<!ELEMENT book (title, chapter+, appendix?)>
]]>
```

This is a method for doing a "turn-on" and a "turn-off" during a development phase.

Here is an example of conditional sections and parameter entities:

```
<!DOCTYPE BOOK CONTROL "bkctl.dtd"[
<!ENTITY % draft 'INCLUDE'>
<!ENTITY % final 'IGNORE'>
]>
```

The percentage symbol (%) designates a parameter entity.

```
<![%draft;[
<!ELEMENT book (query*, title, chapter+, appendix?)>
]]>
<![%final;[
<!ELEMENT book (title, chapter+, appendix?)>
]]>
```

This markup means you can have none or some queries (comments) in the draft of the book, but none in the final version of the book. There should be a title, one or more chapters, and possibly appendices in both the draft and final copies of the book. The draft copy is for an editor, while the final is for the author.

When this technique is used, the processor replaces the content of the PEReference before processing the conditional section. This means you can have two documents referenced by the same external markup declarations.

Warning: A parser may not necessarily support conditional sections.

What are references?

There are two types of references, character and entity: [67] Reference ::= EntityRef | CharRef

Character references manipulate only numbers. Entity references manage names and numbers.

 Warning: While these two reference types look similar, they are not.

What are character references?

A character reference (CharRef) refers to a specific character in the ISO/IEC 10646 character set. A character reference can be for a character not directly accessible from available input devices: [66] CharRef ::= '&#' [0-9]+ ';' | '&#x' [0-9a-fA-F]+ ';'

 Warning: Characters referred to using CharRef must match the Char production.

This rule reads if the character is between 0 and 9 decimal it should read &#n; (n can be any number of characters). If the character is hexadecimal, the CharRef should read &#xn; with x the hexadecimal flag. A legal character <u>must</u> match the production of Char [2].

An example of a character reference is: Type <key>space bar</key> ( ) to get a space.

What are entity references?

An entity reference (EntityRef) refers to a named entity's content. An entity reference is either a parsed general reference or a parameter-entity reference.

What are parsed general references?

Parsed general entity references use as delimiters the ampersand (&) and the semicolon (;): [68] EntityRef ::= '&' Name ';'.

These are the constraints:

- A well-formed document needs no declared amp, lt, gt, apos or quot if it does not have a DTD, only an internal DTD subset, or has a standalone="yes" declaration.
- An entity reference must not contain the name of an unparsed entity.
- A parsed entity must not contain a recursive reference to itself.

> **Warning:** The Name in the entity reference must match that in an entity declaration when the XML document includes an external subset or has external parameter entities.

An example of a parsed general entity reference is:

This document was revised on &docdate; and is considered &final;.

What are parameter-entity references?

Parameter-entity references use as delimiters the percent sign (%) and the semicolon (;): Rule 69: PEReference ::= '%' Name ';'

These are the constraints:

- The Name given in the entity reference must match that in an entity declaration when one of the following conditions is true:
  - The document does not have a DTD.
  - The document has only an internal DTD subset, which contains no parameter-entity references.
  - The document has "standalone="yes"" in the document type PI.
- The Name given in the entity references must match that in an entity declaration (result unpredictable) when in a document with an external subset or external parameter entities with "standalone="no"".
- An entity reference must not contain the name of an unparsed entity. An unparsed entity may be referred to only in an attribute value (rule [10]) declared as type ENTITY or ENTITIES.
- There can be no direct or indirect recursion. A parsed entity must not refer to itself.

How do I use a parameter-entity reference?

Here is an example of a parameter-entity reference also using conditional sections:

```
<!DOCTYPE BOOK CONTROL "bkctl.dtd"[
<!ENTITY % draft 'INCLUDE'>
<!ENTITY % final 'IGNORE'>
]>

<![%draft;[
<!ELEMENT book (query*, title, chapter+, appendix?)>
]]>
<![%final;[
<!ELEMENT book (title, chapter+, appendix?)>
]]>
```

What are processing instructions?

The processing instruction (PI), when implemented correctly, can be of significance because instructions can be sent to applications from a document. PIs are used for communicating with an application without using the DTD. The thinking is that a PI is to be used rarely, but the same thing was said about the HTML tag <blink>.

What are some reasons for using PIs?

Are there valid reasons for using a PI? Here are five possibilities:
- Gives an application explicit instruction(s).
- Vendor's application requires a passed instruction.
- Instruction is unrelated to the document's structure.
- Using a proprietary DTD requires a local instruction.
- There is a special requirement for a unique encoding format.

What are the production rules for PIs?

There are two rules for PIs:

[16] PI ::= '<?' PITarget (S (Char* - (Char* '?>' Char*)))? '?>'
[17] PITarget ::= Name - (('X' | 'x') ('M' | 'm') ('L' | 'l'))

Here are two essential points from these rules:
- PIs are not a part of a document's character data: [14] CharData ::= [^<&]* - ([^<&]* ']]>' [^<&]*)

 Note: Character data is text of a document that is not markup. Markup forms are start-tags, end-tags, empty-element tags, entity-references, comments, CDATA section delimiters, document type declarations, and processing instructions.

- PITarget uses Name [4] and reserves the target names XML and xml:
  [4] Name ::= (Letter | '_' | ':') (NameChar)

 Note: This rule means a name can begin with a letter, an underscore (_), or a colon (:) and be followed by letters, digits, hyphens, underscores, colons, or full stops.

What is an example of a PI?

An example of a special PI that is actually an XML declaration is: <?xml version="1.0"?>.

This is required when the document adheres to the specification. The XML declaration is the first part of the prolog. The XML declaration is governed as follows: [23] XMLDecl ::= '<?xml' VersionInfo EncodingDecl? SDDecl? S? '?>'.

This rule leads to two other rules for encoding: [80] and standalone declarations [32].

What is an encoding declaration?

The rule for encoding is as follows: [80] EncodingDecl ::= S 'encoding' Eq ('"' EncName '"' | "'" EncName "'").

An example using the earlier XML declaration is: <?xml version="1.0" encoding="UTF=8"?>.

In an encoding declaration, there are many options for the value. The rules are:

- When Unicode/ISO/IEC 10646 encodings and transformations are used, the values should be one of the following:
  - UTF-8
  - UTF-16
  - ISO-10646-UCS-2
  - ISO-10646-UCS-4
- When ISO 8859 encoding is used, the value should be "ISO-8859-p" where p equals 1-9.
- When the encoded forms are used from JIS X-0208-1997 (Japanese encoding), one of the following values should be used:

- ISO-2022-JP
- Shift_JIS
- EUC-JP

What is the rule for a standalone declaration?

The rule for a standalone declaration is: [32] SDDecl ::= S 'standalone' Eq (("'" ('yes' | 'no') "'") | ('"' ('yes' | 'no') '"')).

The next enhancement to the XML declaration is: <?xml version="1.0" encoding="UTF=8" standalone="yes"?>.

The "yes" means there are no markup declarations external to the document entity that affect the information passed from the XML processor to the application. The "no" is assumed and means there are external markup declarations.

There are four occasions when the standalone must equal "no." These cases are external markup declarations contain declarations of:

- Attributes with default values, if elements to which these attributes apply appear in the document without specifications of values for these attributes
- Entities (other than amp, lt, gt, apos, quot), if references to those entities appear in the document
- Attributes with values subject to normalization, where the attribute appears in the document with a value that will change as a result of normalization
- Element types with element content, if white space occurs directly within any instance of these types.

  Warning: Failure to adhere to these validity constraints can give unpredictable processing results.

What is language identification?

A special attribute named xml:lang can be used to specify the natural or formal language in which the document's content and its attribute values are written. For a valid document, this attribute must be declared if used. The attribute values when used as language identifiers are found in the Request for Comments (RFC) 1766, "Tags for Identification of Languages."

What rules govern language identification?

LanguageID is governed by production rules [33] — [38].

[33] LanguageID ::= Langcode ('-' Subcode)*
[34] Langcode ::= ISO639Code | IanaCode | UserCode

The Langcode may be:

- A two- or three-letter code as defined by ISO 639, "Codes for the representation of names of languages' [35]
- A language identifier registered with the Internet Assigned Numbers Authority (IANA); begins with the prefix "i-" or "I-" [36]
- A language identifier of private use; begins with the prefix "x-" or "X-" [37]

[35] ISO639Code ::= ([a-z] | [A-Z]) ([a-z] | [A-Z])
[36] IanaCode ::= ('i' | 'I') '-' ([a-z] | [A-Z])+
[37] UserCode ::= ('x' | 'X') '-' ([a-z] | [A-Z])+
[38] Subcode ::= ([a-z] | (A-Z])+

Note: See either of these sites for the ISO 639 and IANA codes:

http://www.ics.uci.edu/pub/ietf/http/related/iso639.txt
ftp://ftp.isi.edu/in-notes/iana/assignments/character-sets

What are the rules for first code segments?

The rules for first code segments are:

- If it consists of two letters, it must be a country code from ISO 3166, "Codes for representation of names of countries."
- If it consists of more than two letters, it has to be an IANA subcode or begin with the prefix "x-" or "X-" as a privately used code.

What are the general language code usage rules?

Here are two general usage rules:

- By custom, a language code is given in lowercase, while the country code is given in uppercase.
- An xml:lang can be overridden by another xml:lang.

What is an example of a simple xml:lang declaration?

Here is an example of a simple xml:lang declaration: xml:lang NMTOKEN #IMPLIED.

Here are examples of xml:lang declarations with default values:

```
<!ATTLIST book xml:lang NMTOKEN 'grc'>
<!ATTLIST gloss xml:lang NMTOKEN 'de'>
<!ATTLIST note xml:lang NMTOKEN 'en'>
```

 Note: This could be the Euclid in the original Greek with glosses in German and with notes in English.

What rules govern character classes?

Character classes are governed by rules [84] – [89]. This is where the character definitions are for the alphabetic characters of the Latin alphabet (BaseChar), ideographic characters such as Chinese (Ideographic), character mixes for diacritics (CombiningChar), digits (Digit), extenders, and enders.

What are the requirements to use UTF-8 or UTF-16 format?

For UTF-8 and UTF-16 format, there is no requirement for an XML encoding declaration. The encoding declaration is a part of the XML declaration. For example, if UTF-4 were to be used, the encoding would look as follows: <?xml version="1.0" encoding="UTF=4"?>.

Chapter 7

XML Dialect Tips

XML is very amenable to special circumstances such as defining chemical formulas. One such dialect is the Chemical Markup Language (CML). This chapter looks at the implications of CML and the importance of other XML dialects to special interest groups.

The chapter discusses some of the earliest developments of specialized XML applications (dialects) both in business and academic environments. This chapter is for readers interested in the development of their own dialect for a specific situation. If your interest is to design and develop general XML DTDs and documents, you might just go to the next chapter.

 Note: A tip is a snippet of advice, a guideline, or a pointer. It is not a full explanation of a subject. It is recognized that the answers here are highly abbreviated and only high points of the topics. A few tips are lengthier than most because of the technical markup responses required.

What is a dialect?

A dialect is a variation of a basic language. For example, British English has American, Canadian, and Indian dialects. British English is the standard. XML has a number of dialects established or as "works in progress." They are specialized language concerns, but their development does show the power of XML. Some, but not all, have a specialized DTD to develop the dialect.

What are some of the important XML dialects?

Here is a very short list of dialects:
- Channel Definition Format (CDF)
- Chemical Markup Language (CML)

- Mathematical Markup Language (MathML)
- Resource Description Framework (RDF)
- Web Interface Definition Language (WIDL)

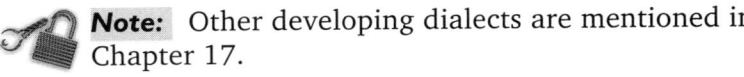 **Note:** Other developing dialects are mentioned in Chapter 17.

What are the three major issues in using dialects?

There are, of course, issues to consider when using these dialects. For example, CML has a unique browser to handle it. Peter Murray-Rust wrote the browser, called Java Universal Molecular Browser for Objects (Jumbo). In addition, these dialects are for highly specialized situations and for specialized discussion groups, such as chemists. The third issue is that the documentation for these dialects may be lacking.

What is Channel Definition Format (CDF)?

Channel Definition Format (CDF) is a proprietary XML implementation by Microsoft. CDF is used to define channels to upload information to a Web site reader. The reader subscribes to the Web site rather than going to the site to get the information. This technology is also called push or Webcasting.

 Note: By doing a search on CDF at http:///msdn.microsoft. com, you can find various examples of this XML implementation.

 Warning: Microsoft CDF (Channel Definition Format) does not currently have available a DTD, or if there is one, it is not easy to find. In addition, the documentation is informal at best. Currently, CDF is only implemented for Internet Explorer.

What is a CDF document?

A CDF document is a unique XML document that is linked to an HTML document on the Web site doing the pushing or Webcasting. The channel definition determines the pages to the reader, and how the pages are sent and transported. A CDF document as an XML document begins with an XML declaration (the condition being that the CDF document adheres to the XML specification) and follows all the production rules including those discussed in Chapters 3 through 5.

What is the extension for a CDF file?

While a CDF file is an XML file, its extension is .cdf rather than .xml.

What is the basic information needed for XML tags and CDF?

The three types of basic CDF information that require XML tags are channel logos, content, and schedules.

What is the basic syntax for the XML declaration of a CDF document?

The basic syntax uses the XML declaration [23] with an external ID [75]. The external ID is the URL for the pushing Web site. The syntax is as follows:

```
<?xml version="1.0"?>
<CHANNEL HREF="http://...">
<ITEM>
<TITLE> Learn XML Tips </TITLE>
<ABSTRACT>Book uses the FAQ format on XML</ABSTRACT>
<LOGO></LOGO>
</ITEM>
</CHANNEL>
```

 Note: Pages are identified using the element ITEM and the associated URL.

What are the subelements of the ITEM element in a CDF document?

The child elements of the ITEM element are TITLE, ABSTRACT, and LOGO.

What does the STYLE attribute for the LOGO element do in a CDF document?

The STYLE attribute for the LOGO element permits you to specify one of three values:

- ICON   16-by-16 pixel icon
- IMAGE   80-by-32 pixel image
- IMAGE-WIDE   194-by-32 pixel image

What is the importance of the SCHEDULE element for a CDF document?

The information in the SCHEDULE element specifies the scheduling information for updates. This element has three attributes: STARTDATE, STOPDATE, and TIMEZONE. The TIMEZONE attribute specifies the difference in hours between the server's time zone and Greenwich Mean Time (GMT or Zulu). In the continental U.S., in standard time from east to west the value may be one of the following four: –5000, –6000, –7000, and –8000.

 Note: There are a number of child elements and attributes associated with the SCHEDULE element. Please see the latest Microsoft implementation for the CDF. Currently, there are a limited number of books on this CDF.

What is Chemical Markup Language (CML)?

Chemical Markup Language (CML) is used to specify complex chemical structures and sequences. It can be used for chemical databases, analysis, and publishing. It has a vocabulary that includes atoms, bonds, crystals, and formulas.

 Note: It was developed by Peter Murray-Rust. It may be the earliest example of an XML application because Peter originally developed this application in SGML and converted it into XML as the XML specification was being developed. For further details on CML, see the site of Venus Internet of London, England at http://www.venus.co /uk/.

What are the advantages of CML?

CML handles searches easier than earlier approaches. It handles complex molecular data on the Web. It also eliminates platform dependency.

What is Jumbo?

Java Universal Molecular Browser for Objects (Jumbo) is a browser created by Peter Murray-Rust to display a CML file. It assigns each XML element to a Java class that knows how to render that element.

 Note: Jumbo, which is distributed with classes for displaying the basic CML elements, is found at http://www.xml-cml.org.

 Warning: You cannot use general browsers to view CML directly.

What are the major development rules from XML used with CML?

CML primarily uses four development rules that are some of the major design constraints of XML:

- Start- and end-tags for each element
- Attributes in quotation marks
- A DOCTYPE declaration
- No white space markup

Can a CML document be edited?

A CML document can be edited in the same fashion as any XML document as long as you adhere to processor and DTD constraints.

What is the major weakness of the CML DTD?

The major weakness of the CML DTD is that it has no comments. You would need to do a comprehensive analysis of the DTD to comprehend the XML declarations.

What are some of the major elements found in the CML DTD?

Eight elements found in the CML DTD are the following:

- `<ARRAY>`
- `<ATOMS>`
- `<BONDS>`
- `<FORMULA>`
- `<MOL>`
- `<XADDR>`
- `<XLIST>`
- `<XVAR>`

What is the basic syntax for a CML document?

The simplest syntax for a CML document is:

```
<!DOCTYPE CML PUBLIC "-//CML//DTD CML//EN">
<CML TITLE=" ... ">
</CML>
```

What is Mathematical Markup Language (MathML)?

Mathematical Markup Language (MathML) is an XML application that describes mathematical notation, that is, its structure and content.

 Note: The latest version of the MathML specification is found at http://www.w3.org/TR/REC-MathML. For further details on MathML, see the MathML Information Center at http://www.webeq.com/mathml.

What are the major categories of MathML elements?

There are six major categories of MathML elements. These categories are:

- Containers   Tokens that indicate numbers and symbols
- Operators   Standard mathematical functions (cos) and operators (plus)
- Qualifiers   Seven specifying qualifiers for twelve operators

- Relations   Canonically empty elements that denote arithmetic and logical relationships
- Conditions   Elements that define "such that" constructions
- Semantic   Element that is the container element for the MathML expression together with its semantic mappings

What is important about the MathML DTD?

An important thing about the MathML DTD is it is highly commented. It is a useful document for learning about an XML DTD.

What is Amaya?

Amaya is a browser from the W3C that implements MathML, which allows browsing of Web pages with mathematical notations.

 Note: For a download, see http://www.w3.org/Amaya.

What is Genealogy Data Markup Language (GedML)?

Genealogy Data Markup Language (GedML) is based on Genealogical Data Communication (GEDCOM), which is a data format for handling genealogical information.

 Note: For more information on GEDCOM, see http://www.tiac.net/users/pmcbride/gedcom/55gcint.htm#S1.

What is Resource Description Framework (RDF)?

Resource Description Framework (RDF) provides an infrastructure to support metadata (data on data) across the Web. Some of the efforts of RDF include site maps, content ratings, digital library collections, and distributed authoring.

What is important about RDF?

RDF permits a community of interest to standardize its vocabulary with others. An example of this activity is the Dublin Core.

What is a potential importance of RDF?

A potential importance of RDF is the possibility for embedding metadata in Web pages. This means the synchronization of site maps and content ratings. This should then evolve into better search mechanisms. The chaotic order of information on the Web should become more ordered and structured.

What is the primary function of RDF?

RDF's primary function is to identify resources. A resource is defined here as anything addressed by a URI (URL). A resource is composed of properties (attributes) such as type and value.

What is Web Interface Definition Language (WIDL)?

Web Interface Definition Language (WIDL) is a forefront Web technology for conceptually developing XML applications. This technology goes hand in hand with the Document Object Model (DOM).

WIDL is an application of XML. It is a metalanguage, a top-level conceptual language, which implements a service-based architecture over the document-based resources of the Web. This Web technology uses HTTP for communication among XML and HTML documents (XML to XML, HTML to HTML, or XML to HTML) by interpreting them as inter-application messages.

 Note: webMethods made a Submission Request to W3C on September 22, 1997 (http://www.w3c.org/Submission/1997/15/). webMethods is a provider of XML-based business-to-business (B2B) integration solutions and holds copyright to the WIDL Specification.

 Warning: When quotation marks are used with the WIDL tips, they are a part of the expected markup. For example the correct markup is "SUCCESS," not SUCCESS.

What are the basic components of WIDL?

The basic components of WIDL version 3.0 are the following:
- WIDL-SPEC DTD

■ WIDL-MAPPING DTD

WIDL defines two types of XML documents: a WIDL specification (WIDL-SPEC) and a WIDL mapping (WIDL-MAPPING). These document types conform to XML document type declarations.

 Note: This URL has links to the WIDL Specifications, the WIDL Specification DTD, the WIDL Mappings, and the WIDL Mapping DTD: http://www.transactnet.com/products/toolkit/userguide/refman/widl/overview.html

What is a WIDL specification?

A WIDL specification is an XML document that provides an abstract description of an application interface. It names the interface and describes the services that are associated with the interface. Different applications may implement the same specification in different ways. WIDL allows any two applications that conform to the same specification to be interchangeable, so clients need not have knowledge of the details of any application's interface. A WIDL specification provides all of the information required for generating code.

 Note: This development shows how one can use XML as an application interface or software template.

What is a WIDL mapping?

A WIDL mapping is an XML document that describes how to map between XML and HTML pages and a WIDL specification. It exposes a Web site or an XML-based application as a set of services. Through a WIDL mapping, a client application may interact with the Web by invoking Web services as if they were implemented as program functions or procedures. WIDL mappings allow applications to interact with the Web without having any knowledge of XML, HTML, or network protocols.

What does the WIDL-SPEC DTD look like?

The comments for this DTD are by the author.

 Warning: In this DTD, there are the attributes NAME and COMMENT under each element. However, they are <u>not</u> identical; they are unique to that element. The

definition of each COMMENT attribute can be phrased in the same manner.

```
<!- - Root element - ->
<!- - any number of sub-elements - ->
<!ELEMENT WIDL-SPEC (METHOD | RECORD)+>
<!ATTLIST WIDL-SPEC
<!- - interface name is case sensitive - ->
<!- - service name for naming or a directory service - ->
  NAME CDATA #REQUIRED
<!- - must be 3.0 - ->
  VERSION CDATA #FIXED "3.0"
  COMMENT CDATA #IMPLIED>

<!- - represents a server operation - ->
<!ELEMENT METHOD EMPTY>
<!ATTLIST METHOD
<!- - a unique method name - ->
  NAME CDATA #REQUIRED
<!- - method's input arguments name - ->
  INPUT CDATA #IMPLIED
<!- - method's output arguments name - ->
  OUTPUT CDATA #IMPLIED
  COMMENT CDATA #IMPLIED>

<!- - similar to a Java class with state variables - ->
<!- - names a collection of fields - ->
<!ELEMENT RECORD (VALUE | RECORDREF)+>
<!ATTLIST RECORD
<!- - unique record name - ->
  NAME CDATA #REQUIRED
  COMMENT CDATA #IMPLIED>

<!- - represents non-nested record fields - ->
<!ELEMENT VALUE EMPTY>
<!ATTLIST VALUE
<!- - unique record name within RECORD - ->
  NAME CDATA #REQUIRED
<!- - 1 = single-dimensional array - ->
<!- - 2 = two-dimensional array - ->
<!- - 0 = a string - ->
  DIM (0 | 1 | 2)  "0"
  TYPE CDATA "STRING"
  COMMENT CDATA #IMPLIED>

<!- - represents nested records - ->
<!ELEMENT RECORDREF EMPTY>
```

```
<!ATTLIST RECORDREF
<!- - unique record name with another record - ->
  NAME CDATA #REQUIRED
<!- - 1 = single-dimensional array - ->
<!- - 2 = two-dimensional array - ->
<!- - 0 = a record - ->
  DIM (0 | 1 | 2) "0"
  RECORD CDATA #REQUIRED
  COMMENT CDATA #IMPLIED>
```

What does the WIDL-MAPPING DTD look like?

The comments for this DTD are by the author.

 Warning: In this DTD, there are the attributes NAME and COMMENT under each element. However, they are not identical; they are unique to that element. The definition of each COMMENT attribute can be phrased in the same manner.

```
<!- - root element - ->
<!- - any number of sub-elements - ->
<!ELEMENT WIDL-MAPPING (SERVICE | INPUT-BINDING |
OUTPUT-BINDING)+>
<!ATTLIST WIDL-MAPPING
<!- - interface name - ->
  NAME CDATA #REQUIRED
<!- - must be 3.0 - ->
  VERSION CDATA #FIXED "3.0"
<!- - URL for various services - ->
  BASEURL CDATA #IMPLIED
<!- - WOM = webMethods Object Model - ->
  DEFAULT-CONTENT (WOM | CONSTANT) "WOM"
  COMMENT CDATA #IMPLIED>

<!- - an empty-element, defines an HTTP request - ->
<!ELEMENT SERVICE EMPTY>
<!ATTLIST SERVICE
<!- - unique service name is case sensitive - ->
<!- - mapping name for naming or directory services - ->
  NAME CDATA #REQUIRED
<!- - input parameters for the service call - ->
  INPUT CDATA #IMPLIED
<!- - output parameters for the service call - ->
  OUTPUT CDATA #IMPLIED
<!- - URL for target document - ->
```

```
  URL CDATA #REQUIRED
<!- - HTTP method specification for service access - ->
  METHOD (GET | POST) "GET"
<!- - HTTP authentication username - ->
  AUTHUSER CDATA #IMPLIED
<!- - HTTP authentication password - ->
  AUTHPASS CDATA #IMPLIED
<!- - sets the HTTP REFERER header variable - ->
  SOURCE CDATA #IMPLIED
<!- - in seconds - ->
  TIMEOUT CDATA #IMPLIED
<!- - number of retries before service failure - ->
  RETRIES CDATA #IMPLIED
  COMMENT CDATA #IMPLIED>

<!- - defines service input parameters - ->
<!ELEMENT INPUT-BINDING (VALUE | BINDINGREF)+>
<!ATTLIST INPUT-BINDING
<!- - identifies the binding for references by SERVICE - ->
<!- - elements cannot have identical binding names - ->
  NAME CDATA #REQUIRED
  COMMENT CDATA #IMPLIED>

<!-  defines service output parameters - ->
<!ELEMENT OUTPUT-BINDING (CONDITION | REGION | VALUE |
BINDINGREF)+>
<!ATTLIST OUTPUT-BINDING
<!- - identifies the bindings by SERVICE and BINDINGREF - ->
<!- - elements cannot have identical binding names - ->
  NAME CDATA #REQUIRED
  COMMENT CDATA #IMPLIED>

<!- - empty element, specifies success and failure - ->
<!- - conditions for data extraction to be returned - ->
<!- - to calling programs in output bindings - ->
<!ELEMENT CONDITION EMPTY>
<!ATTLIST CONDITION
<!- - specifies condition type for a binding attempt - ->
TYPE (SUCCESS | FAILURE | RETRY) "SUCCESS"
<!- - object reference that extracts data from an - ->
<!- - XML document - ->
  REFERENCE CDATA #IMPLIED
<!- - specifies a text pattern for object property - ->
<!- - comparison - ->
  MATCH CDATA #IMPLIED
<!- - in seconds after a service busy error - ->
  WAIT CDATA #IMPLIED
```

```
<!- - specifies a portion of the text that - ->
<!- -REASONREF returns - ->
  MASK CDATA #IMPLIED
<!- - specifies an alternate output binding - ->
  REBIND CDATA #IMPLIED
<!- - specifies a service to invoke with results - ->
<!- - of an output binding - ->
  SERVICE CDATA #IMPLIED
<!- - object reference pointer for an error message - ->
  REASONREF CDATA #IMPLIED
<!- - object reference text for an error message - ->
  REASONTEXT CDATA #IMPLIED
<!- - number of retries before failing the service - ->
  RETRIES CDATA #IMPLIED
  COMMENT CDATA #IMPLIED>


<!- - empty element, out binding defines target of - ->
<!- - a document's sub-regions - ->
<!ELEMENT REGION EMPTY>
<!ATTLIST REGION
<!- - specifies a region's name - ->
  NAME CDATA #REQUIRED
<!- -  beginning of a region - ->
  START CDATA #REQUIRED
<!- - termination of a region - ->
  END CDATA #REQUIRED
<!- - "TRUE" or "FALSE" - ->
<!- - determines if a bind parameter is acceptable - ->
  NULLOK CDATA #IMPLIED
<!- - defines a pattern of elements to match within - ->
<!- - a region - ->
  PATTERN CDATA #IMPLIED
  COMMENT CDATA #IMPLIED>


<!- - represents a string parameter of a binding - ->
<!ELEMENT VALUE (#PCDATA)>
<!ATTLIST VALUE
<!- - identifies the parameter to calling programs - ->
  NAME CDATA #REQUIRED
<! 1 = single-dimensional array - ->
<! 2 = two-dimensional array or table - ->
<! 0 = a string - ->
  DIM (0 | 1 | 2) "0"
<!- - data type of the parameter - ->
  TYPE CDATA "STRING"
<!- - expression type within the element content - ->
<!- - input parameters cannot use WOM - ->
```

149

```
<!- - WOM = webMethods Object Model - ->
  CONTENT (WOM | CONSTANT) #IMPLIED
<!- - specifies the variable name to be submitted - ->
<!- - through the HTTP GET or POST method - ->
  FORMNAME CDATA #IMPLIED
<!- - an optional attribute - ->
  USAGE (DEFAULT | HEADER | INTERNAL) "DEFAULT"
<!- - determines if a bind parameter is acceptable - ->
  NULLOK (TRUE | FALSE) "FALSE"
  COMMENT CDATA #IMPLIED>

<!- - represents a structured record parameter of - ->
<!- - an output binding - ->
<!ELEMENT BINDINGREF (#PCDATA)>
<!ATTLIST BINDINGREF
<!- - identifies the parameter to calling programs - ->
  NAME CDATA #REQUIRED
<!- - 0 = a single binding - ->
<!- - 1 = an array of bindings - ->
<!- - not valid - ->
  DIM (0 | 1 | 2) "0"
<!- - identifies the output binding that the binding - ->
<!- - reference is to nest within its parent output - ->
<!- - binding - ->
  RECORD CDATA #REQUIRED
<!- - identifies the type of expression found within - ->
<!- - the content of the element, where the content - ->
<!- - is the string that resides between the - ->
<!- - BINDINGREF start-tag and end-tag - ->
<!- - WOM = webMethods Object Model - ->
  CONTENT (WOM | CONSTANT) #IMPLIED
<!- - specifies the variable name to be submitted - ->
<!- - through the HTTP GET or POST method - ->
  FORMNAME CDATA #IMPLIED
<!- - an optional attribute - ->
  USAGE (DEFAULT | HEADER | INTERNAL) "DEFAULT"
<!- - determines if a bind parameter is acceptable - ->
  NULLOK (TRUE | FALSE) "FALSE"
  COMMENT CDATA #IMPLIED>
```

 Note: This DTD, in particular the OUTPUT-BINDING element, was reorganized from the Specification to reflect an XML logical structure.

What are some WIDL implications for XML?

WIDL from webMethods describes Web resources so a user can automate all XML and HTML documents and forms interactions. WIDL follows the trend to describe data within documents rather than the documents themselves.

The WIDL specification provides an abstract description for an API to services. While the WIDL mapping provides the interactions among XML and HTML documents.

 Note: A service is a function that resides behind a Web XML or HTML document such as a Common Gateway Interface (CGI) script. An interface is a collection of services.

WIDL describes the location of services at the highest Web level, URL. The input parameters to be submitted to a service are described in the WIDL-MAPPING root element and its SERVICE element with its METHOD attribute. The output parameters to be returned for a service are described likewise.

What is an example of a WIDL-SPEC service interface?

Below is a template example of an XML implementation for a service using WIDL-SPEC. This template can be the basis for developing an interface to a science fiction book catalog service.

```
<WIDL-SPEC NAME="com.cnote.ScFi.catalog" VERSION="3.0">

<METHOD NAME="getbook"
    INPUT="BookList"
    OUTPUT="BookCatalog" />

<RECORD NAME="Title">
  <VALUE NAME="Foundation" />
</RECORD>
<RECORD NAME="Author">
    <RECORDREF NAME="LastName"
        RECORD="Asimov" />
    <RECORDREF NAME="FirstName"
        RECORD="Isaac" />
</RECORD>

</WIDL-SPEC>
```

Note: WIDL is parsed as an XML document. This process extracts relevant data about services declared. To retrieve available services in a given WIDL file, this simple object reference would be used: widl.service[].name.

Chapter 8

Extensible Stylesheet Language (XSL) Tips

XML does not define the look and feel of data. To give XML a functionality similar to HTML such as the tag <b> </b>, XSL was developed. This chapter looks at some of the implications of the XSL specification and some of the latest developments in this area. Relative to the book this chapter is lengthy; however, the current specification has over 300 pages in the HTML format.

 Note: A tip is a snippet of advice, a guideline, or a pointer. It is not a full explanation of a subject. It is recognized that the answers here are highly abbreviated and only high points of the topics.

 Warning: This chapter was probably written six months to a year before the first general reader can read it. In addition, the order of tips is random. This area is the most dynamic area of change and enhancements. One should use this chapter as a foundation for work on styles rather than as the word on the subject.

What is XSL?

Extensible Stylesheet Language (XSL) extends the logical and physical structure of an XML document. XSL includes the visual structure, that is, how one displays the document in any medium and environment. XSL is a markup language for expressing stylesheets. It is a language for transforming XML documents (see Chapter 15 on XSL Transformations) and an XML vocabulary for specifying formatting semantics.

 Note: The tips in this chapter are based on Extensible Stylesheet Language (XSL) Version 1.0 W3C Working Draft (January 12, 2000) found at:

http://www.w3.org/TR/2000/WD-xsl-20000112. The latest version is found at http://www.w3.org/TR/xsl.

What is a stylesheet?

A stylesheet could be a description of an XML document instance that is transformed by a formatting vocabulary.

Why was XSL developed?

XSL was developed because it was expected that XML would outgrow CSS2 and DSSSL. In addition, it was recognized that XML needed its own specialized stylesheet language.

Who developed XSL?

The XSL language was developed by a group of editors from various companies.

What are the basic expectations of the development group for XSL?

The XSL development group expected XSL to do the following:
- Be a declarative language
- Be human-readable
- Be display interface neutral
- Have an extensibility mechanism
- Have DSSSL and CSS2 formatting functionality
- Leverage off other related style recommendations
- Be presentation environment neutral
- Support all levels of formatting tasks
- Support structured and presentation modes
- Support text and data presentations
- Support visual and non-visual presentations
- Consider terseness in XSL markup of minimal importance
- Use minimal options
- Use XML syntax

Note: In summary, any XML document that uses XSL should be displayed in any presentation environment (Internet or any non-electronic environment), with any presentation device (printer or monitor), and in any presentation mode (visual or non-visual).

What is the basis for XSL?

Extensible Stylesheet Language (XSL) is based on Web cascading stylesheets and ISO's DSSSL (pronounced like diesel) standard, 10179.

 Note: For the latest information on CSS2, see http://www.w3.org/TR/REC-CSS2.

For the latest information on Document Style Semantics and Specification Language, see http://www.jclark.com/dsssl.

What is the basic similarity between XSL and CSS?

The basic similarity between XSL and CSS is that both are declarative.

What are some differences between XSL and CSS?

A short listing of differences between XSL and CSS:
- XSL does not have mature browser support, while CSS, of course, does.
- XSL is user-extensible, while CSS is not.
- XSL uses XML notation, while CSS uses its own.

What is the basic similarity between XSL and DSSSL?

The basic similarity between XSL and DSSSL is that both are stylesheet languages.

What are some differences between XSL and DSSSL?

Two differences between XSL and DSSSL are:
- XSL uses a subset of the functionality of DSSSL.

■ XSL focuses on XML documentation, but DSSSL is an international print publishing industry standard.

What are the difficulties in using XSL?

Four of the reasons XSL is difficult to use are:
■ XSL specification has areas to be defined or expanded.
■ Lack of common or standard Web browser support for XML and XSL.
■ There have to be devices that know how to do rendering for both XML and XSL.
■ XSL is only a specialized XML DTD. This means an XML parser must be able to parse the XSL and apply it to the associated XML document.

Is an XSL editor available?

There are a number of XSL editors. Three of these are XSL Editor by ArborText, IBM XSL Editor, and XMLwriter by Wattle Software.

What is the basic structure of the XSL specification?

The XSL specification considers the technical requirements for creating an XSL stylesheet. In addition, it gives information on an area model, property refinement, 32 formatting objects, and 225 properties.

What is the basic content of an XSL stylesheet?

An XSL stylesheet contains an xsl:stylesheet document element. This element may contain xsl:template elements specifying template rules.

What is a template rule?

A template rule consists of a pattern and a template. The pattern is matched against nodes in the source tree. The template forms part of the result tree. A template rule is a rule applied to the source element that has been identified. A template can contain character data, instructions, and literals for creating instructions for result tree fragments. A template rule is specified with the xsl:template element. Its match attribute identifies the applicable source node or nodes. The template is the xsl:template element's content.

What is an example of a template rule?

If you have the following in an XML document: <tag>Stylesheet support <emph>needs</emph> careful study.</tag>

you would need the following stylesheet:

```
<xsl:stylesheet
    xmlns:xsl=
    xmlns:fo=
    result-ns="fo">
  <xsl:template match="emph">
      <fo:inline-sequence font-style="italic">
        <xsl:apply-template/>
      </fo:inline-sequence>
  </xsl:template>
</xsl:stylesheet>
```

 Note: The template rule matches elements of the type emph and has a template that produces a fo:line-sequence formatting with a font-style property of italic.

What is the meaning of fo:?

The fo: prefix is used for referring to elements in an XSL namespace.

What is a pattern?

A pattern is a string that selects a set of nodes in a source document. It is a matched set of elements in the source tree.

What is the simplest pattern?

The simplest pattern is an element type name. An example pattern is author[book="Learn XMLTips"]; this would select author children of the current elements that have a book child with a value equal to Learn XML Tips.

What is a result tree?

A result tree is the result of the association of patterns with templates and uses the formatting vocabulary. See Chapter 15 on XSLT.

 Note: The tree metaphor is a valid one because an XML document's logical structure is based on this metaphor.

What is a source tree?

A source tree is the original arbitrary document structure that can be filtered and reordered. See Chapter 15 on XSLT.

How is a stylesheet represented?

A stylesheet is represented by an xsl:stylesheet element in an XML document.

What is an xsl:stylesheet element?

A stylesheet is represented by an xsl:stylesheet element in an XML document. The element goes immediately after the XML declaration and before any XML element or entity.

 Warning: XSL defined elements are recognized only within the stylesheet.

Are there options for the xsl:stylesheet element?

The xsl:stylesheet element has an optional result-ns attribute (namespace):

- The value must be a namespace prefix.
- If this attribute is specified, all result elements must belong to the namespace identified by this prefix (the result namespace).
- If there is a namespace declared as the default namespace, then an empty string may be used as the value to specify that the default namespace is the result namespace.
- If the result-ns attribute specifies the XSL formatting-objects namespace, then in addition to constructing the result XML tree, the XSL processor must interpret it according to the semantics defined in the specification.

Note: The XSL formatting objects namespace has the placeholder (imaginary) URI http://www.w3.org/TR/WD-xsl/FO.

What is the basic xsl:stylesheet markup?

The most basic xsl:stylesheet markup is the following:

```
<?xml version="1.0"?>
<xsl:stylesheet>
xmlns:xsl=""
xmlns:fo=""
result-ns="fo">
...
</xsl:stylesheet>
```

 Note: The xsl: prefix is for XSL elements. The fo: prefix is for namespaces.

What elements can be included with xsl:stylesheet?

The xsl:stylesheet element can include any of these elements:

- xsl:attribute-set
- xsl:constant
- xsl:id
- xsl:import
- xsl:include
- xsl:macro
- xsl:preserve-space
- xsl:strip-space
- xsl:template

What is an example of the xsl:stylesheet elements?

This example shows the structure of a generic stylesheet. Ellipses (...) indicate where attribute values or content has been omitted. Although this example shows one of each type of allowed element, stylesheets may contain zero or more of each of these elements.

```
<?xml version="1.0"?>
<xsl:stylesheet xmlns:xsl=>
xmlns:fo=""
```

```
result-ns="fo">

<xsl:attribute-set name="...">
...
</xsl:attribute-set>
<xsl:constant name="..." value="...">
...
</xsl:constant>
<xsl:id attribute="..."/>
<xsl:import href="..."/>
<xsl:include href="..."/>
<xsl:macro name="...">
...
</xsl:macro>
<xsl:preserve-space element="..."/>
<xsl:strip-space element="..."/>
<xsl:template match="...">
...
</xsl:template>
</xsl:stylesheet>
```

 Note: The order in which the xsl:stylesheet element's children occur is not significant except for xsl:import elements and for error recovery. Users are free to order the elements as they prefer, and stylesheet creation tools need not provide control over the order in which the elements occur.

What is the xsl:attribute-set element?

The xsl:attribute-set element permits you to define an attribute named set.

How do I use the xsl:attribute element?

For example, you want the CDID element to have a font size of 14pt and to be expanded. The declaration plus template rule would look like this:

```
<xsl:attribute-set name="CDID-style">
  <xsl:attribute name="font-size">14pt</xsl:attribute>
  <xsl:attribute name="font-stretch">expanded</xsl:attribute>
</xsl:attribute-set>
```

```
<xsl:template match="CDIDstyle">
 <fo:inline-sequence>
  <xsl:use attribute-set="CDID-style"/>
  <xsl:apply-templates/>
 </fo:inline-sequence>
</xsl:template>
```

 Warning: Currently, the notion of attribute-set is under question by the specification authors.

 Note: The xsl:use element specifies the attribute-set name.

How would I include xsl:attribute in the markup?

Let us now include xsl:attribute and do the appropriate markup:

```
<?xml version="1.0"?>
<xsl:stylesheet xmlns:xsl=http://www.w3.org/TR/WD-xsl
xmlns:fo="http://www.w3.org/TR/WD-xsl/FO"
result-ns="fo">
<!- CDID style - ->
<xsl:attribute-set name="CDID-style">
   <xsl:attribute name="font-size">14pt</xsl:attribute>
   <xsl:attribute name="font-stretch">expanded</xsl:attribute>
</xsl:attribute-set>
<xsl:template match="CDIDstyle">
   <fo:inline-sequence>
      <xsl:use attribute-set="CDID-style"/>
      <xsl:apply-templates/>
   </fo:inline-sequence>
</xsl:template>
<!- - Bold style - ->
<xsl:template match="emphasis">
   <fo:inline-sequence font-weight="bold">
      <xsl:apply-templates/>
   </fo:inline-sequence>
</xsl:template>
<!- - Italic style - ->
<xsl:template match="italic">
   <fo:inline-sequence font-style="italic">
      <xsl:apply-templates/>
   </fo:inline-sequence>
</xsl:template>
</xsl:stylesheet>
<CD-Library>
```

```
    <CD>
<CDID><CDIDStyle>0001A</ CDIDStyle>
<Composer>John Williams</Composer>
<!- - Use emphasis for title - ->
<Title><emphasis>By Request...</emphasis></Title>
…
<Conductor>John Williams</Conductor>
<Orchestra>Boston Pops Orchestra></Orchestra>
…
<!Use italic for label - ->
<Label><italic>Philips</italic></Label>
…
    </CD>
</CD-Library>
```

What is the use of the xsl:constant element?

One of the uses of the xsl:constant element is defining global string constants. The basic syntax is <xsl:constant name="ABC" value="Npt"/>.

What is an example of the use of the xsl:constant element?

The xsl:constant element would look like this:

```
<xsl:constant name="rmks-font-size" value="8pt"/>
<xsl:template match="para">
    <fo:block font-size="{constant(rmks-font-size)}">
      <xsl:apply-templates/>
    </fo:block>
</xsl:template>
```

What is the function of fo:block?

The use of fo:block (block formatting object) permits you to create a block-level area with text. The markup would look like this if you had a Remarks element: <Remarks><para>...</para></Remarks>.

You would need to have a template rule such as:

```
<xsl:template match="Remarks">
    <fo:block>
        <xsl:apply-templates/>
    </fo:block>
</xsl:template>
```

How do I use the xsl:constant element in markup?

The following markup includes the use of the xsl:constant element:

```
<?xml version="1.0"?>
<xsl:stylesheet xmlns:xsl=http://www.w3.org/TR/WD-xsl>
xmlns:fo="http://www.w3.org/TR/WD-xs /FO"
result-ns="fo">
<!- CDID style - ->
<xsl:attribute-set name="CDID-style">
    <xsl:attribute name="font-size">14pt</xsl:attribute>
    <xsl:attribute name="font-stretch">expanded</xsl:attribute>
</xsl:attribute-set>
<xsl:template match="CDIDstyle">
  <fo:inline-sequence>
     <xsl:use attribute-set="CDID-style"/>
     <xsl:apply-templates/>
  </fo:inline-sequence>
</xsl:template>
<!- - Bold style - ->
<xsl:template match="emphasis">
   <fo:inline-sequence font-weight="bold">
      <xsl:apply-templates/>
   </fo:inline-sequence>
</xsl:template>
<!- - Italic style - ->
<xsl:template match="italic">
   <fo:inline-sequence font-style="italic' >
      <xsl:apply-templates/>
   </fo:inline-sequence>
</xsl:template>
<!- - Style for Remarks element to be added later- ->
<xsl:constant name="rmks-font-size" value="8pt"/>
<xsl:template match="para">
   <fo:block font-size="{constant(rmks-font-size)}">
      <xsl:apply-templates/>
   </fo:block>
</xsl:template>
</xsl:stylesheet>
<CD-Library>
  <CD>
...
  </CD>
</CD-Library>
```

What is the xsl:id element?

The xsl:id element is used to give an element a unique identifier (ID). The basic syntax for xsl:id is <xsl:id attribute="name"/>. It is the value of the attribute that is declared in the DTD as the attribute type ID. No ID-type attribute is used in the CD-Library ID.

 Warning: The xsl:id element must be used when no XML DTD is given.

What are examples of xsl:id element syntax?

The syntax for an ID-type attribute could look like either of these examples:

```
<!ATTLIST CDID
ref ID #IMPLIED
>
<!ATTLIST IDCD
ref ID #REQUIRED
>
```

What is the xsl:macro element?

The xsl:macro element is useful for a text-oriented application. The element allows you to collect result fragments and to reference the composite as a single object.

What is an example of the xsl:macro element?

In this example, a macro is defined for a boxed paragraph with the word "Caution!" preceding the contents. The macro is referenced from a rule for caution elements.

```
<xsl:macro name="caution-note">
    <fo:block-level-box>
        <fo:block>
            <xsl:text>Caution!</xsl:text>
            <xsl:contents/>
        </fo:block>
    </fo:block-level-box>
</xsl:macro>
<xsl:template match="caution">
    <xsl:invoke macro="caution-note">
```

```
        <xsl:apply-templates/>
    </xsl-invoke>
</xsl:template>
```

What is the function of the xsl:preserve-space and the xsl:strip-space elements?

The xsl:preserve-space and xsl:strip-space elements control the preservation or the elimination of white space in text.

What is the xsl:template element?

The xsl:template element has a match attribute that identifies the source node or nodes to which a rule applies. The content of the xsl:template element is the template.

How do I use the xsl:template element?

For example, an XML document might contain: <sentence>This fact is <emphasis>key</emphasis> to listening to Beethoven's Fifth Symphony.</sentence>

 Note: Do I have to use the word "emphasis"? The answer is no. One could use, for example, bold, since this word would be meaningful. Other possibilities that are not necessarily meaningful are "b" or "styleb." However, no matter which one is used, you would get a bold word or phrase when the XML content is expanded.

The following template rule matches elements of type emphasis and has a template that produces a fo:inline-sequence formatting object with a font-weight property of bold:

```
<xsl:template match="emphasis">
    <fo:inline-sequence font-weight="bold">
        <xsl:apply-templates/>
    </fo:inline-sequence>
</xsl:template>
```

 Note: The first line has syntax very similar to a general entity declaration. The value or match equals the markup or tag of emphasis. The second line has two formatting objects. There are 32 formatting objects with 225 properties defined in the current XSL specification.

What formatting objects deal with inline?

The four formatting objects that deal with inline are:

- fo:inline-graphic
- fo:inline-link
- fo:inline-rule
- fo:inline-sequence

What is the purpose of fo:inline-sequence?

The fo:inline-sequence is used here because it can be useful for specifying inherited properties. In the above example, the sequence specifies a font-style property—a bold-emphasis phrase element in a block of text.

What are the possible values for font-weight?

The font-weight="bold" is just one of the options for font-weight. You could also use:

- 100 to 900 in increments of 100
- bolder
- lighter
- normal

What are some other possible font properties?

Other font properties available include the following:

- font-family
- font-size
- font-size-adjust
- font-stretch
- font-style
- font-variant

Note: Each of the properties has a number of allowable values.

What is the function of the xsl:apply-templates element?

The third line of the last example has the xsl:apply-templates element that handles the recursive processing for the source element's children.

How would I use the xsl:stylesheet element in markup?

Using some of the CD-Library markup from Chapter 5, you would include the xsl:stylesheet element right after the XML declaration. The following example includes two templates as they would appear at the beginning of the markup and their inclusion in the markup with the Title and Label elements:

```
<?xml version="1.0"?>
<xsl:stylesheet xmlns:xsl=http://www.w3.org/TR/WD-xsl>
xmlns:fo="http://www.w3.org/TR/WD-xsl/FO"
result-ns="fo">
<!- - Bold style - ->
<xsl:template match="emphasis">
    <fo:inline-sequence font-weight="bold'>
        <xsl:apply-templates/>
    </fo:inline-sequence>
</xsl:template>
<!- - Italic style - ->
<xsl:template match="italic">
    <fo:inline-sequence font-style="italic">
        <xsl:apply-templates/>
    </fo:inline-sequence>
</xsl:template>
</xsl:stylesheet>
<CD-Library>
  <CD>
...
<!- - Use emphasis for title - ->
<Title><emphasis>By Request...</emphasis></Title>
...
<Conductor>John Williams</Conductor>
...
<!Use italic for label - ->
<Label><italic>Philips</italic></Label>
...
```

```
    </CD>
</CD-Library>
```

What is the XSL data model?

The XSL modeling of an XML as a tree is strictly conceptual. There are seven XML node types, but processing instruction and comment nodes are not included in the stylesheet tree. The five nodes in the XSL data model are:

- Root
- Element
- Attribute
- Namespaces
- Text

How are values determined for the tree?

The value criteria are the following:

- Root — Document element
- Element — The string that results from concatenating all characters that are descendants of the element node in the order in which they occur
- Attribute — Normalized value in accordance with the XML specification
- Namespace — Namespace URI
- Text — Character data

What is the meaning of block-progression-direction?

In Western writing systems, the block-progression-direction is "top-to-bottom." The use of block with the specification tries to eliminate absolute indicators. The value of the writing-mode property is used.

What is inline-progression-direction?

In Western writing systems, the inline-progression-direction is "left-to-right." The use of inline with the specification tries to eliminate absolute indicators. The value of the writing-mode property is used.

What is the meaning of color in XSL?

Color is a set of values used to identify a particular color from a color space.

 Warning: Currently, only RGB colors are supported. In addition, there are questions about other color encodes and "named" colors.

What is the meaning of a directly derived trait?

A directly derived trait is a computed value of a property of the same name on the generating formatting object.

What is an indirectly derived trait?

An indirectly derived trait is the result of a computation involving the computed values of one or more properties on the generating formatting object, other traits on this area or other interacting areas (ancestors, parent, siblings, and/or children) and/or one or more values constructed by the formatter.

What is the basic XSL formatting process?

The basic formatting process turns the result of an XSL transformation into a tangible form for the reader or listener. Also, see Chapter 15 on XSLT.

What are formatting objects?

Formatting objects are elements in an area tree, whose names are from the XSL namespace. A formatting object belongs to a class of formatting objects identified by its element name. Some formatting objects are block-level and others are inline-level.

What is an area tree?

An area tree is a hierarchical (genealogical) arrangement or geometric structure that describes a formatted presentation (result). The structure principle is inheritance.

What are the types of formatting objects?

There are three types of formatting objects. The types are based on area generation:

- Generates areas (flow objects)
- Returns areas, but does not generate areas (flow objects)
- Returns areas and generates areas (layout or auxiliary objects)

What is inheritance?

Inheritance is the property that takes the same computed value as the property for the formatting object's parent object.

What are XSL keywords?

XSL keywords provide access to property or calculated values. In the XSL grammar, they are special tokens. The keywords are based on XSL productions [14] – [29].

 Note: These productions are given as a part of the last tip in the chapter.

What is XSL refinement?

XSL refinement is a computational process. It finalizes the properties specification based on the attribute values in the XML result tree. It includes the involvement of property value propagation, evaluation, conversion, and construction. This complex process may involve look-ahead, backtracking, or control splicing with other processes in the formatter.

What is a space-specifier?

A space-specifier is a compound datatype that consists of length or distance constraints (minimum, optimum, and maximum), a Boolean value that controls the limits of a reference area (conditionality), and an integer or the special token force (precedence).

What is the meaning of conditionality?

Conditionality is a Boolean value, which controls whether a space-specifier has an effect at the beginning or end of a reference-area; for a conditional space-specifier this value is true.

What is precedence?

Precedence is a value, which is either an integer or the special token force.

What is the URI for an XSL namespace?

The XSL namespace has the URI http://www.w3.org/1999/XSL/Format.

What are the basic guidelines for establishing a document element?

Here are basic guidelines for establishing a document element:
- A pattern that is just / matches the root.
- A pattern of /div matches the document element when it is a div element.
- A pattern of /* matches the document element, whatever it is.

What is an area model?

An area model has a number of formatting objects that serve as inputs or specifications for a formatter. The formatter using the model constructs a hierarchical arrangement of areas and spaces to produce the formatted results.

What types of areas can be considered in an area model?

A number of area types can be considered within an area model. Some are inclusive, such as rectangular areas, including line-areas that in turn includes inline-area placement.
- Rectangular areas
- Spaces
- Conditions

- Area-containers
- Block-areas
- Line-areas
- Inline-areas
- Stacked inline-areas
- Glyph-areas

What are the various types of formatting objects?

Here is a summary of eight formatting objects. In the parentheses is the number of specific formatting objects for each type.

- Pagination and layout — They are the children of the fo:layout-master-set. The parent defines page geometry and sequences. (16)
- Block-level — They are the basic descriptive document structures such as title, chapters, figure captions, and tables. (2)
- Inline-level — They generate certain portions of text such as header or footer formatting, and generate rules and leaders. (10)
- Tables — They create a table structure for a presentation using a result tree. (9)
- Lists — They create lists (block, item, label, and body). (4)
- Links — They create three different types of links. (6)
- Out-of-line-level — They handle such things as floats and footnotes. (3) This is a dynamic area of discussion.
- Other — They handle anything not handled by the other seven types. (1)

 Note: These formatting objects are based on those that already exist in the print publishing environment. Remember that the XSL specification (a set of standards) is an electronic transition, or a translation, of the print publishing environment.

What is a formatting property?

Properties include such things as border-width and page-margin. There are 225 formatting properties, with each associated with one or more formatting objects.

What are property datatypes?

The datatypes are used with the allowed values of the properties. Currently the datatypes have been organized into eight property groups and nine property clusters. Here is a summary of 30 potential datatypes:

Angle	An integer representing an angle.
Boolean	A Boolean value, where the allowed values are the strings "true" and "false."
Character	A single Unicode character value—white space is not allowed.
Color	A color specification where "#xxxxxx" is an RGB value encoded in hexadecimal.
Coordinate	A pair of signed real values separated by a comma.
Enumeration	An enumerated list of XML NMTOKEN values.
Family-name	A character string that identifies a font.
Font List	A list of font names separated by white space.
Font Name	A string of characters identifying a font.
ID	A character string conforming to the XML NMTOKEN definition that is unique within the stylesheet.
IDREF	A character string conforming to the XML NMTOKEN definition that uses an ID property value used within the stylesheet.
Integer	A signed value that may include an optional "+" or "–".
Language	A character string conforming to the xml:lang attribute value from the XML specification.
Limit Specifier	A semicolon-separated pair of lengths specifying the minimum and maximum lengths.

Name	A character string conforming to the XML NMTOKEN definition.
Number	A signed real number that may include an optional "+" or "−".
Percent	A percentage that is a signed real value (e.g., 45.5 is 455/1000).
Positive Integer	An unsigned integer value, not including zero, which consists of a sequence of digits.
Positive Length	A positive length value, not including zero, where a "length" is a real number plus a unit qualification.
Positive Real	An unsigned real number not including zero, which consists of a sequence of digits followed by an optional "." character and sequence of digits.
Script	A character string that conforms to ISO 15924.
Signed Length	A signed length value where a "length" is a real number plus a unit qualification.
Signed Integer	A signed integer value that consists of an optional "+" or "−" character followed by a sequence of digits.
Signed Real	A signed real number that consists of an optional "+" or "−" character followed by a sequence of digits followed by an optional "." character and sequence of digits.
Space Specifier	A semicolon-separated triplet of lengths specifying the minimum, maximum, and optimal space lengths respectively.
String	A sequence of characters.
Unsigned Integer	An unsigned integer value, including zero, that consists of a sequence of digits.
Unsigned Length	An unsigned length value, including zero, where a "length" is a real number plus a unit qualification.
Unsigned Real	An unsigned real number, including zero, that consists of a sequence of digits followed by an optional "." character and sequence of digits.
URI	A sequence of characters conforming to a URI value as specified in the URI specification.

How would a page sequence for an element be constructed?

The following is an example of a simple XSL stylesheet that constructs a result tree for a sequence of para elements:

```
<xsl:stylesheet
    xmlns:xsl="http://www.w3.org/TR/WD-xsl"
    xmlns:fo="http://www.w3.org/TR/WD-xsl/FO"
    result-ns="fo">
  <xsl:template match="/">
      <fo:page-sequence font-family="serif">
          <xsl:apply-templates/>
      </fo:page-sequence>
  </xsl:template>

  <xsl:template match="para">
      <fo:block font-size="12pt" space-before="11pt">
          <xsl:apply-templates/>
      </fo:block>
  </xsl:template>
</xsl:stylesheet>
```

 Note: The result-ns="fo" attribute indicates that a tree using the formatting object vocabulary is being constructed. The rule for the root node specifies the use of a page sequence formatted with any font with serifs. The para elements become block-formatting objects, which are set in 12-point type with an 11-point space before each block.

How is a block created?

This example creates a block for a chapter element and then processes its immediate children:

```
<xsl:template match="chapter">
    <fo:block>
        <xsl:apply-templates/>
    </fo:block>
</xsl:template>
```

What is a listing of possible formatting objects?

The listing is a potential set of formatting objects. Check the latest XSL specification for the current view.

175

fo:bidi-override
fo:block
fo:block-container
fo:character
fo:conditional-page-master-reference
fo:external-graphic
fo:float
fo:flow
fo:footnote
fo:footnote-body
fo:initial-property-set
fo:inline-container
fo:instream-graphic
fo:layout-master-set
fo:leader
fo:list-block
fo:list-item
fo:list-item-body
fo:list-item-label
fo:multi-case
fo:multi-properties
fo:multi-property-set
fo:multi-switch
fo:multi-toggle
fo:page-number
fo:page-number-citation
fo:page-sequence
fo:page-sequence-master
fo:region-after
fo:region-before
fo:region-body
fo:region-end
fo:region-start
fo:repeatable-page-master-alternatives
fo:repeatable-page-master-reference
fo:root
fo:simple-link
fo:simple-page-master
fo:single-page-master-reference
fo:static-content
fo:table

fo:table-and-caption
fo:table-body
fo:table-caption
fo:table-cell
fo:table-column
fo:table-footer
fo:table-header
fo:table-row
fo:wrapper

What are the common properties?

The common properties are:

- role
- source-document

What are the common absolute position properties?

The common absolute position properties are:

- bottom
- left
- position
- right
- top

What are the common aural properties?

The common aural properties are:

- azimuth
- cue
- cue-after
- cue-before
- elevation
- pause
- pause-after
- pause-before
- pitch
- pitch-range

- play-during
- richness
- speak
- speak-header
- speak-numeral
- speak-punctuation
- speech-rate
- stress
- voice-family
- volume

What are the common border, padding, and background properties?

The common border, padding, and background properties are:

- background
- background-attachment
- background-color
- background-image
- background-position
- background-repeat
- border
- border-after-color
- border-after-style
- border-after-width
- border-before-color
- border-before-style
- border-before-width
- border-bottom
- border-bottom-color
- border-bottom-style
- border-bottom-width
- border-color
- border-end-color
- border-end-style
- border-end-width
- border-left

- border-left-color
- border-left-style
- border-left-width
- border-right
- border-right-color
- border-right-style
- border-right-width
- border-start-color
- border-start-style
- border-start-width
- border-style
- border-top
- border-top-color
- border-top-style
- border-top-width
- border-width
- padding
- padding-after
- padding-before
- padding-bottom
- padding-end
- padding-left
- padding-right
- padding-start
- padding-top

What are the common font properties?

The common font properties are:
- font
- font-family
- font-size
- font-size-adjust
- font-stretch
- font-style
- font-variant
- font-weight

What are the common hyphenation properties?

The common hyphenation properties are:

- country
- hyphenate
- hyphenation-character
- hyphenation-push-character-count
- hyphenation-remain-character-count
- language
- script
- xml:lang

What are the common keeps and breaks properties?

The common keeps and breaks properties are:

- page-break-after
- page-break-before
- break-after
- break-before
- keep-with-next
- keep-with-previous

What are the common margin properties?

The common margin properties are:

- end-indent
- margin
- margin-bottom
- margin-left
- margin-right
- margin-top
- space-after
- space-before
- start-indent

What are the common margin inline properties?

The common margin inline properties are:
- space-end
- space-start

What are the pagination and layout properties?

The pagination and layout properties are:
- blank-page
- column-count
- column-gap
- extent
- flow-name
- force-page-count
- initial-page-number
- master-name
- maximum-repeats
- odd-or-even
- page-height
- page-position
- page-width
- precedence
- region-name

What are the table properties?

The table properties are:
- border-collapse
- border-spacing
- caption-side
- column-number
- column-width
- empty-cells
- ends-row
- may-break-after-row
- may-break-before-row

- number-columns-repeated
- number-columns-spanned
- number-rows-spanned
- starts-row
- table-layout
- table-omit-footer-at-break
- table-omit-header-at-break

What are the character properties?

The character properties are:
- apply-word-spacing
- character
- letter-spacing
- suppress-at-eol
- text-decoration
- text-shadow
- text-transform
- word-spacing

What are the rule and leader properties?

The rule and leader properties are:
- leader-alignment
- leader-length
- leader-pattern
- leader-pattern-width
- rule-style
- rule-thickness

What are the page-related properties?

The page-related properties are:
- page-break-inside
- keep
- orphans
- widows

What are the float-related properties?

The float-related properties are:
- clear
- float

What are the number-to-string conversion properties?

The number-to-string conversion properties are:
- format
- grouping-separator
- grouping-size
- letter-value

What are the properties for links?

The properties for links are:
- auto-restore
- case-name
- case-title
- destination-placement-offset
- dom-state
- external-destination
- indicate-destination
- internal-destination
- show-destination
- starting-state
- switch-to

What are the miscellaneous properties?

Some properties will not fit cleanly into a category. They include:
- baseline-shift
- block-progression-dimension
- clip
- color
- direction
- font-height-override-after

- font-height-override-before
- glyph-orientation-horizontal
- glyph-orientation-vertical
- height
- href
- hyphenation-keep
- hyphenation-ladder-count
- id
- inhibit-line-breaks
- inline-progression-dimension
- last-line-end-indent
- linefeed-treatment
- line-height
- line-height-shift-adjustment
- line-stacking-strategy
- max-height
- maximum-block-progression-dimension
- maximum-inline-progression-dimension
- max-width
- min-height
- minimum-block-progression-dimension
- minimum-inline-progression-dimension
- min-width
- overflow
- provisional-distance-between-starts
- provisional-label-separation
- reference-orientation
- ref-id
- scale
- score-spaces
- size
- space-treatment
- span
- text-align
- text-align-last
- text-indent
- unicode-bidi

- vertical-align
- visibility
- white-space
- white-space-collapse
- white-space-treatment
- width
- wrap-option
- writing-mode
- z-index

How is an HTML table created?

Multiple xsl:apply-templates elements can be used within a single template to do simple reordering. The following example creates two HTML tables. The first table is filled with active comics, while the second table is filled with inactive comics.

```
<xsl:template match="product">
    <TABLE>
            <xsl:apply-templates select="comics/active"/>
    </TABLE>
    <TABLE>
            <xsl:apply-templates select="comics/inactive"/>
    </TABLE>
</xsl:template>
```

For example, given an XML document with this structure:

```
<comics>
    <comic>
  <name>...</name>
  <issue>...</issue>
  <issue>...</issue>
    </comic>
    <comic>
  <name>...</name>
  <issue>...</issue>
  <issue>...</issue>
    </comic>
</comics>
```

the following would create an HTML document containing a table with a row for each comic element:

```
<xsl:template match="/">
 <HTML>
  <HEAD>
   <TITLE>Comics</TITLE>
  </HEAD>
  <BODY>
   <TABLE>
   <TBODY>
    <xsl:for-each select="comics/comic">
     <TR>
      <TH>
      <xsl:apply-templates select="name"/>
      </TH>
      <xsl:for-each select="issue">
      <TD>
       <xsl:apply-templates/>
      </TD>
      </xsl:for-each>
     </TR>
    </xsl:for-each>
   </TBODY>
   </TABLE>
  </BODY>
 </HTML>
</xsl:template>
```

As with xsl:apply-templates the pattern is a select pattern. The select attribute is required.

How is HTML style numbering done?

The following would do HTML style numbering:

```
<xsl:template match="h2">
 <xsl:counter-increment name="h2"/>
 <p>
  <xsl:counter name="h2"/>
  <xsl:text>. </xsl:text>
  <xsl:apply-templates/>
 </p>
 <xsl:counter-reset name="h3"/>
</xsl:template>

<xsl:template match="h3">
 <xsl:counter-increment name="h3"/>
 <p>
  <xsl:counter name="h2"/>
```

```
  <xsl:text>.</xsl:text>
  <xsl:counter name="h3"/>
  <xsl:text>. </xsl:text>
  <xsl:apply-templates/>
 </p>
 <xsl:counter-reset name="h4"/>
</xsl:template>

<xsl:template match="h4">
 <xsl:counter-increment name="h4"/>
 <p>
  <xsl:counter name="h2"/>
  <xsl:text>.</xsl:text>
  <xsl:counter name="h3"/>
  <xsl:text>.</xsl:text>
  <xsl:counter name="h4"/>
  <xsl:text>.</xsl:text>
  <xsl:apply-templates/>
 </p>
</xsl:template>
```

What are the production rules for XSL?

The production rules for XSL are the following:

[1] Expr ::= AdditiveExpr

[2] PrimaryExpr ::= '(' Expr ')' | Numeric | Literal | Color | Keyword |
EnumerationToken | FunctionCall

[3] FunctionCall ::= FunctionName '(' (Argument (',' Argument)*)? ')'

[4] Argument ::= Expr

[5] Numeric ::= AbsoluteNumeric | RelativeNumeric

[6] AbsoluteNumeric ::= AbsoluteLength

[7] AbsoluteLength ::= Number AbsoluteUnitName?

[8] RelativeNumeric ::= Percent | RelativeLength

[9] Percent ::= Number '%'

[10] RelativeLength ::= Number RelativeUnitName

[11] AdditiveExpr ::= MultiplicativeExpr | AdditiveExpr '+' MultiplicativeExpr |
AdditiveExpr '-' MultiplicativeExpr

[12] MultiplicativeExpr ::= UnaryExpr | MultiplicativeExpr MultiplyOperator
UnaryExpr | MultiplicativeExpr 'div' UnaryExpr | MultiplicativeExpr 'mod'
UnaryExpr

[13] UnaryExpr ::= PrimaryExpr | '-' UnaryExpr

[14] ExprToken ::= '(' | ')' | '%' | Operator | FunctionName | EnumerationToken
| Number

[15] Number ::= FloatingPointNumber

[16] FloatingPointNumber ::= Digits ('.' Digits?)? | '.' Digits

[17] Digits ::= [0-9]+

[18] Color ::= '#' AlphaOrDigits
[19] AlphaOrDigits ::= [a-fA-F0-9]+
[20] Literal ::= '"' [^"]* '"' | "'" [^']* "'"
[21] Operator ::= OperatorName | MultiplyOperator | '+' | '-'
[22] OperatorName ::= 'mod' | 'div'
[23] MultiplyOperator ::= '*'
[24] Keyword ::= 'inherit'
[25] FunctionName ::= NCName
[26] EnumerationToken ::= NCName
[27] AbsoluteUnitName ::= 'cm' | 'mm' | 'in' | 'pt' | 'pica'
[28] RelativeUnitName ::= 'em'
[29] ExprWhitespace ::= S

Chapter 9

XML Linking Language (XLink) Tips

There is a requirement to link one XML document with another XML document. This chapter looks at XLink, which handles general links as compared to XPointer that handles links between specific locations between XML documents.

Note: A tip is a snippet of advice, a guideline, or a pointer. It is not a full explanation of a subject. There are dynamic changes in this area. See Chapter 14 on XPath, which is another evolutionary step on linking.

What is the XML Linking Language (XLink)?

XLinks are used to extend an XML document's internal logical and physical structure into the area of bi-directional object links. This chapter covers in detail the XML Linking Language (XLink) W3C Working Draft (December 20, 1999). This version is found at: http://www.w3.org/TR/1999/WD-xlink-19991220.

The latest version is found at http://www.w3.org/TR/xlink.

Why was the XML Linking Language developed?

The XLink Linking Language is a hyperlinking functionality that allows you to establish links in your XML documents and have them recognized as such. In contrast, XPointer allows for the addressing of an element or part of an element.

What is linking?

Linking is the method of establishing a relationship between two linked objects.

What is addressing?

Addressing is the method of finding two linked objects.

What is the developmental origin of the XLink language?

The XLink Linking Language is one of the two divisions of the original XML Linking Language (XLL). The other language is now referred to as XPointer. The goal of both languages is to seek to resolve hypertext-linking issues. XPointer governs the fragment identifier, while XLink governs how you insert your links within an XML document.

What is the fundamental power of the XLink design?

The power of XLink is the concept of "extended links." This means you start from the end of the link and go to any other end in the link, no matter how many. You can store the linking information outside of the source location that does the hooking. This means you only have to update one location rather than updating each link separately.

What is an example of a basic XLink?

A basic XLink might look something like the following within an HTML page:

```
Check out
<a xlink:form="simple" href="http://www.MySite.com">
my home page</a>for further details on XML.
```

What are the essential design goals of XLink?

The nine design principles are obviously similar to the ones in the XML Recommendation. These principles are:

- Usable over the Internet
- Usable by a variety of domain links and applications
- Should use XML
- Design should be quick
- Design should be concise and formal
- Should be human-legible
- Links may reside outside resource documents

- Represent abstract structure and significance of links
- Must be feasible to implement

What are some broad uses for XLinks?

There are a number of broad uses for XLinks. Here are five technical possible uses:

- Aggregate links
- Attributes on links
- Bi-directional links
- Location-independent naming
- Target document link definition (transclusion)

What is some of the need-to-know XLink jargon?

The jargon of XLink comes from the "linking" environment; however, a term may have an XLink "twist." The list below has 13 terms that are used throughout the discussion on XLinks. The various terms are underlined within the definitions to show their interrelationships.

Element tree	A hierarchical representation of the specified XML elements and attributes.
Inline link	Concretely, an inline link is where the linking element's content serves as a participating resource. Abstractly, an inline link is when the link serves as one of its own resources.
Link	An explicit relationship between or among data objects or data object portions.
Linking element	An element that describes a link's characteristics.
Local resource	A local resource is an inline linking element's content.
Locator	The part of a link that identifies a resource.
Multidirectional link	A link whose traversal can be initiated from any of its participating resources.
Out-of-line link	A link that does not serve as one of the link's participating resources. They are generally required for supporting

	multidirectional <u>link</u> <u>traversal</u> and for reading read-only <u>resources</u>.
■ Participating resource	A <u>resource</u> that belongs to a <u>link</u>.
■ Remote resource	Any <u>participating</u> <u>resource</u> of a <u>link</u> is pointed to with a <u>locator</u>.
■ Resource	Concretely, any reachable use of a <u>locator</u> in some <u>linking</u> <u>element</u>. Abstractly, it is any addressable service or unit of information that participates in a <u>link</u>.
■ Subresource	A portion of a <u>resource</u> that is pointed to as the precise <u>link</u> destination.
■ Traversal	The action of using a <u>link</u>, that is, accessing a <u>resource</u>. It can be either user-initiated or under program control.

What production locator syntax is used for XLink?

The formal grammar of the locator syntax is based on Extended Backus-Naur Form (EBNF) notation. There are only four production rules that are used to establish the syntax. However, the rules are more meaningful in the context of the XPointer production rules that are discussed in Chapter 10. This comes out of the original heritage of the two being the same, known as XLL (XML Linking Language). The first three more or less state the three locator types, notation for a connector (# or |), what a URI is, and query definition. The rules are as follows:

[1] Locator ::= URI | Connector (XPointer | Name) | URI Connector (XPointer | Name)
[2] Connector ::= '#' | '|'
[3] URI ::= URIchar*
[4] Query ::= 'XML-XPTR= ' (XPointer | Name)

 Note: A part of the definition of URI inclusion is that a URI includes an optional query component. This is the reason for production rule [4]. It does state the syntax for XML type queries.

What is a locator?

A locator is a URI (Uniform Resource Identifier). The URI specifications used to develop the XLink specification are found in Request for

Comments (RFCs) 1738 and 1808; see http://www.freesoft.org/CIE/RFC/ 1738 or 1808.

What is a value of a locator?

A value of a locator must contain either a URI or a fragment identifier in order to locate an XML document or a part of the document. A fragment identifier is an XPointer.

What is a designated resource?

An entire locator serves to locate a designated resource. The rules that establish the designated resource from the Working Draft are:

- The URI, if provided, locates a resource called the containing resource.
- If the URI is not provided, the containing resource is considered the document in which the linking element is contained.
- If an XPointer is provided, the designated resource is a subresource of the containing resource; otherwise, the designated resource is the containing resource.
- If the Connector is followed directly by a Name, the Name is shorthand for the XPointer "id(Name)"; that is, the subresource is the element in the containing resource that has an XML ID attribute whose value matches the Name. This shorthand is to encourage use of the robust ID addressing mode.
- If the connector is "#", this signals an intent that the containing resource has to be fetched as a whole from the host that provides it and that the XPointer's extraction of the subresource is to be performed on the client-side.
- If the connector is "|", no intent is signaled as to what processing model is to be used for accessing the designated resource.

What are the requirements for link recognition?

The existence of a link is asserted by a linking element. Linking elements must be recognized reliably by application software in order to provide appropriate display and behavior.

How is link recognition accomplished?

Link recognition might be accomplished in a number of ways. Three examples are reserving element type names, reserving attributes, or leaving the matter of recognition entirely up to stylesheets and application software.

What is the purpose of reserving attributes?

Reserving attributes provides a balance between giving users control of their own markup language design and keeping the important structural fact "is a link" explicit within documents.

How are XLink elements recognized?

XLink linking-related elements are recognized based on the use of a designated attribute named xml:link. Values that identify linking elements are simple and extended. Values that identify other related types of elements are locator, group, and document.

An element in whose start-tag such an attribute appears is to be treated as an element of the indicated XLink type that conforms to the XLink specification. For example: <A xml:link="simple" href="http://www.MySite. com/">My Site</A>.

What are the mechanisms used to associate attributes with linking elements?

Two policies (mechanisms) may be used to associate the xml:link and xml:attributes attributes with a linking element. The simpler method is to provide the attribute explicitly in a start-tag. The second method is to use XML's facilities for declaring default attribute values. The following attribute-list declaration indicates that all instances of the HTML <A> element in the current document are XLink simple links: <!ATTLIST A xml:link CDATA #FIXED "simple">.

What are linking element types?

XLink has two types of linking elements:
■ A simple link, which is usually inline and always one-directional.

■ An extended link, which may be either inline or out-of-line and must be used for such link types as multidirectional links and links originating from read-only resources.

 Note: Both kinds of links can have various types of information associated with them.

What types of link information are possible?

The following information can be associated with a link and its resources:

■ One or more locators to identify the remote resources participating in the link; a locator is required for each remote resource
■ Semantics of the link
■ Semantics of the remote resources
■ Semantics of the local resource, if the link is inline

 Note: This information is supplied in the form of attributes on linking elements.

What is a locator string?

A locator string identifies a participating resource. A link must supply a locator for each remote resource. A locator takes the form of an attribute called href. Following is an entity declaration of this attribute, enclosed in a locator.att parameter entity: <!ENTITY % locator.att "href CDATA #REQUIRED">.

What semantic information is possible for a link?

The following semantic information can be provided for a link:

■ When the link is inline, its content counts as a local resource of the link
■ When the link is out-of-line, its content does not count as a local resource
■ The role of the link that identifies the meaning of the link to application software
■ The part that a link plays in representing information

 Note: The link's role is indicated with an attribute called role.

What is an example of link semantic information?

Following is an entity declaration of these attributes, enclosed in a
link-semantics.att parameter entity:

```
<!ENTITY % link-semantics.att
"inline    (true | false)    'true'
 role      CDATA             #IMPLIED">
```

How is a simple link declared?

Because simple links have an attribute called role that has a different
function, they cannot have a role attribute for link semantics. Following
is a simple-link-semantics.att parameter entity declaration for use in sim-
ple linking elements: <!ENTITY % simple-link-semantics.att "inline (true |
false) 'true'">.

What is the semantic information for a remote resource?

For a remote resource of a link, the following semantic information can
be provided:

- The role of the resource that identifies to application software the
  part it plays in the link
- Role information can be optionally provided in an attribute called role
- A title for the resource that serves as a displayed caption that explains
  to users the part the resource plays in the link
- Title information can be optionally provided in an attribute called title
- Behavior policies to use in traversing to this resource
- The attributes show and actuate, which communicate general policies
  concerning the traversal behavior of the link, can be optionally used

What is a show attribute?

The show attribute can have one of three values: new, replace, or embed.

What is an actuate attribute?

The actuate attribute can have one of two values: auto or user.

What is a behavior attribute?

The behavior attribute is used to communicate detailed instructions for traversal behavior.

What is an example of a remote resource declaration?

Following is an entity declaration of these attributes, enclosed in a remote-resource-semantics.att parameter entity:

```
<!ENTITY % remote-resource-semantics.att
"role           CDATA                      #IMPLIED
title           CDATA                      #IMPLIED
show            (embed | replace |new)     #IMPLIED
actuate         (auto | user)              #IMPLIED
behavior        CDATA                      #IMPLIED">
```

What is the semantic information for a local resource?

For a local resource of an inline link the following semantic information can be provided:

- The role of the resource that identifies the part it plays in the link to application software
- Role information can be optionally provided in an attribute called content-role
- A title for the resource that serves as a displayed caption that explains to users the part the resource plays in the link
- Title information can be optionally provided in an attribute called content-title

What is an example of a local resource declaration?

Following is an entity declaration of attributes, enclosed in a local-resource-semantics.att parameter entity:

```
<!ENTITY % local-resource-semantics.att
"content-role  CDATA    #IMPLIED content-title  CDATA     #IMPLIED">
```

What is a simple link?

Simple links can approximate the functionality of a basic HTML <A> element. A simple link has one locator, thus combining the functions of a linking element and a locator into a single element. Because of this combination, the simple linking element offers both a locator attribute and all the link and resource semantic attributes.

What is an example of a simple link declaration?

Following is a declaration example for a simple link, showing the possible XLink-related attributes. The xml:link attribute value for a simple link must be simple.

```
<!ELEMENT simple ANY>
<!ATTLIST simple
xml:link   CDATA       #FIXED "simple"
%locator.att;
%remote-resource-semantics.att;
%local-resource-semantics.att;
%simple-link-semantics.att;>
```

Attributes relevant to remote resources are expressed on the corresponding contained locator elements. Each remote resource can have its own semantics in relation to the link as a whole.

 Note: In the above declaration, it is given a content model of ANY to indicate that any content model or declared content is acceptable. In a valid document, every element that is XLink-related must conform to the constraints expressed in its governing DTD.

What is an example of a simple link markup?

Following is an example of a simple link markup:

```
<link1 xml:link="simple" title="Learn XML Tips"
href="http://www.MySite.com/xml/..." show="new"
content-role="Reference">XML FAQ. (2000)</link1>
```

 Note: This example link1 element might have the following element and attribute-list declarations:

```
<!ELEMENT link1            (#PCDATA)>
<!ATTLIST link1
xml:link        CDATA     #FIXED "simple"
href            CDATA     #REQUIRED
content-role    CDATA     #IMPLIED>
```

What is an out-of-line simple link?

An out-of-line simple link is called "one-ended" and associates discrete semantic properties with locations. The properties might be expressed by attributes on the link, the link's element type name, or in some other way, and are not considered full-fledged resources of the link.

What is an extended link?

An extended link differs from a simple link in that it can connect any number of resources, rather than a single optional local resource and one remote resource. An extended link is more commonly out-of-line than a simple link.

Why may an extended link be required?

Extended links are required for the following reasons:

- Enables outgoing links in documents that cannot be modified to add an inline link
- Creates links between resources in formats with no native support for embedded links
- Applies and filters sets of relevant links on demand
- Enables advanced hypermedia capabilities

 Note: An extended link contains a series of child elements that serve as locators. Because an extended link can have more than one remote resource, it separates out linking itself from the mechanisms used to locate each resource. The linking element itself retains those attributes relevant to the link as a whole and to its local resource, if any.

What is an example of an extended link declaration?

Following is a declaration example for an extended link. The xml:link attribute value for an extended link must be extended.

```
<!ELEMENT extended ANY>
<!ATTLIST extended
xml:link CDATA    #FIXED "extended"
%link-semantics.att;
%local-resource-semantics.att;>
```

What is a locator element?

The content of a linking element typically consists only of locator elements; however, the declaration as ANY indicates that any other content may be added. Only locator elements that are direct children of the linking element define resources linked by that linking element.

What is an example of a locator element declaration?

Following is a declaration example for a locator element, showing the possible XLink-related attributes it may have. The xml:link attribute value for a locator element must be locator.

```
<!ELEMENT locator ANY>
<!ATTLIST locator
xml:link   CDATA    #FIXED "locator"
%locator.att;
%remote-resource-semantics.att;>
```

 Note: Defaults for the semantic attributes on locator elements can be specified on the linking element that contains them. If any attribute is omitted from a locator element, the value of the containing linking element is to be used.

What is an example of markup for an out-of-line extended link?

Following is an example of an out-of-line extended link:

```
<book xml:link="extended" inline="false">
<locator href="ignatius2.1" role="Author"/>
<locator href="dracula1.4"  role="Editor"/>
<locator href="picasso3.2"  role="Designer"/>
</book>
```

What is an example of an extended link with attributes?

Following is a declaration example for an extended link showing the possible XLink-related attributes it may have, including the remote resource semantics attributes:

```
<!ELEMENT extended ANY>
<!ATTLIST extended
xml:link   CDATA   #FIXED "extended"
%link-semantics.att;
%local-resource-semantics.att;
%remote-resource-semantics.att;>
```

What is an extended link group element?

An extended link group element, a special extended link, can store a list of links to other documents that together constitute an interlinked group. Each document is identified by means of an extended link document element, a special locator element.

What are examples of extended link group and document elements?

Following are declaration examples for extended link group and extended link document elements, showing the possible XLink-related attributes. The xml:link attribute value for an extended link group element must be group, and the value for an extended link document element must be document.

```
<!ELEMENT group (document*)>
<!ATTLIST group
xml:link     CDATA     #FIXED "group"
steps        CDATA     #IMPLIED>
<!ELEMENT document EMPTY>
<!ATTLIST document
xml:link     CDATA     #FIXED "document"
%locator.att;>
```

 Note: The steps attribute deals with the situation where an extended link group directs application software to locate another document that proves to contain an extended link group of its own. The steps attribute should have a numeric value that serves as a flag to any link processor as to how many steps of extended link group processing should be undertaken. It does not have any normative effect. For example, should a group of documents be organized with a single "hub" document containing all the out-of-line links, it is logical for each non-hub document to contain an extended link group containing only one reference to the hub document. In this case, the best value for steps would be 2.

What is the meaning of link behavior?

Link formatting and link behavior are relational twins. Formatting focuses the appearance or treatment of the link prior to any user action, such as choice of font, color, icons, and other devices to show that a link is present. Behavior focuses on what happens when the link is traversed, such as opening, closing, or scrolling windows or panes; displaying the data from various resources in various ways; testing, authenticating, or logging user and context information; or executing various programs.

How can XLink handle formatting issues?

XSL (XML Stylesheet Language) should be for formatting issues. However, XLink does provide certain basic behavior policies based on major or invariant semantics of link types. XLink permits you to signal certain intentions as to the timing and effects of traversal. Such intentions can be expressed along two axes, show and actuate. These are used to express policies rather than mechanisms.

 Note: Any link-processing application software is free to devise its own mechanisms, best suited to the user environment and processing mode, to implement the requested policies.

What is the "show axis"?

The show attribute expresses a policy as to the context in which a "traversed to" resource should be displayed or processed. This attribute can have of one of the following three values for the purposes of display or processing:

- Embed   Indicates that upon link traversal, the designated resource should be embedded in the body of the resource and at the location where the traversal started.

- Replace   Indicates that upon link traversal, the designated resource should replace the resource where the traversal started.

■ New   Indicates that upon traversal of the link, the designated resource is in a new context, not affecting that of the resource where the traversal started.

What is the "actuate axis"?

The actuate attribute expresses a policy as to when traversal of a link should occur. This attribute can be one of the following two values:

■ Auto   Indicates that the resource in question should be retrieved when any of the other resources of the same link is encountered. The display or processing of the initiating resource is not considered complete until this is done. All auto resources are retrieved in the order specified.

■ User   Indicates that the resource should not be presented until there is an explicit external request for traversal.

What are the potential impacts of a show and actuate combination?

Each combination of the show and actuate attributes is meaningful. Perhaps the least obvious is show="replace" combined with actuate="auto"; this could be used in "forwarding" type applications, where when one anchor is display, the other(s) are to replace it without user intervention. Since XLink provides only the most general semantics for links, details of presentation, such as a time delay or beep before forwarding, can be specified on a per-application basis using a style language.

What are the requirements for attribute remapping?

To avoid collisions among attributes with the same name, these attribute names can be mapped to the default names using the xml:attributes attribute.

There are three requirements for a conforming attribute. They are the following:

■ The attribute must contain an even number of white-space-separated paired names.

■ The first name must be one of the default XLink names:
  ■ role
  ■ href

- title
- show
- inline
- content-role
- content-title
- actuate
- behavior
- steps
- The second name, when recognized in the document, is treated as though it were playing the role assigned to the first.

How do I use XLink in a DTD?

For example, consider a DTD with the following declaration:

```
<!ELEMENT BOOK ANY>
<!ATTLIST BOOK
title            CDATA       #IMPLIED
role  (PRIMARY | SUPPORTING) #IMPLIED>
```

To have a simple link, it is necessary to remap the attributes. This could be accomplished in the internal subset:

```
<!ATTLIST BOOK
xml:link         CDATA       #FIXED "simple"
xml:attributes   CDATA       #FIXED "title xl-title role xl-role">
```

The following would be recognized as a simple link with the document:

```
< BOOK title="Learn XML Tips"
      role="PRIMARY" xl-title="FAQ on XML and its family."
      xl-role="ONLINE-PURCHASE"
      href="/cgi/auth-search?q="+Doss"/>
```

What is required to have an XML document conform also to XLink?

A document or an application conforms to the XLink specification if:

- The element has an xml:link attribute that has prescribed attribute values.
- The element and its attributes and content adhere to the syntactic requirements imposed by the xml:link attribute value.

- The element and attributes conform to the XML Working Draft and the other associated specifications.

Chapter 10

XML Pointer Language (XPointer) Tips

Because there was a requirement to link one XML document with another XML document, a linking markup language was created and it was split into two general and specific markup languages. This chapter looks at XPointer, which handles links between specific locations between XML documents as compared to XLink (Chapter 9), which handles general links.

 Note: A tip is a snippet of advice, a guideline, or a pointer. It is not a full explanation of a subject. It is recognized that the answers here are highly abbreviated. As with XLink, XPointer is a dynamic evolutionary area of XML.

What is the XML Pointer Language (XPointer)?

The XML Pointer Language is used to extend an XML document's internal logical and physical structure by providing a specific reference to elements, character strings, and other XML instances. This chapter covers in detail the XML Pointer Language (XPointer) W3C Working Draft (December 6, 1999). This version is found at: http://www.w3.org/TR/1999/WD-xptr-19991206

The latest version is found at http://www.w3.org/TR/xptr.

Why does the XML Pointer Language exist?

XPointer addresses the deficiencies of the <A> element of HTML that can only point to the top of a document or to a predefined internal anchor. It can point to (address into) any arbitrary location of an XML document. It permits both relative and absolute locations. A conforming browser might even highlight the links.

What is addressing?

Addressing is the method of finding two linked objects.

What is linking?

Linking is the method of establishing a relationship between two linked objects.

What is the developmental origin of XPointer?

XPointer is one of the two divisions of the original XML Linking Language (XLL). The other language is now referred to as XLink. The goal of both languages is to seek to resolve hypertext-linking issues. XPointer governs the fragment identifier, while XLink governs how you insert your links within an XML document.

What are the design principles of XPointer?

The eight design principles are obviously similar to the ones in the XML specification. A summary of these principles is:

- Addressing should be into XML documents
- Usable over the Internet
- Usable into Uniform Resource Identifiers (URIs)
- Design should be quick
- Design should be concise and formal
- Should be human-legible
- Should be optimized for usability
- Should have feasible implementation

What is fundamental XPointer jargon?

Besides the jargon (keywords) associated with absolute and relative locations, there are a few other terms one needs to know in the context of XPointer. They are the following:

- **Element tree**   A relevant or hierarchical structure that is an abstraction that shows the "genealogy" of the XML elements, attributes, and any other markup constructs.

- **Link**   An explicit relationship between or among data objects or portions of data objects.
- **Linking element**   An element that describes a link's characteristics.
- **Locator**   The link's part, usually a Uniform Resource Identifier (URI), which identifies a resource.
- **Resource**   Concretely, it is anything that can be reached by a locator. Abstractly, it is an informational address unit such as a file, an image, or a document.
- **Subresource**   The precise resource portion that points to a specific link destination.

What is meant by the XPointer "structure"?

XPointer uses the "tree" as defined by the elements and other markup in a DTD. That is, the parent-child paradigm is used to establish a relative location. The technique used to establish an absolute location is a keyword. There are four possible types (forms) of keywords used to frame the XPointer structure:

- root
- origin
- id
- html

 Note: All these keywords are in small letters.

What is meant by the location term?

The location term is the basic unit for addressing information. A combination of location terms results in a precise location specification. The location term, of course, is the XPointer. There are three XPointer production rules that establish its structure. They are the following:

[1] XPointer ::= AbsTerm '.' OtherTerms | AbsTerm | OtherTerms
[2] OtherTerms ::= OtherTerm | OtherTerm '.' OtherTerm
[3] OtherTerm ::= RelTerm | SpanTerm | AttrTerm | StringTerm

How can an XPointer be classified?

The three production rules [1] – [3] establish that an XPointer can be classified in:

■ Absolute terms
■ Relative terms
■ Spanning terms
■ Attribute terms
■ String data terms

How is an absolute location point declared?

An absolute location points to one or more elements or XML document locations without any reference to another source. There are three production rules used to establish an absolute location. They are the following:

[4] AbsTerm ::= 'root()' | 'origin()' | IdLoc | HTMLAddr
[5] IdLoc ::= 'id(' Name ')'
[6] HTMLAddr ::= 'html(' SkipLit ')'

What are the keywords used to describe an absolute location point?

These production rules can be explained in the context of four keywords (all in small letters):

■ root   Location source or the root element
■ origin   Subresource location source

> **Warning:** Do not use origin() where a URI provides and identifies a containing resource different from source location.

■ id   Location source has an attribute having a declared type of ID and a value matching the given Name.
■ html   Location is the <A> element that has an attribute called NAME whose value is the same as the supplied NAMEVALUE or the same as the HTML "#" fragment identifier.

What are some examples of the use of the root() keyword?

To develop an absolute location using root() and perhaps including a third child that is of the type H2, one can state root().child(3,H2), or child(3,H2) since the root element is the default when omitted. However, to have a fuller specification one needs to consider the XLink production rules [1] and [2]. The fuller specification could look like this:

DocQ.htm#root().child(3,H2)

or

DocQ.htm#child(3,H2)

 Note: The XLink production rules [1] and [2] are as follows:

[1] Locator ::= URI | Connector (XPointer | Name) | URI Connector (XPointer | Name)
[2] Connector ::= '#' | '|'

In the above examples the octathorpe (#) can be replaced by the vertical bar (|). Child could be replaced when appropriate by any of the other six keywords (descendant, ancestor, preceding, following, psibling, or fsibling) for a relative location term. The 3 could be any positive or negative number. The H2 could be any valid type such as para.

What is an example of the use of the origin() keyword?

The origin absolute location can only point to a place within the same document. In this example, the pointer is to the second place preceding the origin: href=#origin().preceding(-2,#element)

 Note: The markup follows a similar syntax to the one for root().

What is an example of the use of the id() keyword?

To point to a location source that is an element in the containing resource with an attribute having a declared type ID and a value matching the given Name, in this case canine, one would specify: id(canine).

What is an example of the use of the html() keyword?

This locator was designed to use with <A .../>. A document that points to <A NAME = "top"/> element would be specified in a similar manner to the following: <mylink> xml:link="simple" href="MyDocument.htm#htm(top)> link name</mylink>.

What is a relative location point?

A relative location points to one or more elements or XML document locations with a reference to another source, a location source. If none is given, the root element of the containing resource is it. Direction can be up, down, forward, or backward.

What are the production rules for relative location points?

There are eight production rules that can be used to establish a relative location. The eight rules are as follows:

```
[7] RelTerm ::= Keyword? Arguments
[8] Keyword ::= 'child' | 'descendant' | 'ancestor' | 'preceding' | 'following' |
'psibling' | 'fsibling
[9] Arguments ::= '('InstanceOrAll (',' NodeType (',' Attr ',' Val)*)? ')'
[10] InstanceOrAll ::= 'all' | Instance
[11] Instance ::= ('+' | '-')? [1-9] Digit*
[12] NodeType ::= Name | '#element' | '#pi' | '#comment' | '#text' | '#cdata' |
'#all'
[13] Attr ::= '*' | Name       <!- - any attribute type - ->
[14] Value ::= '#IMPLIED'      <!- - no value specified, no default - ->
             | '*'             <!- - any value, even defaulted - ->
             | Name
             | SkipLit         <!- - exact match - ->
```

What are the genealogical keywords for relative locations?

Production rule [8] has a set of keywords that identify a sequence of elements or other XML nodal types that determine the location source. The following are the seven "genealogical" keywords:

- child   Identifies the location source's <u>direct</u> child nodes.
- descendant   Identifies nodes <u>within</u> a location source's content.
- ancestor   Identifies the nodes that <u>contain</u> a location source.

- preceding   Identifies the nodes that appear <u>before</u> a location source.
- following   Identifies the nodes that appear <u>after</u> a location source.
- psibling   Identifies the sibling (same parent) nodes that appear <u>before</u> a location source.
- fsibling   Identifies the sibling (same parent) nodes that appear <u>after</u> a location source.

Note: If a keyword is omitted, it is treated as though it were the preceding keyword.

Warning: The keyword must not be omitted from the first location of any relative location XPointer.

What are the possible values for a relative location?

Production rule [12] has values rather than keywords that identify the nodal type (XML declaration type) source. The values are the Arguments of production rule [7]. The following are the seven values:

- Name   Selects a particular XML element type.
- #element   Identifies an XML element is the default value when no NodeType is specified.
- #pi   Identifies an XML processing instruction and is meaningful when a PI location source is a string (rule [3]).
- #comment   Identifies an XML comment and is meaningful when the comment location source is a string (rule [3]).
- #text   Selects among text regions inside elements and CDATA sections and is meaningful when the text-region location source is a string (rule [3]).
- #cdata   Selects among text regions inside CDATA sections and is meaningful when the CDATA region location source is a string (rule [3]).
- #all   Selects from among the above nodes; however, when there is an attribute, it is the same as #element.

Note: Elements can contain other node types; all the other node types can only contain strings.

213

Can I mix and match keywords and arguments?

When you mix and match keywords and arguments you can specify a pointer up, down, forward, backward, or even at the same location. You may be able specify within one element to within another element. You can use positive or negative numbers to point downward or upward in the markup.

How can I use the child keyword?

XPointer can be as simple as the example that identifies the sixth child element of any type: Root()child(6).

Since root absolute location term is the default when omitted, the specification could also be: child(6).

The third option is to specify using #all: child(6,#all).

XPointer can be complex, as the following snippet uses only elements of the specified type. This example identifies the fourth paragraph of the third subdivision of the second major division of the source location: child(4,DIV1).child(3,DIV2).child(2,P).

The above example could also be written as follows, because when the keyword is omitted, the preceding keyword is assumed: child(4,DIV1).(3,DIV2).(2,P).

What does a descendant keyword do?

The descendant location term selects a specified node by looking through trees of subelements in order to end at the node type requested (not included are PIs, comments, or text regions). The search for matching node types occurs from the first start-tag of an element on to the next as they occur in the XML parse flow. This search method is called a depth-first traversal.

How do I use the descendant keyword?

The following example selects the second TYPE element with a WILD attribute whose value is WOLF, occurring within the element with an ID attribute whose value is canine: id(canine).descendant(2,TYPE,WILD, WOLF).

When the number is positive, the search is depth-first and left-to-right. However, if the number is negative, the search is depth-first but right-to-left, in which the right-most, deepest matching element is numbered -1.

 Note: The examination order corresponds to the ordering of the first tag encountered. The following example chooses the last TYPE element in the document, the rightmost end-tag: root().descendant(-1,TYPE).

If the last TYPE is nested within another TYPE, the containing one is chosen, not the subelement.

How do I use the ancestor keyword?

The following example first chooses the innermost element (nearest ancestor) properly containing the location source and having attribute WILD with value WOLF, and then the smallest DIV element properly containing that ancestor: ancestor(1,#element,WILD,WOLF).(WOLF,DIV).

A positive number counts upwards from the parent of the location source to the root of the containing resource. The negative number counts downwards from the root to the direct parent.

 Warning: The ancestor can never select the location source itself.

 Note: The node type parameter for ancestor should be #element. If the current location source is an attribute, the attribute's element is the first ancestor.

How do I use the preceding keyword?

The preceding keyword selects a node of the specified type from among those that occur or begin before (precede) the location source. The following example designates the third node type that occurs or starts before the element that has an ID of canine: id(canine).preceding(3,#all).

A positive number counts left from the location source. A negative number counts right from the root element of the containing resource. The first delimiter or tag encountered, whether starting or ending, counts as a node occurrence.

How do I use the *following* keyword?

The following keyword selects a node of the specified type from among those that occur or end after (follow) the location source. This example designates the first comment that occurs after the element that has an ID of canine: id(canine).following(1,#comment).

A positive number counts right from the location source. A negative number counts left from the end-tag of the root element of the containing resource. The first delimiter or tag encountered, whether starting or ending, counts as a node occurrence.

What is the use of the *psibling* keyword?

The psibling keyword selects a node of the specified type from among those that precede the location source within the same parent element. The nodes of the same parent element are siblings. Elder siblings are those that precede the location source. Younger siblings are those that follow the location source.

How do I use the *psibling* keyword?

This example designates the fifth element immediately preceding the element with an ID of canine, as long as they share the same parent: id(canine).psibling(5,#element).

A positive number counts left from the most recent elder sibling to the eldest sibling. A negative number counts right from the eldest sibling. The location term fails if the location source does not have at least as many elder siblings as the absolute value of the given number.

If the location source has at least one elder sibling, then the following location term designates the very eldest sibling: psibling(-1,#element).

This location term is the same as this example: ancestor(1,#element). child(1,#element).

The following example designates the set of elements preceding the element that has an ID of canine and are contained by the same parent: id(canine).psibling(all,#element).

What is the use of the fsibling keyword?

The fsibling keyword selects a node of the specified type from among those that follow the location source within the same parent element. The nodes of the same parent element are siblings. Elder siblings are those that precede the location source. Younger siblings are those that follow the location source.

How do I use the fsibling keyword?

This example designates the element immediately following the parent element with an ID of canine: id(canine).fsibling(1,#element).

A positive number counts right from the most recent younger sibling to the youngest sibling. A negative number counts left from the youngest sibling. The location term fails if the location source does not have at least as many younger siblings as the absolute value of the instance number.

If the location source has at least one younger sibling, then the following location term designates the very youngest sibling: fsibling(-1, #element).

This location term is the same as the following: ancestor(1,#element). child(-1,#element).

How do I use the Name argument?

This example selects from within the element with the ID="canine" the third node (element) with the name: canistype: id(canine).child(3, canistype).

How do I use the #element argument?

This example selects from within the canine element the second node (element): id(canine).child(2,#element). This might be the case or it could be the same relative location as specified in the prior example.

How do I use the #pi argument?

When the processing instruction (PI) is a string, you can specify as with #element: id(canine).child(1,#pi).

This example selects the first PI within the element canine.

How do I use the #comment argument?

When a comment is a string, you can specify as with #element: id(canine).child(2,comment).

This example selects the second comment with the canine element.

How do I use the #text argument?

When a text region, any section containing unmarked up text, is a string, you can specify as with #element: id(canine).child(5,#text).

This example selects the fifth text region within the element canine.

How do I use the #cdata argument?

When the text regions of CDATA sections are strings, then you can specify as follows: id(canine).child(3,#cdata).

This example selects the third text region within CDATA sections of the element canine.

How do I use the #all argument?

The following example selects the second child node within the canine element regardless of the node type: id(canine).child(2,#all).

What is the meaning of spanning a location?

An important design or development consideration is that a span cannot be treated as a set or list of elements. A span may locate partial elements. The span keyword locates a subresource starting at the beginning of the data selected by its first argument and continues through to the end of the data selected by a second argument. There is only one production rule for spanning: [15] SpanTerm ::= 'span(' XPointer ',' XPointer ')'.

How do I declare a span?

This example shows how to span the fourth to the fifth child node for the element with the ID of canine: id(canine).span(child(4).child(5).

How do I locate a point by attribute?

The attr keyword permits selection only by attribute name and the attribute's value is returned. There is only one production rule to handle attribute location. It is: [16] AttrTerm ::= 'attr('Name')'.

Because only an element has an attribute, only the nodal types of Name and #element are valid. To point to the third element that had the attribute called WILD with a value of WOLF you would specify the following example: child(3,#element,WILD,"WOLF").

 Note: One can do a wild card either for an attribute or value by using an asterisk (*) as a replacement.

What is a string data location term?

A string data term is similar to a relative term because it also specifies a location using another location. The string keyword permits selection of one or more strings or positions between strings in the location source. There are three production rules that control the string data location term:

[17] StringTerm ::= 'string('InstanceOrAll ',' SkipLit (',' Position (',' Length')?)?)'
[18] Position ::= ('+' | '-')? (1-9) Digit* | 'end'
[19] Length ::= [1-9] Digit*

What are the meanings of the values for a StringTerm production?

The meanings of the values for a StringTerm production are:

- InstanceOrAll Identifies the plus or minus *n*th occurrence of the specified string.
- SkipLit Identifies the candidate string to be found within the location string.

■ Position   Identifies a positive or minus character offset from the start of the candidate string(s) to the beginning of the desired final string match.

■ Length   Specifies the number of characters to be selected and when zero or omitted, it is a precise point preceding the character indicated by Position.

What are the steps for a string location search?

When the location source is either a PI or a comment, string operates on that node's content.

There are four steps in a search involving a string location term. They are the following:

1. Select the search string.
2. Select the "for" string.
3. Select where to start the return.
4. Select how much to return.

How do I declare a string location search?

The following example identifies the fifth character in the first text region of the element with the ID of canine: id(canine).string(5,"").

 Warning: You need to consider in your count that an XML line break is one character and a tab is counted as a character.

How does XPointer handle complex nodes?

XPointer can go beyond the usual or common expectation for selecting a single element. Here are four scenarios where this expectation has multiplicity:

■ If a string location term has markup within it, the result matched content may include portions of multiple elements.

■ If a string location term has the instance value of all, the result may be a list of (non-sharing) portions of string data.

■ If a relative location term has the instance argument of all, the result may consist of a vector of non-adjacent nodes, rather than a subtree.

■ A spanning XPointer may include partial elements.

How does the use of an ID assist link persistence?

It is not possible to guarantee a link will never break. The most robust locator uses only an ID. When an element does not have an ID, then the preferred locator is one that points to the nearest element with an ID and then uses the child location term to go down the element tree. This is robust for four reasons:

- No outside editing of the element with the ID can change the reference.
- Failure will be obvious.
- It has a more clear reference.
- It improves the detection possibility of a cause for failure.

How is XPointer document conformance achieved?

There is document conformance when the string adheres to the syntax as defined by the XML Pointer Language (XPointer) Working Draft. The specification does not require a string to actually point to an existing resource.

XML Namespaces Tips

Because there was a need to give XML tag sets and markup languages unique names in an Internet environment, namespaces were developed. This chapter looks at the importance of namespaces in XML documents. Tags with the same name in multiple document environments may need unique names.

 Note: A tip is a snippet of advice, a guideline, or a pointer. It is not a full explanation of a subject. It is recognized that the answers here are highly abbreviated.

What is a definition of XML namespaces?

Namespaces associate certain names within XML documents using Uniform Resource Identifiers (URIs). An XML namespace is a collection of names and should not be considered in the same sense as a non-XML namespace, which is a name set. In addition, in order for URIs to be identical they must be the same character-for-character.

 Warning: URIs are not identical even if they are functionally the same.

 Note: This chapter raises questions about namespaces in XML World Wide Consortium (January 14, 1999). The URL is http://www.w3.org/TR/1999/REC-xml-names-19990114. The latest version of this specification is found at http://www.w3.org/TR/REC-xml-names.

What is the reason for namespaces?

A given markup might have a special meaning to a given user, but the meaning may not be conveyed to any other user. Consider this markup: <title>...</title>.

This could be a job title with various implications, a book title, a composition, etc. By associating a URI, real or fiction, one could clearly give a narrow meaning to the <title> element that carries both a local and global meaning.

 Note: The general principle or guideline for a namespace is you can associate these URIs with the <title> element and its attributes if they exist to make it unique. For example, with a job title one might associate the URIs www.university.edu or www.hospital.com to distinguish between the title of "doctor." For a book <title> element, one might use www.MyBookStore.com. For the composition <title> element, one might use www.MyMusicStore.com.

What is the basic syntax for an XML namespace?

The basic syntax is:

```
xmlns:[prefix]="[URI of namespace]"
<prefix:element>...</prefix:element>
```

What is a specific namespace definition?

A namespace is an XML convention that uses processing instructions (PIs) to assign unique names in a document to URIs. A URI is a reference to a section of a document that defines an element's parser and storage format.

Why were namespaces developed?

Namespaces were developed with the intent that they would be used in cases where there were files with common markup structure (vocabulary). A file name could be declared within a document without having to specifically include this markup structure. Many different applications could use a common markup structure by declaring a namespace. This idea does require that documents have universal names that have a scope extending beyond a given document.

What are the production rules for declaring a namespace attribute?

There are five production rules to declare namespace attribute names. They use the EBNF notation and are the following:

[1] NSAttName ::= PrefixedAttName | DefaultAttName
[2] PrefixedAttName ::= 'xmlns:' NCName
[3] DefaultAttName ::= 'xmlns'
[4] NCName ::= (Letter | '_') (NCNameChar)*
[5] NCNameChar ::= Letter | Digit | '.' | '-' | CombiningChar | Extender

What is the purpose of the NSAttName production?

Production rule [1] means that the namespace name identifies the namespace as a URI reference, the attribute's value. The attribute value of NSAttName should be unique and persistent. In developing a naming syntax to meet this goal, the Request for Comments (RFC) 2141, *Uniform Resource Names*, should be considered. RFC 2141 is located at ftp://nic.ddn.mil/rfc/rfc2141.txt.

What is the purpose of the PrefixedAttName production?

Production rule [2] reflects the use of an XML restricted name. Notice the colon (:) that distinguishes between the prefixed and default attribute names. The NCName is the namespace prefix used to associate an element and its attribute names with the namespace name. The namespace name cannot be empty. The key idea put forth here is name associations.

What is the purpose of the DefaultAttName production?

Production rule [3] also uses a restricted XML name. The default name namespace is the namespace name in the attribute value. The default value, however, can be empty.

What is the purpose of the NCName production?

Production rule [4] shows that a NCName found in production rule [2] can begin either with a letter or an underscore (_) followed by zero or more occurrences of a NCNameChar. To comprehend this rule one must

225

look at the associated XML production rules beginning with: [84] Letter ::= BaseChar | Ideographic.

 Note: XML production rules [85] and [86] define BaseChar and Ideographic. The complete rules are found in Appendix C.

What is the purpose of the NCNamechar production?

Namespace production rule [5] states that a NCNamechar can be a period (.) or an underscore (_) or an expression defined by XML production rules [84], [88], [87], and [89]:

[84] Letter ::= BaseChar | Ideographic
[88] Digit ::= [#x0030-#x0039] | [#x0660-#x0669] |
[#x06F0-#x06F9] | [#x0966-#x096F] | [#x09E6-#x09EF] |
[#x0A66-#x0A6F] | [#x0AE6-#x0AEF] | [#x0B66-#x0B6F] |
[#x0BE7-#x0BEF] | [#x0C66-#x0C6F] | [#x0CE6-#x0CEF] |
[#x0D66-#x0D6F] | [#x0E50-#x0E59] | [#x0ED0-#x0ED9] |
[#x0F20-#x0F29]
[87] CombiningChar ::= [#x0300-#x0345] | [#x0360-#x0361] |
[#x0483-#x0486] | [#x0591-#x05A1] | [#x05A3-#x05B9] |
[#x05BB-#x05BD] | #x05BF | [#x05C1-#x05C2] | #x05C4 |
[#x064B-#x0652] | #x0670 | [#x06D6-#x06DC] |
[#x06DD-#x06DF] | [#x06E0-#x06E4] | [#x06E7-#x06E8] |
[#x06EA-#x06ED] | [#x0901-#x0903] | #x093C |
[#x093E-#x094C] | #x094D | [#x0951-#x0954] |
[#x0962-#x0963] | [#x0981-#x0983] | #x09BC | #x09BE |
#x09BF | [#x09C0-#x09C4] | [#x09C7-#x09C8] |
[#x09CB-#x09CD] | #x09D7 | [#x09E2-#x09E3] | #x0A02 |
#x0A3C | #x0A3E | #x0A3F | [#x0A40-#x0A42] |
[#x0A47-#x0A48] | [#x0A4B-#x0A4D] | [#x0A70-#x0A71] |
[#x0A81-#x0A83] | #x0ABC | [#x0ABE-#x0AC5] |
[#x0AC7-#x0AC9] | [#x0ACB-#x0ACD] | [#x0B01-#x0B03] |
#x0B3C | [#x0B3E-#x0B43] | [#x0B47-#x0B48] |
[#x0B4B-#x0B4D] | [#x0B56-#x0B57] | [#x0B82-#x0B83] |
[#x0BBE-#x0BC2] | [#x0BC6-#x0BC8] | [#x0BCA-#x0BCD] |
#x0BD7 | [#x0C01-#x0C03] | [#x0C3E-#x0C44] |
[#x0C46-#x0C48] | [#x0C4A-#x0C4D] | [#x0C55-#x0C56] |
[#x0C82-#x0C83] | [#x0CBE-#x0CC4] | [#x0CC6-#x0CC8] |
[#x0CCA-#x0CCD] | [#x0CD5-#x0CD6] | [#x0D02-#x0D03] |
[#x0D3E-#x0D43] | [#x0D46-#x0D48] | [#x0D4A-#x0D4D] |
#x0D57 | #x0E31 | [#x0E34-#x0E3A] | [#x0E47-#x0E4E] |
#x0EB1 | [#x0EB4-#x0EB9] | [#x0EBB-#x0EBC] |
[#x0EC8-#x0ECD] | [#x0F18-#x0F19] | #x0F35 | #x0F37 |
#x0F39 | #x0F3E | #x0F3F | [#x0F71-#x0F84] |

[#x0F86-#x0F8B] | [#x0F90-#x0F95] | #x0F97 |
[#x0F99-#x0FAD] | [#x0FB1-#x0FB7] | #x0FB9 |
[#x20D0-#x20DC] | #x20E1 | [#x302A-#x302F] | #x3099 |
#x309A
[89] Extender ::= #x00B7 | #x02D0 | #x02D1 | #x0387 | #x0640 | #x0E46 |
#x0EC6 | #x3005 | [#x3031-#x3035] | [#x309D-#x309E] | [#x30FC-#x30FE]

What is an example of a namespace prefix declaration?

An example of a namespace prefix declaration, which associates the namespace prefix pfx with the namespace name http://www.MySite.com/mypurpose, is as follows:

```
<zzz xmlns:pfx="http://www.MySite.com/mypurpose">
<!- - the prefix "pfx is bound to the URL. - ->
<!- - for the "zzz" element and its contents - ->
</zzz>
```

What is an example of a namespace default declaration?

The following example shows the use of the default namespace:

```
<?xml version="1.0"?>
<!-- default elements are in the HTML namespace -->
<html xmlns="http://www.w3.org/TR/REC-xml-names">
<head><title>Namespaces</title></head>
<body><p>Moved to
<a href="http://www.MySite.com">location</a></p></body>
</html>
```

 Warning: A default namespace applies to an element where it is declared if the element has no namespace prefix declaration. In addition, default namespaces do not apply directly to attributes. If there are non-prefixed elements in the declaration's scope, they are not considered to be in a namespace.

What is an example of a namespace non-prefixed declaration?

The following is an example of the use of non-prefixed elements:

```
<?xml version="1.0"?>
<!—non-prefixed element types are from "books" -->
```

```
<book xmlns="urn:loc.gov:books" xmlns:isbn="urn:ISBN:1-55622-715-9">
<title>Learn Red Hat Linux OS Tips</title>
<isbn:number>0-12345-678-9</isbn:number>
</book>
```

 Note: The specification uses "unprefixed," which is not correct because this implies that the prefix is being undone, rather than not having one to begin with.

What areas must be considered when declaring qualified names?

The four areas one needs to consider when declaring qualified names are:

- Qualified name declarations
- Element types
- Attributes
- Qualified names in declarations

When can a qualified name be declared?

A qualified name may be declared when an XML document is in conformance to the Namespaces in XML specification. A name (a construct corresponding to the non-terminal Name (XML production [5]) may be declared as a qualified name. In the XML specification, Name is declared by:

```
[5] Name ::= (Letter | '_' | ':') (NameChar)*
[4] NameChar ::= Letter | Digit | '.' | '-' | '_' | ':' | CombiningChar | Extender
```

The namespace production rules for a qualified name are the following:

```
[6] QName ::= (Prefix ':')? LocalPart
[7] Prefix ::= NCName
[8] LocalPart ::= NCName
```

The optional Prefix [7] provides the namespace prefix part of the qualified name, and must be associated with a namespace URI reference in a namespace declaration. The prefix functions only as a placeholder for a namespace name. The LocalPart [8] provides the local part of the qualified name. NCName is defined in namespaces production [4].

What are the rules for element type qualified names?

Element types can give qualified names if an XML document conforms to the Namespaces in XML specification. The production rules for the element type qualified names are as follows:

[9] Stag ::= '<' QName (S Attribute)* S? '>' [NSC: Prefix Declared]
[10] Etag ::= '</' QName S? '>' [NSC: Prefix Declared]
[11] EmptyElemTag ::= '<' QName (S Attribute)* S? '/>' [NSC: Prefix Declared]

 Warning: The Namespace Constraint (NSC), Prefix Declared, states, "The namespace prefix, unless it is xml or xmlns, must have been declared in a namespace declaration attribute in either the start-tag of the element where the prefix is used or in an ancestor element (i.e., an element in whose content the prefixed markup occurs). The prefix xml is, by definition, bound to the namespace name http://www.w3.org/XML/1998/namespace. The prefix xmlns is used only for namespace bindings and is not itself bound to any namespace name."

What is an example of a qualified name serving as an element type?

The following is an example of a qualified name serving as an element type:

```
<zzz xmlns:von="http://www.MySite.com/pages">
<!- - the "page_count" element's namespace is - ->
<!- -http://www.MySite.com/pages - ->
<pfx:page_count="body">372</pfx:page_count>
</zzz>
```

What is the rule for attributes declared with namespaces?

Attributes are either namespace declarations or their names are given as qualified names. The production rule for attributes is as follows:

[12] Attribute ::= NSAttName Eq AttVa ue| QName Eq AttValue [NSC: Prefix Declared]

What is an example of a qualified name serving as an attribute name?

An example of a qualified name serving as an attribute name is:

```
<zzz xmlns:von="http://www.MySite.com/pages">
<!- - the "number" attribute's namespace is - ->
<!- -http://www.MySite.com/pages - ->
<chapter pfx:number="11">XML Namespaces Tips</chapter>
</zzz>
```

What are the rules for the use of qualified names in an XML DTD?

Element names and attribute types are also given as qualified names when they appear in declarations in the DTD. The production rules for qualified names in declarations are the following:

```
[13] doctypedecl ::= '<!DOCTYPE' S QName (S ExternalID)? S? ('['
(markupdecl | PEReference | S)* ']' S?)? '>'
[14] elementdecl ::= '<!ELEMENT' S QName S contentspec S? '>'
[15] cp ::= (QName | choice | seq) ('?' | '*' | '+')?
[16] Mixed ::= '(' S? '#PCDATA' (S? '|' S? QName)* S? ')*' | '(' S? '#PCDATA'
S? ')'
[17] AttlistDecl ::= '<!ATTLIST' S QName AttDef* S? '>'
[18] AttDef ::= S (QName | NSAttName) S AttType S DefaultDecl
```

What is the scope of a namespace declaration?

The scope of a namespace declaration is two-fold:

- The namespace declaration applies to an element in all of its instances until overridden by another namespace declaration.
- A single element can have multiple namespaces declared as attributes.

What are the guidelines for developing namespace defaults?

There are four guidelines for namespace defaults. They are the following:

- A default namespace applies to an element at the point of declaration.

- Any element without a prefix and within the content of another element has the default namespace apply to it also.
- A default namespace does not apply directly to an attribute, only the attribute's element.
- A default namespace can be set to an empty string.

What is an example of the use of a default string namespace?

Here is an example that uses default string namespaces:

```
<?xml version="1.0"?>
<music>
<!- - HTML is the default namespace - ->
<table xmlns="http://www.w3.org/TR/REC-html4.0">
<th><td><Composer></td><td>Country</td><td>Composition</td></th>
<tr>
<!- - no default namespaces within the table cells - ->
<td><LastName xmlns="">Rachmaninov</LastName></td>
<td><origin xmlns="">Russia</origin></td>
<td>
<data xmlns=""><title>Concerto No. 1</title>
        <instrument>piano</instrument>
            <opus>1</opus>
</data>
</td>
</tr>
</table>
</music>
```

What are the guidelines for having a unique attribute?

There are two guidelines to ensure attribute uniqueness. They are the following:

- No element (tag) can have two attributes with the same name.
- No qualified name with the same prefix and local part can have been bound to identical namespaces.

What is an example of the illegal use of a qualified namespace?

The following example shows an illegal use of qualified names:

```
<!- - http://www.MySite.com is bound to nameA and nameB - ->
<element xmlns:nameA="http://www.MySite.com"
        xmlns:nameB="http://www.MySite.com">
        <incorrect a="1" a="2"/>
        <incorrect nameA:a="1" nameB:a="2"/>
</element>
```

What is an example of the legal use of a qualified namespace?

The following snippet shows a legal use of qualified names:

```
<!- - http://www.MySite.com is bound to nameA and it is the default - ->
<element xmlns:nameA="http://www.MySite.com"
        xmlns:http://www.MySite.com">
        <correct a="1" b="2"/>
        <correct a="1" nameA:a="2"/>
</element>
```

What are the guidelines to ensure document conformance?

There are five guidelines to ensure document conformance when using namespaces. They are the following:

- Element types and attribute names must match the production of QName [6].
- The Namespace Constraint, Prefix Declared, must be adhered to (quoted after namespace production [11] above).
- All document tokens must match the XML production for Name (XML production [5]) and the namespace production for NCName [4]).
- Any element type or attribute name can contain either zero or one colon.
- An entity name, PI target, or notation name cannot contain a colon.

Chapter 12

Scalable Vector Graphics (SVG) Tips

There have been two major efforts to specify the requirements for graphics in XML documents. This chapter looks at the first effort, Scalable Vector Graphics (SVG). The next chapter looks at Vector Markup Language (VML), the second effort. While the current specification has added significant information on Data Object Model (DOM) interfaces, this chapter has limited tips because of the specific focus of the book, which is to give general tips on XML implementation. This area requires a background in the implications of DOM2.

The basis for the tips in this chapter is the Scalable Vector Graphics (SVG) 1.0 Specification W3C Working Draft (December 3, 1999) found at http://www.w3.org/TR/1999/WD-SVG-19991203. The latest version is found at http://www.w3.org/TR/SVG. The development of graphic manipulation for XML is taking a staged developmental approach. According to the SVG Specification, "It is inappropriate to use this document as reference material or to cite it as other than 'work in progress'." This work in progress is currently over 300 pages in length.

 Note: A tip is a snippet of advice, a guideline, or a pointer. It is not a full explanation of a subject. It is recognized that the answers here are highly abbreviated.

Warning: SVG elements are currently defined as 'name' rather than <name> as in earlier specifications.

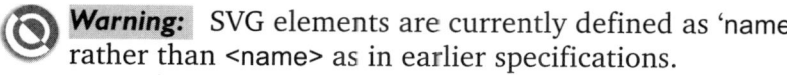

What is the purpose of scalable vector graphics?

SVG describes two-dimensional graphics in XML. SVG permits three graphic object types: vector graphics, images, and text. This means these graphic types can be created by a browser based on plain text instructions. In addition, the graphical objects can be labeled: grouped, styled, transformed, and composited. In addition, the feature set includes nested transformations, clipping paths, alpha masks, filter effects, and template objects.

What is a scalable vector graphic?

Scalable means a uniform increase or decrease of an object to present a different resolution from the original. A vector graphic is a linear geometric object such as a set of lines or curves.

 Note: Scalable can be defined in a broader sense, because of Internet technology, as the increase or decrease in a set of graphics, users, applications, or files.

What is an image?

An image is a graphic that requires stored information on all pixels.

What are grouped graphical objects?

The use of grouped graphic objects is the rendering technique to group the child elements to produce a temporary paint canvas. The result is that when the canvas is painted onto the ancestor element, it appears that the standard rendering rules are used.

 Note: SVG uses the 'g' element. A snippet of the 'g' element:

```
<g style="fill:blue">
    <rect x="50" y="50" width="75" length="25">
    <rect x="100" y="100" width="25" length="75">
</g>
```

What are styled graphical objects?

SVG objects use either CSS2 or XSL for styling. Styled SVG objects use the 'style' element. Styling includes the use of font and text properties.

 Note: A snippet of the 'style' element:

```
<g style="fill:red">
    ...
</g>
```

 Warning: You should not use both CSS2 and XSL in the same document.

What are transformed graphical objects?

Transformed graphical objects are SVG objects that are established in a new user space through operations such as rotation, scaling, and translation. A coordinate system is used.

What are composited graphical objects?

SVG only supports alpha blending compositing. Alpha blending is a rendering technique that uses a set of very simple formulas. A composite object is an object made up of distinct components.

What are nested transformations?

SVG permits multiple levels of transformations via nesting. SVG uses the 'transform' element.

 Note: A snippet of nested transformation is as follows:

```
<svg ...>
    ...
<g transform="...">
  <g style="...">
    ...
  </g>
  <text ...>
  (transform 1)
  </text>
<g transform="...">
  <g style="...">
    ...
  </g>
  <text ...>
  (transform 2)
  </text>
<g transform="...">
  <g style="...">
    ...
  </g>
  <text ...>
  (transform 3)
  </text>
```

```
      </g>
      </g>
      </g>
   </svg>
```

What is a clipping path?

A clipping path is a technique to restrict a painting region. A specific SVG definition is a clipping path which is a 1-bit mask. The SVG 'clip' property is the same as CSS2 clip. The clipping path is specified by the 'clip-path' property on the ancestor elements.

What are alpha masks?

An alpha mask is used to composite an object into a background. A mask is defined by a 'mask' element, while it is referenced by a 'mask' property.

 Note: While this answer may be unclear upon first reading or even second reading, it does reflect the technical language of the specification. This is another example where the area of "what-I-need-to-know" is very broad. Perhaps one does not need to know the theory to practice the use of having vector graphics in an XML document, but this knowledge might help to do troubleshooting of complex XML documents.

What are filter effects?

SVG filter effects use "processing nodes." Each processing node uses a primitive graphic set, processes them, and then generates a revised primitive graphic set. Filter effects are defined by the 'filter' element.

Note: A snippet of the 'filter' element is as follows:

```
<svg ...>
    ...
   <defs>
      <filter id="...">
         <!- - Filter definition - ->
      </filter>
   </defs>
</svg>
```

What are template objects?

Template objects are used to establish default attributes. The 'symbol' element is used with template objects.

How does SVG relate to XML?

SVG is considered an XML application. SVG provides the capability for structured vector descriptions. A goal of SVG is to conform to the XML, XLink, XPointer, and XML Namespaces Recommendations. It also conforms to Cascading Style Sheets, level 2 (CSS2), and Document Object Model (DOM), levels 1 and 2. The goal is to ensure that SVG serves as a grammar component of HTML 4.0 and its future versions.

Why can SVG be important to you as a Web author?

There are four reasons that SVG would be important to a Web author:
- SVG is plain text.
- Code can reside inside of HTML.
- Graphic positional control is CSS2.
- It is written in XML.

What are the major intended uses of SVG?

SVG has two intended uses:
- Support standalone SVG that represents complete drawings. The drawings should be developed by a graphics authoring package and be for use on the Web.
- Support SVG "fragments," that is, graphics snippets included in the body of a Web document.

What is a list of the SVG elements?

SVG elements include the following:

a	animateMotion
altGlyph	animateTransform
altGlyphDef	circle
animate	clip-path
animateColor	cursor

defs	polygon
desc	polyline
ellipse	radialGradient
feImage	rect
fill	script
filter	set
font	src
foreignObject	stop
g	stroke
glyph	style
glyphSub	svg
hkern	switch
image	symbol
line	text
linearGradient	textPath
marker	title
mask	tref
missing-glyph	tspan
object	use
path	view
pattern	vkern

What is an example of standalone SVG?

An example of a standalone SVG is:

```
<?xml version="1.0"?>
<g xmlns="http://www.MySite.com/...">
<!- - Drawing elements here - ->
</g>
```

 Note: The 'g' is an SVG element for grouping and naming drawing element collections.

What is an example of a basic drawing element?

An example of a basic drawing element is:

```
...
<g style="fill:green">
```

```
<rect x="250" y="250" width="50" height="75" />
</g>
```

 Note: The color can be one of 16 named colors or a numerical RGB specification. The valid named colors include red, white, blue, black, and gray. Both color specifications are defined in HTML 4.0.

 Warning: The syntax of the style attribute depends on the stylesheet language.

What are the predefined SVG graphics objects?

SVG has six predefined graphic objects. They are defined as the elements rect, circle, ellipse, line, polyline, and polygon.

Why are SVG drawings easier to handle than images?

SVG drawings can be handled more easily than images because:

- Text strings are represented as XML character data rather than as bitmap images.
- Descriptive material can be handled in the form of a title.
- SVG conforms to CSS2. SVG has the ability to develop personal style sheets and do color adjustments.

What is the basic SVG document structure?

The range of an SVG document is from a single SVG graphic drawing element <g> ... </g> to a series of nested elements. An SVG document can be embedded as a fragment within a parent document. It can be a standalone self-contained document (file). The following example shows this type of file:

```
<?xml version="1.0" standalone="yes"?>
<g xmlns="http://www.MySite.com/.../">
<rect x="50" y="50" width="25" height="25" />
<rect x="125" y="125" width="40" height="30" />
<rect x="200" y="200" width="35" height="45" />
</g>
```

How can I add attributes to elements?

The next example shows how you can add common attributes for a collection of elements:

```
<?xml version="1.0"?>
<g xmlns="http://www.MySite.com/.../">
<!- - 1. Color two of the rectangles. - ->
<g style="fill:green">
<rect x="50" y="50" width="25" height="25" />
<rect x="125" y="125" width="40" height="30" />
</g>
<!- - 2. Add no special color for the top rectangle - ->
<rect x="200" y="200" width="35" height="45" />
</g>
```

 Note: Snippet 1 shows how you could color fill a set of SVG drawing elements using the style attribute. Essentially, you have an XML element with an attribute and then two empty elements. Snippet 2 shows that while one color fills some of the SVG drawing elements, one could choose not to color other shapes on the canvas.

How do I declare a group's common attribute or attributes?

It is possible to name a group in a similar manner to establish a common attribute for a group:

```
<?xml version="1.0"?>
<g xmlns="http://www.MySite.com/.../">
<!- - 1. Group 1 needs two rectangles. - ->
<g id="Group1">
<rect x="20" y="20" width="25" height="25" />
<rect x="125" y="125" width="40" height="30" />
</g>
<!- - Group 2 needs an ellipse - ->
<g id="Group2">
<ellipse rx="125" ry="50" style="fill:gray" />
</g>
</g>
```

What is the meaning of the SVG rendering model?

The SVG rendering model permits a continuous tone rasterization phase. This means that an image can have multiple processing that affects color and coverage channels.

What is clipping?

Clipping is the functionality or path that permits the "inside" of an outline to show, while the "outside" does not show. For example, you could put a text clipping path on a waterfall image and it would look as if your text is being filled by water.

What is masking and compositing?

Masking and compositing are functions that permit a semi-transparent mask for compositing foreground objects into the current background. A mask is established by specifying its properties. This is close to the PhotoShop-style techniques on the Web.

How does SVG relate to CSS2 properties?

In designing SVG, criteria were established to determine which parts would be expressed as XML elements and attributes and which parts would be expressed as CSS2 properties. The CSS2 criteria for properties are as follows:

- Visual parameters such as attributes that define how an object is to be painted, for example, fill and stroke colors
- Font-family and font-style for text styling
- Parameters that permit the crossing of XML grammar lines such as transformations
- Parameters that impact rendering, for example, clipping paths

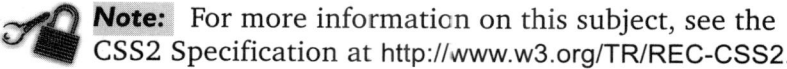 **Note:** For more information on this subject, see the CSS2 Specification at http://www.w3.org/TR/REC-CSS2.

What is the meaning of a coordinate system?

A coordinate system determines how coordinates (X- and Y-axes) and attributes are mapped onto the canvas, that is, the location where SVG graphical objects are drawn or rendered.

What is the meaning of transformation?

How one modifies the location of a SVG drawing is transformation. Transformation operations include:

- Rotation
- Scaling
- Skewing
- Translation

What is the meaning of units within SVG?

Units are the coordinates and lengths in SVG. Units correspond closely to those defined by CSS2.

What is the meaning of filling and stroking?

Filling means painting an object's interior, while stroking means painting an object's outline. With either one, SVG can paint:

- A single color
- A gradient (linear or radial)
- A pattern (image or vector)
- Custom

How do I use the 'linearGradient' element?

To use a paint server you would first define a gradient using the 'linearGradient' element with a 'defs'. Second, you would assign a gradient ID. Third, you would reference the ID with a property. In this example, the fill style gradient is used:

```
<g>
  <defs>
    <linearGradient id="Gradient1"... >
      <!- - Gradient defined here - ->
```

```
    </linearGradient>
  </defs>
<rect style="fill:url(#Gradient1)".../>
</g>
```

What are the fill properties?

There are three fill properties. They are the following:

- fill (<paint>)
- fill-rule (evenodd | nozero | inherit)
- fill-opacity (<opacity-value> | inherit)

What are the defined stroke properties?

There are eight defined stroke properties. They are:

- stroke (<paint>)
- stroke-width (<width> | inherit)
- stroke-linecap (butt | round | square | inherit)
- stroke-linejoin (miter | round | bevel | inherit)
- stroke-miterlimit (<miterlimit> | inherit)
- stroke-dasharray (none | <dasharray> | inherit)
- stroke-dashoffset (<dashoffset> | inherit)
- stroke-opacity (<opacity-value> | inherit)

What are gradients?

Gradients, whether linear or radial, consist of continuously smooth color transitions across a vector. Gradients are specified with 'defs' and then with either a fill or a stroke property. A basic linear gradient and stroke example is as follows:

```
<g>
  <defs>
      <linearGradient id="Gradient1"... >
          <!- - Linear gradient defined here - ->
      </linearGradient>
  </defs>
<rect style="stroke:url(#Gradient1)".../>
</g>
```

Why is a gradient stop declared?

Gradient stops are used to transition colors by percentage. Here is an example of a linear gradient definition that consists of a transition in thirds from red to orange to yellow:

```
<linearGradient id="red-to-orange-to-yellow">
    <stop offset="0%"   style="stop-color:red"/>
    <stop offset="34%" style="stop-color:orange"/>
    <stop offset="67%" style="stop-color:yellow"/>
</linearGradient>
```

What is the meaning of a pattern?

A pattern is a predefined graphic object used to fill or stroke an object. The 'pattern' element defines the pattern used. To use a pattern, the <url> parameter has to be set on either fill or stroke properties to name the pattern. Here is a snippet where a pattern "catsanddogs" is defined and the declaration for using the pattern to fill a rectangle is given:

```
<g>
   <defs>
      <pattern id="catsanddogs"...>
         <!- - Standard graphic elements defined here. - ->
      </pattern>
   </defs>
<rect style="fill:url(#catsanddogs)" .../>
</g>
```

What is a path?

A path is a current point that can be changed and for which an object outline (open or closed) can be defined. Path objects can be filled, stroked, a clipping path, or a combination of the three. An object's outline might be defined in any of these terms:

- moveto (sets a new current point, notated by an M)
- lineto (draws a straight line, notated by an L)
- curveto (draws a curve)
- arc (circular or elliptical)
- closepath (draws a line to last moveto, notated by a z)

Note: A 'path' element contains a d="path data" attribute that includes one or more of the terms given above. For example, to define a closed triangle, you would do the following: <path d="M 250 250 L 400 200 L 300 400 z" />.

How does SVG handle text?

SVG allows text to be inserted in a drawing. The same attributes available for paths and vector graphic shapes are usable with the 'text' element.

What is the functionality of a 'text' element?

The 'text' element adds text to a drawing. All text data must be specified using this element. SVG has three ways to specify how text strings are to be drawn:

- <text> standard XML character data </text>
- A 'text' element string attribute
- A <src href="..."/>

Here is an example that includes correct and incorrect uses of these three specifications:

```
<g>
<!- - CAGE will not be drawn because it is within a defs element - ->
    <defs>
        <text id="MyText">CAGE</text>
    </defs>
<!- - LION is drawn - ->
    <text>LION</text>
        <!- - WOLF is drawn - ->
        <text string="WOLF"/>
    </text>
<!- - CAGE will be drawn - ->
    <src xml:link="simple" show="embed" actuate="auto" href="#MyText"/>
</g>
```

How do I use the 'tspan' element?

The 'tspan' element defines the selection for multiple 'text' elements. This element allows SVG generators to specify text order even when the text contents are located randomly on the canvas. The following example has two tspans and four strings. S1 (with string "Cherries") and S3

245

(with string "Grapes") belong to one tspan. S2 (with string "Lions" and S4 (with string "Wolves") belong to another tspan.

```
<g>
  <defs>
    <tspan id="TFA">
        <tf xml:link="simple" href="S1"/>
        <tf xml:link="simple" href="S3"/>
    </tspan>
    <tspan id="TFB">
        <tf xml:link="simple" href="S2"/>
        <tf xml:link="simple" href="S4"/>
    </tspan>
  </defs>
<text x="75" y="150" id="S1"><tf xml:link="simple"
href="TFA"/>Cherries</text>
<text x="75" y="250" id="S2"><tf xml:link="simple" href="TFB"/>Lions</text>
<text x="125" y="150" id="S3"><tf xml:link="simple"
href="TFA"/>Grapes</text>
<text x="125" y="250" id="S4"><tf xml:link="simple"
href="TFB"/>Wolves</text>
</g>
```

What is interactivity?

Interactivity is concerned with links and event handling. For the links, there is the 'a' element. The 'a' element is similar to HTML's <A> tag. The 'a' element may also be considered an XLink.

Event handling involves user interface events.

What are the elements used to handle backward browser compatibility, descriptions, and titles?

For handling alternate representation of an event, you can use either the 'switch' element with XML grammar or the 'object' element with HTML.

To what degree has SVG specified DOM interfaces?

The current SVG specified has described 68 interfaces. These interfaces are based on SVG elements and attributes. SVG DOM includes complete support for DOM2 core, views, and stylesheets. It also includes the relevant aspects of the DOM2 CSS object model and the DOM event model. It also supports DOM2 traversal and range features.

What is the basic syntax for a DOM interface?

The delimiters for an SVG DOM interface are as follows:

```
interface SVGname {
 <! -definition - ->
};
```

How do I handle a situation where SVG functions with DOM?

SVG has an exception DOM interface. It is as follows:

```
exception SVGexception {
    unsigned short code;
    {;
    // SVGExceptionCode
    const unsigned short SYNTAX_ERR                    =0;
    const unsigned short SVG_INVALID_MODIFICATION_ERR  =1;
    const unsigned short SVG_NO_GRAPHICS_ELEMENTS      =2;
    const unsigned short SVG_MATRIX_NOT_INVERTABLE     =3;
```

How is the SVG DOM accessed?

The SVG DOM is accessed using supplemental scripting language.

What are some of the specific relationships between SVG and XML?

The following listing is not all-inclusive, but does give many of the specific relationships between SVG and XML:

■ An important interchange feature is to ensure that a higher-level print metafile XML grammar could use SVG as its page-imaging operator.

■ An SVG document fragment can be embedded inline as a fragment within a parent XML document.

■ An SVG specification is designed to make SVG files as small as possible and yet retain the benefits of XML.

- An XMLNS prefix may indicate an XML namespace for an SVG attribute name.
- Because SVG is an XML application, it supports Unicode encodement.
- SVG aural media represents an XML grammar style.
- SVG fills a hole in XML by providing the capability for structured descriptions of vector graphics.
- SVG filters do not use XML IDs for results.
- SVG handles white space in text using the XML attribute xml:space.
- SVG is an XML grammar for stylable graphics and is usable for XML namespaces.
- SVG is intended as a component of a multiple namespace XML application.
- SVG models graphic objects in a similar manner as XML models document objects.
- SVG text strings are represented as XML character data.
- Synchronized Multimedia Integration Language (SMIL) is a future consideration for use with SVG and XML grammar.
- The attributeType attribute used in specifying a namespace has as one of its values "XML."
- The 'svg' element can be either the root of an XML document tree or a component of a parent XML grammar.
- The use of the 'switch' element is the recommended technique for an alternate presentation to SVG content.

What is the specific URL for the SVG DTD?

The current URL for the SVG DTD is as follows: http://www.w3.org/TR/1999/WD-SVG-19991203/svgdtd.html.

Vector Markup Language (VML) Tips

There have been two major efforts to specify the requirements for graphics in XML documents. This chapter looks at the second effort, Vector Markup Language (VML). Scalable Vector Graphics, the first effort, was looked at the last chapter.

VML is an early XML application development. It interacts with both XML and HTML 4.0.

The version of the initial draft specification used for the tips in this chapter is Vector Markup Language (VML) World Wide Web Consortium Note (May 13, 1998) found at http://www.w3.org/TR/1998/NOTE-VML-19980513. The latest version is found at http://www.w3.org/TR/NOTE-VML.

Most of the members that wrote the earliest version of the VML specification were representatives from Microsoft Corporation. Microsoft made an early commitment to VML implementation. The examples in this chapter reflect this implementation of VML with Internet Explorer 5. For specific details on this implementation, see Chapter 18.

For the examples to work correctly the VML has to be placed within the <BODY> region of an HTML Web page. You should also include in the <HEAD> region:

```
<style>
v:* ( behavior: url(#VMLRender); )
</style>.
```

 Note: A tip is a snippet of advice, a guideline, or a pointer. It is not a full explanation of a subject. It is recognized that the answers here are highly abbreviated and only high points of the topics. Do not confuse VML with VRML.

What are the basic functions or characteristics of VML?

The basic functions or characteristics of VML are the following:

- Supports vector graphic markup in a similar manner as HTML supports text markup
- Uses CSS2, as does HTML
- Uses path transformations to describe how lines and curves should be connected
- Uses XML syntax
- Parses similarly to XML
- Describes objects as shapes or collections of shapes, also known as groups

What is the purpose of path transformations?

Path transformation means that VML generates locations, related information for vector paths, and related objects.

 Note: The use of path transformations is a distinct difference from HTML, since HTML uses character layout.

Where does parsing come into the VML workflow?

Parsing is the first step in the VML workflow.

What is the essential VML structure?

The VML structure can be summarized by the XML definitions of the two primary elements: shape and group.

What is the function of the <shape> element?

A <shape> element defines a visible vector graphic element.

What is the function of the <group> element?

A <group> element defines a collection of shapes so they can be transformed as one.

What is an example of the use of the <shape> element?

The basic syntax for shape is the following:

```
<v: shape ...>
<v: path .../>
</v:shape>
```

This example shows that the <shape> element uses the XML syntax for elements.

 Note: The "v:" is a notation to identify VML.

What is an example of the use of the <group> element?

The basic group syntax is: <v:group .../>.

The <group> element uses the XML syntax for empty element.

 Note: You can differentiate between SVG and VML by group declaration. SVG uses <g> ... </g> while VML uses <v:group .../>. Design goals may be the same, but implementation can be significantly different even when using the same fundamental rules for syntax.

What are the essential design goals of VML?

If you know the design goals of VML from the specification, you can see its parameters or delimiters. Here is a brief listing of some of the essential design goals:

- Allow for an application not to use the full set of VML functionality
- Be backward compatible with browsers
- Provide efficient vector graphic representations
- Retain high-level information for editing
- Support data interchange between applications
- Support hand-editing
- Use existing HTML and CSS2 mechanisms

 Note: To achieve the first goal above, VML would have two types of implementation, viewer and editor. A viewer implementation is for full implementation, while editor implementation is for a VML subset.

How does VML use CSS2?

As a part of its workflow, VML uses the CSS Box Model. Each box is determined by shape. This is in contrast to HTML, where a box's position (layout) is the determining factor.

How do I use the style attribute?

The style attribute uses the syntax of the Visual Rendering Model (VRM) of CSS2. Positioning can be either absolute or relative. Both the <shape> and <group> elements make full utilization of the VRM. The following example is a basic use of style to define a rectangle that is described as a square filled with silver:

<v:rect style='width:120pt;height:80pt' fillcolor="silver"/>.

 Note: Besides using rect you may use arc, curve, image, oval, line, polyline, and roundrect. For a fillcolor besides silver, you may use aqua, black, blue, fuchsia, gray, green, lime, maroon, navy, olive, purple, red, teal, white, and yellow. In addition, color can be expressed as either an RGB decimal triplet or an RGB hexadecimal triplet.

What is the function of local coordinate space?

A local coordinate space for a shape or a group permits you to define the specific space on the canvas. To do this you use the coordsize and coordorigin property attributes with style. Coordsize determines the shape's width and height, while coordorigin determines the top left corner of the shape.

What is an example of local coordinate space?

Here is an example that uses local coordinate space, fill, stroke, and path:

<v:shape style='position:absolute;left:10pt;top:5pt; width:100pt;height:100pt'
coordsize="10800,10800" path="m5900,010,5900,10800,10800,5900e"
fillcolor="gray" strokecolor="navy" strokeweight="3.5">

 Note: Only one shape is involved, so it is v:shape. If there had been more than one shape it would be v:group. The local coordinate space size is defined in units coordsize="10800,10800". A unit is equivalent to 1/108 point (10800 units divided by 100pt, width and height). The path defines the shape as a diamond. The "m" starts the path, while the "e" denotes the current point as the end-point.

What are the top-level elements in VML?

There are four top-level elements in VML. They are the following:

- shape (describes a shape)
- shapetype (describes a shape so it can be referenced at a later point in a document)
- group (describes a set of shapes as a unit)
- background (describes the fill of a page's background using vector graphic fills)

How do I use the *<shapetype>* element?

The following example shows the creation of a <shapetype> element with property attributes and the use of a shape instance that inherits the attributes from the <shapetype> element:

```
<v:shapetype id="#Shape1" fillcolor="blue" strokecolor="navy"...>
</v:shapetype>
...
<v:shape type="#Shape1" style='width=75pt;height=125pt'/>
```

What is the *<background>* element?

The <background> element can be used to customize a Web page.

How do I use the *<background>* element?

Here is a simple example that has to be put in the <BODY> region that draws a gradient-filled background:

```
<v:background fillcolor="navy">
<v:fill type:"gradient"/>
</v:background>
```

What is the <group> element?

The <group> element makes it possible to transform two or more shapes as one.

How do I use the <group> element?

This example shows the basic syntax for using the <group> element:

```
<v:group id="Group1" style='...' ...>
<v:shape id ="ShapeQ" ...></v:shape>
<v:shape id ="ShapeZ" ...></v:shape>
</v:group>
```

What elements are used to advance the properties of shapes?

There are nine elements and their associated subelements that are used to advance the properties of shapes. Each of these elements has a series of attributes and in some cases, related commands. The nine elements are:

- path   Uses a string that contains a rich collection of pen movement commands that define the path that makes up a shape
- formulas   Varies a shape's path
- handles   Defines user interface elements that can vary the adjustable values of a shape
- fill   Defines a fill within a shape other than a solid color
- stroke   Specifies a color and weight for a shape's outline
- shadow   Defines the shadow effect for a shape
- textbox   Defines text that is to appear inside a shape
- textpath   Defines a vector path based on the supplied text data, font, and font styles
- imagedata Defines a picture to be rendered on top of a shape

What are the predefined shapes for VML?

There are eight predefined shapes. They have the same properties as the <shape> element, except the type attribute is not permitted. The predefined shapes are:

- arc   Draws an oval segment
- curve   Draws a cubic bézier curve
- image   Draws a bitmap retrieved from an external source
- line   Specifies a line
- oval   Draws an oval as defined by the CSS2 content width and height
- polyline   Specifies a shape of connected line segments
- rect   Draws a simple rectangle
- roundrect   Draws a rectangle with rounded corners

How do VML and SVG compare to each other?

There are a number of similarities and differences between VML and SVG. The differences are more a result of the fact that VML was developed prior to the completion of the XML Recommendation 1.0. In addition, a comparison is more a contrast between the requirements of the two technologies than their implementations.

A big difference between these two is the level of completion of the two specifications.

A second difference is that while VML is considered an XML application it was based on existing (1998) HTML capabilities. SVG reflects in more depth the definitions of the latest XML Recommendation.

An obvious similarity is that both specifications are available to the public. A subtle similarity is that both specifications need to resolve the critical extensible issue.

The majority of the members that wrote the VML specification were from Microsoft Corporation. Perhaps because of this there was an early commitment on Microsoft's part to implement VML. The commitment is expressed in VML implementation with Internet Explorer 5. The implementation of SVG has a wider base of vendors.

While SVG and VML may in some cases have identical element names, the syntax for each of them is probably different. They both have similar functionality such as grouping, but handle it in significantly different ways to get essentially the same result. Each has a different set of predefined shapes.

What is a major issue between VML and HTML for the use of graphics?

A DTD is a concept, while markup is how it is expressed. In HTML 4.0 it is okay to have an <img> element (tag); however, in XML to have a well-formed document one must use <img.../>. This is an important difference between concept and practice.

At HTML's beginnings, there was no standard HTML DTD to establish a consistent or standard environment. The early versions of browsers tried to consider the many random type styles.

XML, SVG, and VML have been developed to work within a standard environment. There has been the desire of the authors of the various recommendations associated with XML to have a consistent syntax, while there may be inconsistency in implementation. This is true of the vector graphic area. The two vector graphic specifications in their design considered the possibilities and limitations of the segments of the HTML 4.0 DTD.

What types of graphics are impacted by a strict HTML DTD?

The three sections of the strict HTML DTD that deal with graphics are:
- Client-side image maps
- Images
- Object

Below are the three sections from the HTML DTD you need to know while working with both SVG and HTML.

```
<!--============ Client-side image maps =======================-->

<!-- These can be placed in the same document or grouped in a separate
document although this isn't yet widely supported -->

<!ELEMENT MAP - - ((%block;)+ | AREA+) -- client-side image map -->
<!ATTLIST MAP
  %attrs;                            -- %coreattrs, %i18n, %events --
  name      CDATA      #REQUIRED     -- for reference by usemap --
  >

<!ELEMENT AREA - O EMPTY            -- client-side image map area -->
<!ATTLIST AREA
```

```
%attrs;                                -- %coreattrs, %i18n, %events --
shape        %Shape;     rect          -- controls interpretation of
                                          coords --
coords       %Coords;    #IMPLIED      -- comma separated list of
                                          lengths --
href         %URI;       #IMPLIED      -- URI for linked resource --
nohref       (nohref)    #IMPLIED      -- this region has no action --
alt          %Text;      #REQUIRED     -- short description --
tabindex     NUMBER      #IMPLIED      -- position in tabbing order --
accesskey    %Character; #IMPLIED      -- accessibility key character --
onfocus      %Script;    #IMPLIED      -- the element got the focus --
onblur       %Script;    #IMPLIED      -- the element lost the focus -->
```

```
<!--============ Images ====================================-->
```

```
<!-- Length defined in strict DTD for cell padding/cellspacing -->
<!ENTITY % Length       "CDATA"    -- nn for pixels or nn% for
                                      percentage length -->
<!ENTITY % MultiLength  "CDATA"    -- pixel, percentage, or relative -->

<!ENTITY % MultiLengths "CDATA"    -- comma-separated list of
                                      MultiLength -->

<!ENTITY % Pixels       "CDATA"    -- integer representing length in
                                      pixels -->
```

```
<!-- To avoid problems with text-only UAs as well as to make image content
understandable and navigable to users of non-visual UAs, you need to provide
a description with ALT, and avoid server-side image maps -->
<!ELEMENT IMG - O EMPTY            -- Embedded image -->
<!ATTLIST IMG
  %attrs;                                -- %coreattrs, %i18n, %events --
  src        %URI;       #REQUIRED     -- URI of image to embed --
  alt        %Text;      #REQUIRED     -- short description --
  longdesc   %URI;       #IMPLIED      -- link to long description
                                          (complements alt) --
  height     %Length;    #IMPLIED      -- override height --
  width      %Length;    #IMPLIED      -- override width --
  usemap     %URI;       #IMPLIED      -- use client-side image map --
  ismap      (ismap)     #IMPLIED      -- use server-side image map --
  >
```

```
<!-- USEMAP points to a MAP element which may be in this document or an
external document, although the latter is not widely supported -->
```

```
<!--============== OBJECT ====================================-->
<!--
```

```
    OBJECT is used to embed objects as part of HTML pages
    PARAM elements should precede other content. SGML mixed content
    model technicality precludes specifying this formally ...
    -->

    <!ELEMENT OBJECT - - (PARAM | %flow;)* -- generic embedded object -->
    <!ATTLIST OBJECT
      %attrs;                              -- %coreattrs, %i18n, %events --
      declare     (declare)      #IMPLIED  -- declare but don't instantiate flag
                                           --
      classid     %URI;          #IMPLIED  -- identifies an implementation --
      codebase    %URI;          #IMPLIED  -- base URI for classid, data,
                                              archive--
      data        %URI;          #IMPLIED  -- reference to object's data --
      type        %ContentType;  #IMPLIED  -- content type for data --
      codetype    %ContentType;  #IMPLIED  -- content type for code --
      archive     %URI;          #IMPLIED  -- space separated archive list --
      standby     %Text;         #IMPLIED  -- message to show while loading --
      height      %Length;       #IMPLIED  -- override height --
      width       %Length;       #IMPLIED  -- override width --
      usemap      %URI;          #IMPLIED  -- use client-side image map --
      name        CDATA          #IMPLIED  -- submit as part of form --
      tabindex    NUMBER         #IMPLIED  -- position in tabbing order --
      %reserved;                           -- reserved for possible future use
                                           --
      >

    <!ELEMENT PARAM - O EMPTY              -- named property value -->
    <!ATTLIST PARAM
      id          ID             #IMPLIED  -- document-wide unique id --
      name        CDATA          #REQUIRED -- property name --
      value       CDATA          #IMPLIED  -- property value --
      valuetype   (DATA|REF|     DATA      -- How to interpret value --
                   OBJECT)
      type        %Content       #IMPLIED  -- content type for value when
    Type;                        valuetype=ref
      -->
```

Chapter 14

XML Path Language (XPath) Tips

To simplify the task of addressing, there was a requirement for a new specification. This specification is the XML Path Language (XPath). This chapter considers some of the potential general questions about XPath that might be raised by someone already knowledgeable in XML. For additional insight in this area, you need to consider at least two other chapters. Chapter 9 looked at XLink, which handles general links. Chapter 10 looked at XPointer, which handles links between specific locations between XML documents.

The XML Path Language (XPath) Version 1.0 W3C Proposed Recommendation (October 8, 1999) is found at http://www.w3.org/TR/1999/PR-xpath-19991008. The latest version is found at http//www.w3.org/TR/xpath.

 Warning: The XPath specification is at the proposal stage and is not to be considered a reference document. It should be considered a "work in progress" document.

 Note: A tip is a snippet of advice, a guideline, or a pointer. It is not a full explanation of a subject. It is recognized that the answers here are highly abbreviated. These tips are more theoretical than practical.

What is the XML Path Language (XPath)?

XPath was developed to simplify document addressing. It was designed to function with the XSL Transformations (XSLT) (Chapter 15) and the XML Pointer Language (XPointer) (Chapter 9).

 Note: Addressing is the method of finding two linked objects, that is, specific XML document internal locations as compared to linking, that is, for document level locations.

What is an essential characteristic of XPath?

XPath uses path navigation with a notation similar to the one for URLs.

What are the basic functions of XPath?

XPath's primary function is to handle addressing to internal XML document parts. Second, XPath provides the capabilities for string, number, and Boolean manipulations.

In what part of an XML document does XPath function?

XPath operates within an XML document's logical structure.

How does XPath model an XML document?

XPath models an XML document using a tree node. The node types are:

- Element
- Attribute
- Text

What is an element node?

Each element in a document has an element node. A precise definition from the XPath Proposed Recommendation [section 5.2] is "An element node has an expanded-name computed by expanding the QName of the element specified in the tag in accordance with the XML Namespaces Recommendation."

What are examples of an attribute node?

Two available attribute nodes are xml:lang and xml:space. An attribute node has an expanded-name and a string-value.

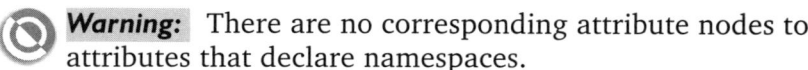 **Warning:** There are no corresponding attribute nodes to attributes that declare namespaces.

What is a text node?

A text node is a grouping of character data. A group may only consist of one character. An example of a text node is a CDATA section.

Does XPath support XML namespaces?

XPath fully supports XML namespaces.

How do namespaces function with XPath?

Namespace declarations are maps between prefixes and namespace URIs.

What is the basic syntactic construct for XPath?

The basic syntactic construct for XPath is the expression that consists of the production Expr. This construct has its beginnings with production [14] Expr ::= OrExpr

This production is clarified by further productions that are discussed later in the chapter.

What types of expression objects are possible?

There are four basic types of expression objects:
- Boolean
- Node-set (can be unordered)
- Numeric (floating-point)
- String (UCS characters)

What is the meaning of the core function library?

It is the library that must be included with any XPath implementation. The types of functions that must be included are those that support the expression objects.

Where is a common location for XPath expressions in an XML document?

Probably the most common location for XPath expressions is within XML attributes.

What is a location path?

A location path is an expression that selects a node-set relative to the context node. A location path consists of the following production: [1] LocationPath ::= RelativeLocationPath | AbsoluteLocationPath

The location path is the most important construct in Xpath.

 Note: This production involves productions [2], [3], [10], and [11]. A listing of the productions is given in the answer to the last tip in the chapter.

What are the two types of syntax for location paths?

The two types of syntax for location paths are abbreviated and unabbreviated.

What are some examples of abbreviated location paths?

Here are five examples of abbreviated location paths for a mytag element:

- mytag
- */mytag
- //mytag
- .mytag
- mytag[3]

What are some examples of unabbreviated location paths?

Here are five examples of unabbreviated location paths for a mytag element:

- child::mytag
- descendant::mytag
- child::*/child::mytag

- child::mytag[position()=last()]
- /descendant::mytag[position()=13]

What are the steps in processing a location path?

The parts of a "location step" are:
- Axis
- Node test
- Predicates (can be zero)

What is an axis?

An axis is defined by production [6] AxisName. The 13 axes are primarily based on ancestry.

 Note: The complete list of axes is found in the answer to the last tip in the chapter.

What is a node test?

A general definition of a node test is a test is true if the declared axis has its appropriate principle node type.

What is a predicate?

A predicate acts as a node-set filter. A predicate's related production rules are:

[8] Predicate ::= '['PredicateExpr']'
[9] PredicateExpr ::= Expr

What are the document conformance requirements?

There are not specified document conformance requirements for XPath. However, since XPath relies on XML, XPointer, and XSLT specifications, then the document conformance requirements in those specifications must be followed.

What are the production rules for XPath?

There are 39 production rules in the XPath Proposed Recommendation. The syntax is based on the EBNF:

[1] LocationPath ::= RelativeLocationPath | AbsoluteLocationPath

[2] AbsoluteLocationPath ::= '/' RelativeLocationPath? | AbbreviatedAbsoluteLocationPath

[3] RelativeLocationPath ::= Step | RelativeLocationPath '/' Step | AbbreviatedRelativeLocationPath

[4] Step ::= AxisSpecifier NodeTest Predicate* | AbbreviatedStep

[5] AxisSpecifier ::= AxisName '::' | AbbreviatedAxisSpecifier

[6] AxisName ::= 'ancestor' | 'ancestor-or-self' | 'attribute' | 'child' | 'descendant' | 'descendant-or-self' | 'following' | 'following-sibling' | 'namespace' | 'parent' | 'preceding' | 'preceding-sibling' | 'self'

[7] NodeTest ::= NameTest | NodeType '(' ')' | 'processing-instruction' '(' Literal ')'

[8] Predicate ::= '[' PredicateExpr ']'

[9] PredicateExpr ::= Expr

[10] AbbreviatedAbsoluteLocationPath ::= '//' RelativeLocationPath

[11] AbbreviatedRelativeLocationPath ::= RelativeLocationPath '//' Step

[12] AbbreviatedStep ::= '.' | '..'

[13] AbbreviatedAxisSpecifier ::= '@'?

[14] Expr ::= OrExpr

[15] PrimaryExpr ::= VariableReference | '(' Expr ')' | Literal | Number | FunctionCall

[16] FunctionCall ::= FunctionName '(' (Argument (',' Argument)*)? ')'

[17] Argument ::= Expr

[18] UnionExpr ::= PathExpr | UnionExpr '|' PathExpr

[19] PathExpr ::= LocationPath | FilterExpr | FilterExpr '/' RelativeLocationPath | FilterExpr '//' RelativeLocationPath

[20] FilterExpr ::= PrimaryExpr | FilterExpr Predicate

[21] OrExpr ::= AndExpr | OrExpr 'or' AndExpr

[22] AndExpr ::= EqualityExpr | AndExpr 'and' EqualityExpr

[23] EqualityExpr ::= RelationalExpr | EqualityExpr '=' RelationalExpr | EqualityExpr '!=' RelationalExpr

[24] RelationalExpr ::= AdditiveExpr | RelationalExpr '<' AdditiveExpr | RelationalExpr '>' AdditiveExpr | RelationalExpr '<=' AdditiveExpr | RelationalExpr '>=' AdditiveExpr

[25] AdditiveExpr ::= MultiplicativeExpr | AdditiveExpr '+' MultiplicativeExpr | AdditiveExpr '-' MultiplicativeExpr

[26] MultiplicativeExpr ::= UnaryExpr | MultiplicativeExpr MultiplyOperator UnaryExpr | MultiplicativeExpr 'div' UnaryExpr | MultiplicativeExpr 'mod' UnaryExpr

[27] UnaryExpr ::= UnionExpr | '-' UnaryExpr

[28]   ExprToken   ::=   '(' | ')' | '[' | ']' | '.' | '..' | '@' | ',' | '::' | NameTest | NodeType | Operator | FunctionName | AxisName | Literal | Number | VariableReference

[29]   Literal   ::=   '"' [^"]* '"' | "'" [^']* "'"

[30]   Number   ::=   Digits ('.' Digits?)? | '.' Digits

[31]   Digits   ::=   [0-9]+

[32]   Operator   ::=   OperatorName | MultiplyOperator | '/' | '//' | '|' | '+' | '-' | '=' | '!=' | '<' | '<=' | '>' | '>='

[33]   OperatorName   ::=   'and' | 'or' | 'mod' | 'div'

[34]   MultiplyOperator   ::=   '*'

[35]   FunctionName   ::=   QName - NodeType

[36]   VariableReference   ::=   '$' QName

[37]   NameTest   ::=   '*' | NCName ':' '*' | QName

[38]   NodeType   ::=   'comment' | 'text' | 'processing-instruction' | 'node'

[39]   ExprWhitespace   ::=   S

Chapter 15

XSL Transformations (XSLT) Tips

There was a requirement for the capability to convert one XML document into another based on a stylesheet. The specification on XSL Transformations (XSLT) is in response to this issue. This chapter considers some of the potential general questions about XSLT that might be raised by someone who is already knowledgeable about XML and XSL. Look at Chapter 8 for details on XSL, which is a formatting language.

XSL Transformations (XSLT) Version 1.0 W3C Recommendation (November 16, 1999) is found at http://www.w3.org/TR/1999/REC-xslt-19991116. The latest version is found at http://www.w3.org/TR/xslt.

 Warning: The specification can be considered a reference document more than a "work-in-progress" document. Its function is to express the syntax and semantics of the XSLT namespace. A significant part of the specification is devoted to processing issues, which are not covered in this chapter. The chapter focuses on the general nature of XSLT, that is, basic syntax and semantics.

Note: A tip is not a full explanation of a subject. There is no detailed description. It is recognized that the answers here are highly abbreviated and only high points of the issues. Many answers given here have further technical and processing ramifications. The information in the specification of about 80 pages is essential to the responses.

What are XSL Transformations?

The XSL Transformations are of the nature to do transformations for documents that adhere to the XSL specification rather than of a general XML nature. Transformations have the purpose of converting an input tree to an output tree. Both trees are normally XML documents.

Transformations are not for converting the logical and physical structure of one XML document into another one. Specifically, a transformation is a stylesheet.

The practical application is to move data from one XML document to another without worrying about presentation, that is, the rendering of a human-readable display. This is accomplished by using a fine granular view of an XML document's tree structure.

What is a tree?

A tree is a data structure that begins with a node, called a root, and then has a series of connecting nodes. This tree is similar to a genealogical chart with ancestors and descendants. Nodes without children, descendants, are called leaves. Likewise, a single node without a child is a leaf.

What is an XML tree?

An XML tree consists of elements and their content. However, XSL extends the notion of nodes so there are seven node types:

- Root
- Element
- Text
- Attribute
- Namespace
- Processing instruction
- Comment

What is the distinguishing characteristic of XSLT-defined elements?

XSLT-defined elements must belong to a specific XML namespace. The namespace used in the specification is XSLT namespace.

How is a transformation achieved?

A transformation is achieved by associating patterns with templates.

What is a pattern?

A pattern is matched against elements in the input tree.

What are some examples of patterns?

Here are three examples of patterns:

- mytag   Matches any mytag element
- chapter//mytag   Matches any mytag element with a chapter ancestor element
- mytag [3]   Matches any mytag element in the third mytag child element of its parent

What is a template?

A template is used to create part of the output tree.

What is a stylesheet?

A stylesheet contains a set of template rules. A template rule contains a pattern and a template.

What is a template rule?

A template rule has a pattern that applies to the input trees and a template that produces output trees when the pattern is matched. An xsl:template element is a template rule.

What is the xsl: prefix?

The xsl: prefix identifies XSL elements. Within the xsl:template are instructions that have this prefix. An example instruction is xsl:attribute.

 Note: Elements that are XSL instructions are also part of the XSL namespace.

269

What is the basic syntax for a template rule?

The basic syntax for the xsl:template is:

```
<xsl:template
    match = pattern
    name = qname
    priority = number
    mode = qname>
</xsl:template>
```

The xsl:template element is a top-level one.

What is a qname?

A qname (production QName [Namespaces 6]) is a qualified name for an internal XSLT object.

What are the internal XSLT objects?

There are seven internal XSLT objects:
- Named templates
- A mode
- An attribute set
- A key
- A decimal-format
- A variable
- A parameter

What is a named template?

A named template is any template that can be invoked by name. The instruction syntax is:

```
<xsl:call-template
    name = qname>
    <!- - Content: xsl-with-parm* - ->
</xsl:call-template>
```

 Warning: It is an error if a stylesheet contains more than one template with the same name and the same import precedence.

What is a mode?

A mode permits multiple processing of an element. Each result is different.

What is an attribute set?

An attribute set is defined by using the xsl:attribute element. The name of an attribute set is defined by the xsl:attribute-set element.

What is a key?

A key handles an implicit cross-reference structure within a document. An explicit cross-reference structure uses the XML ID, IDREF, and IDREFS attribute types. A key requires a node, name, and a value.

What is a decimal-format?

The decimal-format determines the meaning of special characters for a pattern. The syntax is based on JDK 1.1.

 Warning: It is an error if the stylesheet does not contain a decimal-format declaration with an expanded-name specification.

What is a variable?

A variable is a name that may be bound to a value. The basic syntax for a variable is:

```
<!- - Category: top-level-element - ->
<!- - Category: instruction - ->
<xsl:variable
     name = qname
     select = expression>
     <!- - Content: template - ->
</xsl:variable>
```

What is a parameter?

A parameter is a default value of a binding. The basic syntax for a parameter is:

```
<!- - Category: top-level-element - ->
<xsl:parm
    name = qname
    select = expression>
    <!- - Content: template - ->
</xsl:parm>
```

How do I apply a template rule?

You would use an instruction to apply a template with the following syntax:

```
<xsl:apply-templates
    select = node-set-expression
    mode = qname>
    <!- - Content: (xsl:sort | xsl:with-parm)* - ->
</xsl:apply-template>
```

When you use the instruction you are telling the formatter to process the root element's children.

What are the capabilities of a template?

A template:

■ Creates structures of arbitrary complexity
■ Pulls string values out of arbitrary locations within a source tree
■ Generates structures that are repeated according to the occurrence of the element within a source tree

 Note: XPath is used for selecting elements for processing, for conditional processing, and for generating text.

How can I override a template rule?

You can override a template rule by using this instruction:
`<xsl:apply-imports>`.

What is the URI for the XSLT namespace?

The XSLT namespace URI is http://www.w3.org/1999/XSL/Transform.

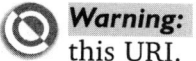 **Warning:** Currently, Internet Explorer does not accept this URI.

May I include any element in the XSLT namespace?

No. All the specified XSLT-defined elements are listed in Appendix B of the specification. There are some two dozen elements defined. Two examples are:

```
<!- - Category: instruction - ->
<xsl:attribute
    name = (qname)
    namespace = (uri-reference)>
    <!- - Content: template - ->
</xsl:attribute>

<!- - Category: top-level-element - ->
 <xsl:attribute-set
    name = qname
    use-attribute-sets = qnames>
    <!- - Content: xsl:attribute* - ->
</xsl:attribute-set>
```

What is the purpose of the xsl: prefix?

The xsl:prefix identifies elements within the XSLT namespace. The prefix can actually be anything as long as it adheres to specification requirements.

What is a top-level element?

A top-level element is any element that is a child of an xsl:stylesheet element.

How do I create an element?

To create an element within a stylesheet, you use the instruction:

```
<xsl:element
    name = (qname)
    namespace = (uri-reference)
    use-attribute-sets = qnames>
    <!- - Content: template - ->
</xsl:element>
```

273

How do I create an attribute?

To create an attribute within a stylesheet you use the following instruction:

```
<xsl:attribute
    name = (qname)
    namespace = (uri-reference)
    <!- - Content: template - ->
</xsl:attribute>
```

What is the purpose of xsl:transform?

Xsl:transform is a synonym for xsl:stylesheet. The xsl:stylesheet element is used to represent a stylesheet in an XML document. The following are identical in nature:

```
<xsl:stylesheet
    version = number>
...
</xsl:stylesheet>

<xsl:transform
    version = number>
...
</xsl:transform>
```

 Note: The version attribute is used to indicate the version of XSLT. Currently, the only valid number is 1.0.

What are the available element types that can be within a stylesheet?

The following 12 XSL elements can be contained in a stylesheet. All are prefixed by xsl:

- attribute-set
- decimal-format
- import
- include
- key
- namespace-alias
- output

- param
- preserve-space
- strip-space
- template
- variable

 Note: For more information on these element types, see Chapter 8.

What types of mechanisms are used to combine stylesheets?

XSLT uses two mechanisms for combining stylesheets:
- Inclusion   Allows combining without changing the semantics of either stylesheet
- Import   Allows for the stylesheets to override each other

What is the basic syntax for a stylesheet inclusion?

The basic syntax for a stylesheet inclusion is:

```
<xsl:include
    href = uri-reference />
```

What is the basic syntax for a stylesheet import?

The basic syntax for a stylesheet import is:

```
<xsl:import
    href = uri-reference />
```

Can an XSLT stylesheet be embedded within a resource?

Yes. The two methods are:
- The stylesheet is embedded textually within the non-XML resource.
- The xsl:stylesheet element may occur in an XML document other than as a document element.

What type of data model is used by XSLT?

XSLT uses the XPath data model.

What is a base node?

A base node is a node's URI that resolves attribute values that represent relative URIs into absolute URIs.

What is the meaning of an XSLT expression?

An XSLT expression uses the XPath production Expr. See Chapter 14 for details on the Expr production.

What are some of the purposes of an XSLT expression?

Here are three purposes of an XSLT expression:

■ Generates text for inclusion in the result tree
■ Selects nodes for processing
■ Specifies methods for node processing

How do I copy the current node?

To copy the current node you use the instruction:

```
<xsl:copy
    use-attribute-sets = qname>
    <!- - Content: template - ->
</xsl:copy>
```

How do I compute generated text?

An example of generating text is extracting text from the source tree. To handle this type of function you use the instruction:

```
<xsl:value-of
    select = string-expression
    disable-output-escaping = "yes" | "no" />
```

How do I insert a formatted number into the result tree?

To insert a formatted number into the result tree you use the instruction:

```
<xsl:number
    level = "single" | "multiple" | "any"
    count = pattern
    from = pattern
    value = number-expression
    format = (string)
    lang = (nmtoken)
    letter-value = ("alphabetic" | "traditional")
    group-separator = (char)
    group-size = (number) />
```

How do I do a sort?

To do a sort, you specify xsl:sort elements as children of an xsl-apply-templates or xsl:for-each element. The xsl:sort element instruction is:

```
<xsl:sort
    select = string-expression
    lang = (nmtoken)
    data-type = ("text" | "number" | gname-but-not-ncname)
    order = ("ascending" | "descending")
    case-order = ("upper-first" | "lower-first") />
```

You can have multiple levels of sorts. The first specified xsl:sort element is primary.

What is the basic syntax for creating output as HTML?

The basic syntax for creating output as HTML might look like this:

```
<xsl:stylesheet version="1.0"
        xmlns:xsl="http://www.w3.org/1999/XSL/Transform">

<xsl:output method="html"/>

<xsl:template match="/">
    <html>
      <xsl:apply-templates/>
    </html>
</xsl:template>
...
</xsl:stylesheet>
```

 Warning: There are a number of conditions have to be met to achieve your expectations.

Warning: The HTML used must meet XML well-formedness constraints.

What are the production rules for XSLT?

The production rules for XSLT are as follows:

[1] Pattern ::= LocationPathPattern | Pattern '|' LocationPathPattern
[2] LocationPathPattern ::= '/' RelativePathPattern? | IdKeyPattern (('/' | '//')
RelativePathPattern)? | '//'? RelativePathPattern
[3] IdKeyPattern ::= 'id' '(' Literal ')' | 'key' '(' Literal ',' Literal ')'
[4] RelativePathPattern ::= StepPattern | RelativePathPattern '/'
StepPattern | RelativePathPattern '//' StepPattern
[5] StepPattern ::= ChildOrAttributeAxisSpecifier NodeTest Predicate*
[6] ChildOrAttributeAxisSpecifier ::= AbbreviatedAxisSpecifier | ('child' |
'attribute') '::'

Chapter 16

Tools

This chapter is an overview of the generalized roles of three types of tools for XML: editors, parsers, and browsers. The focus here is on Web implementations rather than on non-Web implementations, because the first of the ten design goals for XML, according to the XML specification, is "XML shall be straightforwardly usable over the Internet."

However, the second design goal from the XML specification states "XML shall support a wide variety of applications." Many tools or applications that use XML do not have to be used on the Web. One example of this is Microsoft's implementation of XML in Office 2000. Another example is XML Authority by Extensibility, Inc. in Chapel Hill, North Carolina, which seeks to use XML for CORBA networking integration. Each of these examples requires specific vendor tools. This chapter includes checklists of things you need to consider when using any vendor product.

In addition, some available vendor products and shareware are considered. A brief description is included for each product.

 Note: A tip is a snippet of advice, a guideline, or a pointer. It is not a full explanation of a subject. It is recognized that the answers here are highly abbreviated.

What is the role of an editor?

The editor is for XML DTD and document creations. The editor's primary functions are for entering and tagging the data. Any word processor can be used from Notepad, not to be confused with Microsoft's XML Notepad, to Microsoft Word or Corel WordPerfect to input a document type definition (DTD) or markup. When using Word, save the file with the text-only option. Rename the file with either the extension .DTD or .XML. The file should never include carriage returns.

Warning: You can do XML markup in a text editor or word processor, but it is never advantageous to do so since there XML editors available that enforce structure and automate tagging.

If you have an extensive amount of XML markup, you should look at an XML editor. This type of editor adds the markup as you desire and it enforces document rules.

An editor can check for simple errors such as omitting a right (>) or left angle (<). Some color the markup. Some are even smart enough to check your DTD and determine if your document is well formed and valid.

What is the role of a parser?

The parser is for validating an XML document. The parser is also for validating the XML markup. A parser does two fundamental actions. The first action is to recognize that the structural elements of a document are consistent with the well-formedness constraints of the XML specification. These constraints are discussed in detail in an earlier chapter. An example of a well-formedness constraint is, "The Name in an element's end-tag must match the element type in the start-tag."

The second action of a parser is to validate the grammar of the XML based on rules given in the document type definition (DTD). Validation requires either an explict or an implict DTD. A validating parser also checks for adherence to the validity constraints of the XML specification. An example of a validity constraint is, "Values of type ENTITY must match the Name production, and values of type ENTITIES must match Names; each Name must match the name of an unparsed entity declared in the DTD."

A parser is one of the two parts of an XML processor. The other part is the display mechanism or device. There are two types of parsers: non-validating and validating. A non-validating parser only checks a document against the XML production rules to see that it is well-formed, proper markup. A validating parser verifies that a document conforms to a specific DTD.

When is a validating parser required?

A validating parser is required only when there is an associated DTD. It looks for the following:

- There is an XML declaration that includes a required (as compared to implied) markup declaration.
- All elements and their attributes and entities adhere to the correct syntax.
- Within a single DOCUMENT entity (type), all the elements and their contents are properly nested.
- Any entities within document must be declared within the DTD.
- For the latest information you might look at "XML Software Guide: XML Parsers" at http://www.wdvl.com/Software/XML/parsers.html. Here are other sites where one might also get additional information:
    - W3C's site   See Appendix B.
    - Robin Cover's site   See Appendix B.
    - Tim Bray's site   See Appendix B.

 Note: Java-based processors (parsers) run on a computer with a Java runtime environment. See Appendix B for the URL where the PC version of the Java runtime environment is found. Anyone using either Microsoft's Internet Explorer or Netscape's Communicator has the Java runtime environment.

What is the role of a browser?

The browser is for online viewing of an XML document. Remember the cliché "garbage in, garbage out" because a browser cannot correctly process or display an XML document if the document does not conform to its XML DTD. The principle used here is the same as any language, markup, or object-oriented programming.

 Warning: The status of XML implementation is not standard among the browsers.

 Note: There are special browsers for XML dialects such as the Chemical Markup Language (CML). Peter Murray-Rust wrote the browser and it is called Jumbo, Java Universal Molecular Browser for Objects.

Microsoft has incorporated a Microsoft XML (MSXML) parser into Internet Explorer since version 4.01. It allows, of course, for the browsing of Channel Definition Format (CDF) files. The use of IE for vector graphics (VML) is discussed in Chapter 18.

What are some of the functions I should look for in an editor?

Here are some specific features one might look for in an XML document editor:

■ Automated formatting	Enables rule-based formatting, that is, the ability to import a new formatting template
■ Correctability	Corrects errors easily
■ Customization	Gives flexibility to handle local issues
■ Flexibility	Enters information in any order, but still maintains validity
■ Guided editing	Gives a visual view of the elements so that you do not have to work directly with tags
■ Interactive formatting	Permits the fine tuning of a document's format
■ Publishing capabilities	Capabilities to publish to either the Web or paper
■ Well-formedness support	Identifies tag issues

 Note: Editing is really two phases. The first phase is entering the markup. Does the editor support well-formedness validation? The second phase is for the parser to check if you have a valid XML document. Is the parser a validating one? Is it in full adherence to the XML specification? Does it give optional user-friendly error messages?

What are the general issues in viewing an XML document?

When you want to view an XML document, how difficult is the viewing process? If you are using a browser, can you click on an XML file and have it become viewable? Do you have to open the browser and then, through several steps, get to the point where the document can be viewed? To what degree is the browser compliant to the XML specification? Do you have to have special markup with the XML document or outside of the document so you can use the browser as a viewer?

An example of a non-browser that permits you to view your XML document is Microsoft Notepad.

What is a major concern with printing an XML document?

You should be able to print not only your markup, but also your output. Remember that XML content is non-formatted text until you introduce XSL.

What are the processing capabilities between XML and Java?

In Java, native XML support lets you have full XML processing capabilities. This means you can read and manipulate XML data as it moves among applications or platforms.

What are some of the processing issues for XSL?

The XSL utility or processor should support the latest version of the XML and XSL specifications. The XSL specification is discussed in detail in Chapter 8. Currently XSL is a "work in progress," so it is advisable to view the latest version at http://www.w3.org/TR/xsl.

Any XSL product needs to support the transformation of data in XML documents and the specification of formatting semantics.

Any XSL support product should:
- Have an easy method for the application of style sheets
- Be dynamic
- Be flexible
- Be easy to customize

Any XSL product should also support patterns. A pattern is a set of rules that map markup to produce the final HTML. A pattern is also a string that identifies a specific XML node at a point in the XML tree.

 Warning: If one uses Microsoft's XSL command-line utility, one should remember that it transforms your XML data files and XSL spreadsheets into HTML files.

What are some of the support issues for XLink?

The XLink specification is discussed in detail in Chapter 9. Currently, XLink is also a "work in progress," so it is advisable to view the latest version at: http://www.w3.org/TR/xlink.

A vendor product should support bi-directional object links.

What are some of the support issues for XPointer?

The XPointer specification is discussed in detail in Chapter 10. Currently, XPointer is also "work in progress," so it is advisable to view the latest version at: http://www.w3.org/TR/xptr.

A vendor product should support XPointers that provide a specific reference to elements, character strings, and other XML instances. The product should have the XPointer capability to point to (address into) any relative or absolute location in an XML document.

A conforming browser might even highlight the links.

What are some of the support issues for XML namespaces?

There is one critical question about XML namespace support. Is the vendor's validating engine, the parser, in full adherence to the XML specification and the XML Namespaces specification? In particular, does the engine permit you to qualify elements uniquely on the Web, thus avoiding element name conflicts?

 Warning: The XML Namespaces specification does not require real URIs, only locations that have a valid appearance definition.

The XML Namespaces specification is discussed in detail in Chapter 11. Currently, XML namespaces specification is also a "work in progress," so it is advisable to view the latest version at: http://www.w3.org/TR/REC-xml-names.

What are some of the support issues for vector graphics?

The Scalable Vector Graphics (SVG) specification is discussed in detail in Chapter 12. The Vector Markup Language (VML) specification is discussed in detail in Chapter 13. Currently, the graphic specifications are a "work in progress," so it is advisable to view the latest version at: http:// www.w3.org/TRSVG or http://www.w3.org/TR/NOTE-VML.

 Note: Microsoft's Internet Explorer 5 does support the VML specification. Look at Microsoft's site for the latest support documentation.

Why is there a requirement for schema support?

Whatever the situation, the product should have schema support, that is, the ability to define the rules that govern element and attribute relationships using the stated syntactical standards. In particular, the schema support should include that for data types and namespaces.

What is the meaning of the concept "data islands"?

Microsoft has developed the notion of "data islands." A data island is an XML document or fragment within an HTML page. This concept is supported specifically within a Microsoft environment. This is done using either a script or the <OBJECT> tag.

What are some of the miscellaneous areas of concern for XML support?

Other areas that might be considered are the following:
- Capabilities to handle queries
- Collection messaging
- CORBA support
- Document security
- Drivers for database connections
- Sample templates

What are some companies that have authoring, editing, and publishing support?

Companies that have tools for authoring, editing, and publishing include:
- ArborText
- Inso

- Interleaf
- SoftQuad

What are some of the companies that provide DTD and XML schema generation?

Companies that provide tools for generating DTDs and XML schema include:

- Design Microstar
- Extensibility, Inc.

What are some of the companies that provide for database publishing and management?

Companies that provide tools based on XML for database publishing, content management, and data management include:

- DataChannel, Inc.
- Sequoia Software
- UserLand Software
- Vignette Corp.

What are some of the companies that provide for XML data storage?

Companies that provide storage for XML data include:

- Chrystal Software
- Object
- POET

What is the design trend for programming tools?

The design trend for these programming tools is to be visualization tools and software code libraries that authors can use to create and manipulate XML content. These tools tend to also have language-neutral interfaces.

What is the development trend for new XML applications?

The current trend for the development of applications is to support new XML vocabularies such as Microsoft "data islands." Many of the products are being designed for interoperability within an application class, as well as across application classes.

Is there a list of some of the available vendors and shareware tools?

Here is a short list of available vendor and shareware tools:

ADEPT Editor 7.0 Permits authors to write text, place graphics, and create books, manuals, catalogs, encyclopedias, and similar types of information. By ArborText, Inc.

Ælfred For use by Java programmers to add XML support to their applets and applications. By Microstar.

Astoria An authoring support system for complex technical and content publishing environments. By Chrystal Software.

Balise An XML/SGML application programming environment that builds information exchange and translation systems. By AIS Software.

Clip A visual editor that includes capabilities for validating, advanced searching and replacing, and applying markup through dialog boxes. By Techno 2000 Project.

DataChannel XML Development Kit A collection of XML parsers, viewers, APIs, and documentation for XML developers. By DataChannel.

DXP DataChannel XML Parser A validating parser written in Java. It is for server-side applications that require XML capabilities. It is a parser for the professional because it is such a powerful tool. By DataChannel.

DynaBase An integrated content management and dynamic publishing system for the development of large dynamic Web sites. By Inso.

expat XML Parser Toolkit written in C as a non-validating parser. It is a part of Netscape's solution to XML support. It includes user-defined style sheets. By James Clark.

Frontier A cross-platform Web scripting environment built around an object database whose structure mirrors the structure of XML. By UserLand Software.

287

HEX HTML Enable XML Parser   It is a parser written in Java and is a validating parser. By Anders Kristensen.

Lark   Lark is a non-validating parser written in Java by the senior editor of the XML specification. Bray developed it to test the validity of the recommendation. By Tim Bray.

Larval   Larval is a validating parser written in Java. By Tim Bray.

LT XML   A set of tools that includes a parser for checking for well-formed documents. By Language Technology.

MSXML (Microsoft XML)   It is a validating parser written in Java. By Microsoft.

Near and Far   An editor that includes the ability to import SGML documents and convert them to well-formed or valid documents. By Microstar.

POET Content Management Suite   Includes the POET Object Server and the SGML/XML parser, the SGML/XML Navigator, and the POET Content Management Suite programmer's API. By POET.

Real-time XML Editor   A validating XML editor written in DHTML for Internet Explorer 5. By archiTag.

SAX   A standard interface for event-based XML parsing. It is free. By Microstar.

Tango Enterprise Version 3.1 "Generation X"   This product automatically generates XML documents from business logic and the values of changing business data in SQL or ODBC databases. By EveryWare Development Corp.

tdtd   A set of macros built specifically for the Emacs text editor. You should be an experienced user of Emacs. By Mulberry Technologies.

Visual XML   A Java-based editor. It has a tree-based representation of a document's content and markup. By Pierre Morel.

Web Automation Toolkit   This toolkit uses XML for data exchange so companies can connect applications to existing Web sites and utilize Web protocols to integrate business applications directly over the Web. By webMethods, Inc.

XED   It checks for valid documents. It has error messages, so it is good for a new XML user. By Henry S. Thompson.

XML <PRO>   An XML editor with a user interface that allows users to create and edit XML-based documents. By Vervet Logic.

XML Spy   An XML and DTD editor with a structured approach for Microsoft Windows 95, Microsoft Windows 98, and Microsoft Windows NT written in C++. By XML Spy.

xmlproc   Python XML parser written in Python that may be a validating parser. By Lars Marius Carshol.

XP XML Parser   A validating parser written in C. By James Clark.

Chapter 17

XML Applications and Initiatives Tips

This chapter looks at some of the interesting methods that XML and its related technologies are using in applications and some of the initiatives that will lead to further XML development and enhancements. Some of the applications have a new vision above data handling, while others are considering the modification of applications limited because of their use of HTML or SGML or the need for a new function.

Most of the discussed applications and initiatives in the chapter should be considered more as proposals rather than finished work because of the evolving nature of the XML technologies. One of the first books on XML was on the designing of XML Internet applications. It is important to consider the active work is designing, not the implementing of XML Internet applications.

As has been said in other places in the book, the truth made today may be the untruth of tomorrow. It is very important to see what actions others are taking in this area so that one will not reinvent the wheel. We all build on the successes and failures of others. No failure should be condemned if we can learn from it. Each person's dream today may be another person's reality tomorrow.

Because of the flux of the specifications for XML, XSL, XLink, XPointer, and XML namespaces, and the newness of XPath and XSLT specification, you cannot necessarily develop a logical set of criteria for quality and authenticity. The information given here may only be at a level of demonstration or proof-of-concept. It should be recognized that the developers of these initiatives are working their products through stages. As with many of the specifications, you should consider these applications "works-in-progress" or dreams.

As has been said elsewhere, the markup for an XML application is based on a dialect, any specialized instance of a language. Many of the initiatives briefly identified in this chapter are primarily dialects. Any book has a page limitation, and thus, so does any chapter. For links and more

detailed descriptions for most of these initiatives, see
http://www.oasis-open.org/cover/xmlIntro.html/xml#applications.

 Note: A tip is a snippet of advice, a guideline, or a
pointer. It is not a full explanation of a subject. It is
recognized that the answers here are highly abbreviated
and only high points of the topics. In the descriptions of
the initiatives or proposals, only a very brief statement of
the purpose is given.

What is the Astronomical Markup Language (AML)?

The Astronomical Markup Language (AML) aims at being a standard
exchange format for metadata in astronomy. AML supports the following objects (in the object-oriented sense): astronomical object, article,
table, set of tables, image, and person. A Java-based AML browser can
be used to retrieve AML documents and browse them with a common
user interface.

What is the Bank Internet Payment System (BIPS)?

The Bank Internet Payment System (BIPS) specification includes a protocol for sending payment instructions to banks over the Internet and a
payment server architecture for processing these payment instructions.
BIPS instruction messages and their responses conform to the XML
specification. Each BIPS message begins with an XML header that
includes the XML version number, document type, a reference to the
BIPS DTD file, and the BIPS version number.

What is the Bioinformatic Sequence Markup Language (BSML)?

The Bioinformatic Sequence Markup Language (BSML) is a public
domain protocol for Graphic Genomic Displays. The project goals are,
in some respects, similar to those of the Chemical Markup Language
except for genome research. Goals are to describe the features of
genetic sequences through graphic objects and established procedures
for assigning graphic objects to sequence features.

What is the BIOpolymer Markup Language (BIOML)?

The BIOpolymer Markup Language (BIOML) is to be used for the annotation of biopolymer sequence information. It allows the full specification of all experimental information known about molecular entities (a physical object) composed of biopolymers, for example, proteins and genes. It is an implementation of a basic design of XML, data transfer among computers.

What is the Capability Card?

The Capability Card is a kind of attribute certificate designed from a secure communication framework on the Internet. The goal is for users to have the capability to handle various types of data in capability cards visually with an XML viewer.

How is XML being used with CASE?

The CASE Data Interchange Format (CDIF) addresses the problem of interoperability faced by both users and vendors of Visual Modeling tools and Computer Aided Software and Systems Engineering (CASE) tools. CDIF lays out a single architecture for exchanging information between modeling tools and between repositories, and defines the interfaces of the components to implement this architecture. The CDIF Technical Committee is preparing a specification called the CDIF XML-based Transfer Format. Any CDIF Transfer file employing the Transfer Format is also a legal XML file.

What is the Clinical Trial Data Model?

The Clinical Trial Data Model is being used to accelerate Clinical Trial Data Exchange Standards. It is an effort by Phase Forward Incorporated to establish an XML-based data model of its InForm Web-based clinical trial data collection and management software to key industry standards organizations.

What is Coins?

Coins is a programming project undertaken by Bill la Forge. One of the operations of a Coins program is the binding of XML element types to specific Java classes. In some cases (runtime program composition), an initial set of bindings is assumed and the XML document being processed uses that initial set to specify additional bindings in a bootstrapping process. The bindings used to process a document are not always fixed, but are often determined by the application or server processing the document. In these cases, the XML document is simply a vehicle for moving information between applications, and the Coins technology simply provides the means for processing that document.

What is the Cold Fusion Markup Language (CFML)?

The Cold Fusion Markup Language (CFML) provides a generalized markup language for handling the richness of programming, logic, and integration required for full-scale applications on the Web platform. It allows developers to build reusable components that can be easily dropped into a dynamic Web application. These tags are processed by the Cold Fusion server.

What is Commerce XML (cXML)?

Commerce XML (cXML) is an open Internet-based standard for e-commerce that is a set of XML DTDs. It facilitates the exchange of content and transactions over the Internet. It was developed by more than 40 companies.

What is the CommerceNet industry initiative?

The CommerceNet initiative is to close the time gap between the development of industry standards and implementation of open, interoperable applications in the electronic commerce arena. A goal is to accelerate the adoption of XML as an important technology for the realization of efficient Internet Commerce. The CommerceNet program includes the strategic project for the development of XML catalogs and DTDs.

What is the initiative by the Customer Support Consortium?

The Customer Support Consortium has a subgroup developing a set of mappings for open exchange standard specifications using XML. It is a group of over 70 technology companies. Their purpose is to improve customer support.

What is the DocBook XML DTD?

The DocBook XML is an XML version of the DocBook DTD. DocBook is an SGML DTD maintained by the DocBook Technical Committee of OASIS. It is particularly well suited to books and papers about computer hardware and software.

What is the Document Content Description for XML (DCD) proposal?

The Document Content Description for XML (DCD) W3C proposal is from International Business Machines Corporation (IBM) and Microsoft Corporation. It defines a vocabulary for describing constraints upon XML documents. More specifically, it proposes a structural schema facility, Document Content Description (DCD), for specifying rules covering the structure and content of XML documents.

What is an initiative to use EDI and XML?

The Electronic Data Interchange (EDI) effort provides a standard format to describe different types of data so that the information can be decoded, manipulated, and displayed consistently and correctly by implementing EDI dictionaries. The XML-EDI Group is an organizational part of the Graphic Communications Association Research Institute (GCARI).

What is the Educom Instructional Management Systems Project (IMS)?

The Educom Instructional Management Systems Project (IMS) is a metadata XML-based specification. It specifies how learning materials should flow over the Internet and how organizations and individual learners should manage the learning process.

What is Encoded Archival Description (EAD)?

The EAD (Encoded Archival Description) initiative is an effort of the U.S. Library of Congress and several research level institutions. These institutions use the EAD DTD to encode their archival finding aids using the Standard Generalized Markup Language (SGML) or in XML. This standard is maintained by the Network Development and MARC Standards Office of the Library of Congress (LC) in partnership with the Society of American Archivists.

What is the Extensible Log Format (XLF) Initiative?

The XLF (Extensible Log Format) Initiative was organized by Don Park, CTO of Docuverse. The XLF Initiative's short-term goal is to design the XML-based Web server log format. Its long-term goal is to design a universal log format based on XML.

What is the Extensible User Interface Language (XUL)?

The Extensible User Interface Language (XUL) is an XML-based language for describing the contents of windows and dialogs. XUL has language constructs for all of the typical dialog controls, as well as for widgets like toolbars, trees, progress bars, and menus.

What is the HTTP Distribution and Replication Protocol (DRP)?

The HTTP Distribution and Replication Protocol (DRP) uses a data structure, called an index, specified using XML. The index describes metadata for:

- Content identifiers, using the existing URI specification
- An index format that describes a set of files
- A new HTTP header field, Content-ID, that obtains the correct version of a file by specifying a content identifier
- A new HTTP header field, Differential-ID, that obtains a differential update for a file

What is iCalendar?

The iCalendar XML DTD defines an XML document type definition (DTD) that corresponds to the iCalendar calendaring and scheduling core object format defined by RFC 2445.

What is the IEEE Standard DTD?

The purpose of the IEEE Standard DTD is to create and edit IEEE standards of all sorts.

What is the purpose of ISO 12083 XML DTD?

The International Standard 12083 DTD provides a set of building blocks for the structuring of books, articles, serials, and similar publications in print and electronic form. This International Standard provides a document architecture to facilitate the creation of various application-specific document type definitions.

What is Java Speech Markup Language (JSML)?

The Java Speech Markup Language (JSML) allows applications to annotate text with additional information that can improve the quality and naturalness of synthesized speech. JSML documents can include structural information about paragraphs and sentences. Sun Microsystems, Inc. has worked in partnership with leading speech technology companies to define the specifications.

What is the XML Legal Working Group?

The XML Legal Working Group's purpose is to develop one or more model document type definitions (DTDs) for the filing and exchange of legal documents using XML standards.

What is NuDoc technology?

NuDoc from Bitstream, Inc. describes, edits, and permits the viewing of highly designed pages for print and online distribution. NuDoc uses a document object made of style, content, and page layout subobjects. NuDoc reads and writes XML content files during the authoring process.

How is OASIS using XML?

OASIS, the Organization for the Advancement of Structured Information Standards (formerly SGML Open), is trying to represent all the possible forms of XML as documents, data and metadata, and any new class of information systems that allows data or objects to be reused with any application. The members include: Allaire, Andersen Consulting, Arbor Text, BTG, DataChannel, Daylight Software, Informix, Inso, NexGen SI, OmniMark Technologies, Online Computing Library Center, PLATINUM Technology Solutions, POET Software, NC Focus, Sybase, Thomson Corporation, Wall Data, and webMethods.

What is Open Content Syndication (OCS)?

Open Content Syndication (OCS) uses a directory format to enable channel listings to be constructed for use by portal sites, client-based headline software, and other similar applications.

What is the Open Software Description Format (OSD)?

The Open Software Description Format (OSD) was developed by Marimba, Inc. and Microsoft. The format has an XML-based vocabulary for describing software packages and their dependencies for heterogeneous clients.

What is the Open Trading Protocol (OTP)?

The Internet Open Trading Protocol (OTP) provides an interoperable framework for Internet commerce where the payment system roles are performed by different parties or by one party. OTP messages are XML documents physically sent between the different organizations involved in a trade.

What is OpenMLS?

OpenMLS is a Web-based real estate listing management system. OpenMLS uses the real estate listing search technology called Xsearch!. Xsearch! is based entirely on XML. The use of XML adds meaning to mark-up. The DTD(s) is (are) designed to work with several different user types:

- Those making MLS entries using custom software (such as OpenMLS)
- Those making MLS entries with standard XML editors
- Those simply making a Web site (separate from MLS entry)

What is the P3P Syntax Specification?

The Platform for Privacy Preferences (P3P) Syntax Specification specifies for P3P applications the capability to enable sites to automatically declare their privacy practices in a way that is understandable to users' browsers. P3P uses RDF/XML for the exchange of structured data and assertions.

What is the Precision Graphics Markup Language (PGML)?

The Precision Graphics Markup Language (PGML) is an effort of W3C.

The vendor leaders in this effort are Adobe Systems, Inc., International Business Machines Corporation, Netscape Communications Corporation, and Sun Microsystems, Inc. PGML is a 2-D scalable graphics language designed to meet both the simple vector graphics needs of casual users and the precision needs of graphic artists.

What is the Question and Answer Markup Language (QAML)?

The Question and Answer Markup Language (QAML) provides a specific format for documents dealing with questions and answers. QAML is meant for Frequently Asked Questions (FAQs).

What is RosettaNet?

RosettaNet is a global business consortium creating the electronic commerce framework to align processes in the IT supply chain. webMethods announced in August 1999 the first commercial use of RossettaNet with Marshall Industries, a distributor of industrial electronic components.

What is SABLE?

The Standard for Text-to-Speech Synthesis Markup (SABLE) is an XML/SGML-based markup scheme for text-to-speech synthesis. It was developed to address the need for a common TTS control paradigm.

What is Simple Workflow Access Protocol (SWAP)?

The Simple Workflow Access Protocol (SWAP) allows for interoperability between workflow systems and between workflow systems and other applications. The protocol defines four primary interfaces, which are used to manage, monitor, initiate, and control the execution of processes on external workflow systems.

What is the smartX Markup Language (SML)?

The smartX Markup Language (SML) enables automation of interactions with XML documents providing general methods to represent a set of smart device functions. SmartX is a descriptive language to describe the application protocol, SML (Smart Markup Language), that implements XML for the smart card industry.

What is the XML effort of the Society of Automotive Engineers (SAE)?

The Society of Automotive Engineers (SAE) has adopted a number of standards under the SAE J2008 family of standards designed to provide easy access to emission-related automotive service information. The Society is developing a data model for automotive service information. Among the efforts of the Society is the development of a standard XML version of the SAE J2008 DTD for the data model.

What is the Synchronized Multimedia Integration Language (SMIL)?

The Synchronized Multimedia Integration Language (SMIL) is an effort of W3C. SMIL allows for the integration of a set of independent multimedia objects into a synchronized multimedia presentation. Using SMIL, an author can describe the temporal behavior of a presentation, describe the layout of the presentation on a screen, and associate hyperlinks with media objects.

What is the Talk Markup Language (TalkML)?

The Talk Markup Language (TalkML) is used for applications with context free grammars, so more flexible voice interaction dialogs can be developed. The goal is to make it easy to create dual access Web sites, which can be accessed through visual or voice browsers. TalkML is an experimental XML language for voice browsers. It was developed by HP Labs.

What is Telecommunications Interchange Markup (TIM)?

The TIM document type definition (DTD) describes the logical structure of telecommunications and other technical documents. It is based on early versions of the DocBook DTD developed by the Davenport Group.

What is the Text Encoding Initiative (TEI)?

The Text Encoding Initiative (TEI) is an international consortium that is developing guidelines for encoding research textual materials in electronic form. The main URL is http://www.tei-c.org. To download one of two DTDs you can go to http://www.uic.edu/orgs/tei/ed/teixml.dtd or http://www.uic.edu/orgs/tei/lite/teilte.dtd. The TEIXML DTD has approximately 122 elements for defining the logical structure of a research document type.

What is the User Interface Markup Language (UIML)?

The User Interface Markup Language (UIML) is used to describe the user interface in generic terms and then use a style description to map the interface to various operating systems (OSs) and appliances. It reduces the work in porting the user interface to another platform.

What is the vCard electronic business card proposal?

This is the effort to use XML for a vCard format that will be the standard format for electronic business card data, useful for exchange of personal directory data across the Internet, as well as in non-Internet environments. The vCard XML DTD defines an XML document type definition (DTD) that corresponds to the vCard, an electronic business card format defined by VCard.

What is the Virtual Hyperglossary (VHG)?

The Virtual Hyperglossary (VHG) project endeavors to enhance knowledge with terminological services for individuals and groups, especially learned societies who want to provide their services on the Web or intranets. It is based upon ISO standards for terminology (ISO FDIS 12620, MARTIF—Machine Readable Terminology Interchange Format). It employs such concepts as clickable concept maps. Its XML DTD uses terminology based on ISO 12620 (Data Categories for Terminology).

What is the WAP Wireless Markup Language specification (WML)?

The Wireless Application Protocol (WAP) Wireless Markup Language (WML) is to be used for specifying content and user interfaces for narrow band devices, including cellular phones and pagers.

What is the Weather Observation Markup Format (OMF)?

The Weather Observation Markup Format (OMF) is used to encode weather observation reports. The goal of the OMF system is to annotate and augment standard weather reports with derived, computed quantities, and to recast the essential information in a markup format that is easier to interpret, yet completely accurate.

What is Web Collections?

Web Collections uses metadata syntax. It can be expressed inside HTML documents or standalone. It is stylistically similar to HTML. Potential uses of Web Collections include Web maps, HTML e-mail threading, PIM functions, scheduling, content labeling, and distributed authoring.

What is the WebBroker's effort for Distributed Object Communication on the Web?

The WebBroker effort from DataChannel, Inc., attempts to unify interface technology used in existing distributed object systems like CORBA, DCOM, and RMI but is based on XML, HTTP/1.1, and traditional CGI technology. This effort comes under the umbrella of W3C.

What is WebDAV?

WebDAV stands for Web-based Distributed Authoring and Versioning. It is a set of extensions to the HTTP protocol, which allows users to collaboratively edit and manage files on remote web servers. WebDAV uses XML.

What is the XML DTD for Phone Books?

XML DTD for Phone Books was developed by Siemens AG and Microsoft Corporation. It describes the information to be included in the standard phone book for roaming applications.

What is the XML Metadata Interchange Format (XMI)?

The XML Metadata Interchange Format (XMI) from the Object Management Group (OMG) has a goal of unifying XML and related W3C specifications with object and component modeling standards.

What is XML-F (XML for FAX)?

VSI (V-Systems Inc.) developed the XML Interface for FAX, XML-F (XML for FAX). It is to be used for connecting fax servers to applications, other fax servers, and fax service providers. XML-F Specifications include XML DTDs. XML-F uses six XML document types to implement features, requests, and responses.

XML and IE Tips

The emphasis of this chapter is on the general implementation of XML technologies by Microsoft and its impact on your XML document design and development. Second, the tips are given to provide an overview of the basic support structure in Microsoft Internet Explorer 5 (IE5) for XML and its family members, such as XSL. In addition, for additional insights into this implementation, the introduction of support for XML in IE4 is included.

 Note: A book larger than this one could probably give the details one would need to technically comprehend Microsoft's implementation of XML within IE5.

Many of the questions raised in this chapter may have been generated because of Microsoft's implementation of VML. However, in many instances, you might replace the acronym "VML" with "vendor-specific implementation." One of the features supported by IE5 is the XML-Data schema, which is considered by Microsoft and other vendors as a replacement for the XML DTD as highlighted in this chapter.

Chapter 13 looked at the Vector Markup Language (VML) specification. In Chapter 13, the examples are based on an implementation of VML by Microsoft. The word "an" is used in the previous sentence because this is an area of dynamic development and you should check Microsoft's Web site for the latest on this technology.

 Note: A tip is a snippet of advice, a guideline, or a pointer. It is not a full explanation of a subject. It is recognized that the answers here are highly abbreviated and only high points of the topics.

What is the major issue in working with the IE implementation of VML?

While Microsoft has made a commitment to full standards-level support, it is not there currently. This implementation may or may not be a gateway to resolving XML compatibility in a way that was not done with HTML. You have to consider such things as incompatibility with other browsers and the use of XSLT.

 Warning: It was mentioned in Chapter 7 that there was currently no known public DTD for Channel Definition Format (CDF) which was introduced with IE4. You have to consider this point in the context of an "open architecture" for XML technologies for any vendor implementation.

What type of support was introduced in IE4 for XML?

IE4 used a series of ActiveX controls and Java applets to support XML. This support could be embedded into a Web page. The page could be parsed and its data content could be displayed within an XML-format file. The basic design principle was to turn an XML file into an HTML file.

What is the major XML design issue that involves this implementation?

XML (Chapters 2 through 6) was designed to be transported effectively and efficiently over the Web. The focus of the XML specification was on data and text manipulation rather than data and text appearance. Because of the concerns for the style formatting and transforming, two additional specifications were developed for XSL (Chapter 8) and XSLT (Chapter 15). Running in parallel was the need for graphics. In addition, two more specifications have been developed for SVG (Chapter 12) and VML (Chapter 13). The limitation for graphics is the use of vectors. In this dynamic environment, Microsoft has sought to introduce public viable implementations of XML technologies.

 Note: It is important not to forget the place of Document Object Model (DOM) in this mix.

What areas of information do I need to know about to work with this implementation?

To work effectively with this implementation, you need to know about a number of areas of information. Some of these are:

- XML productions
- XSL stylesheets
- VML graphic design
- ActiveX controls
- Java applet design
- Web page creation
- XML document structure
- IE5 capabilities and use
- HTML programming techniques
- Dynamic HTML programming techniques

Is there any issue with DTD access?

The basic XML design principle was to have the capability for anyone to access the same DTD. The first issue to arise out of this design principle was common markup that had different meanings such as <title> </title>. The use of this markup would be different for a hospital and a university for the position of doctor. This issue was resolved by the introduction of namespaces in XML. Second, since any markup is a part of an XML document, what are the implications of vendor-specific markup such as Microsoft's for the use of VML? One has to consider processing issues based on the local DTD and markup. The metaquestion (a conceptual question of meaning of the highest level) being raised here is "Does any XML application or implementation become a dialect of the XML language?"

Is there any issue of interoperability?

XML was designed to work across platforms. This means the specific features of a platform were to be irrelevant to XML data transport. The concept was to give you the capability to build client/server or Web-based applications. This concept becomes important when you upgrade, enhance, or extend an application or add more clients. A browser has to be considered a platform. What are the interoperability

307

implications when an XML implementation will only work effectively on one browser?

Is there an issue of general accessibility?

The basic XML design principle was for an XML document to be considered a source of data for a variety of applications and Web pages. The data must be within a self-describing format. This format has to be read by a number of tools including parsers and browsers. Without a set of global standards for handling and manipulating this format, you might expect inconsistencies. This issue becomes more complex as your XML document evolves from data only to the inclusion of styles, and then to the inclusion of graphics.

What is the major hurdle to a standard data interchange methodology?

The major hurdle to a standard data interchange methodology is that XML has the capability for markup to mean whatever the author wants it to mean. While this is an exciting idea, the design, development, testing, and implementation of an XML document or application requires project management. This means one needs to be systematic in thinking out the issues. HTML does not have this problem because there is a fixed set of predefined tags that are also supposed to have predefined meanings. However, the interpretation of these meanings is an issue from browser to browser.

Why should I consider XML, XSL, and VML on IE5?

Any new technology requires a shakedown. That is, any technology goes through a developmental period where there are implementations before there are standards for the technology. These developments add to the knowledge of the technology and assist in raising solutions that might ultimately become a part of the standards. You must recognize that any implementation may not be compatible with "all the current standards." You have to comprehend the degree of "feature creep" of the implementation. You should try the XML implementations on IE5 for the sake of comprehending the technology and the related issues. You should not try these implementations because you think this is the solution.

Note: Microsoft has put a "stake in the ground." Its approach may be correct or incorrect. However, in the past, Microsoft's implementations have influenced the outcomes of Web standards.

What is the level of XML support in IE5?

As this book is being written, published, and distributed, there are dynamic changes going on with the many XML specifications and Microsoft's implementation of VML. The level of support discussed in this chapter is what is known currently, early in the year 2000. This book is also putting a "stake in the ground." There are two converging environments, XML standards and Microsoft's developmental interpretations of these standards. Hopefully, any tips given will be useful to the reader.

What is the importance of design conditions?

Usually, a small forgotten condition can produce a disastrous result. In addition, a condition given as absolute may not be absolute. For example, it might be a given that in HTML when you type <BODY BGCOLOR="#6F4242">, you will always get salmon as the background color. The author may state this "fact" as absolute; however, the outcome might be different under conditions omitted by the author.

 Warning: This tip means any design statement should always be considered conditional.

What is the difference between IE4 and IE5 XML support?

IE5 has built-in XML support. IE4 did not have this type of support. This means that IE5 is supposed to render an XML document as the original.

 Note: To get the latest information on IE try Microsoft's Web site at http://www.microsoft.com/windows.ie. The latest on XML specifications can be found at http://www.w3.org. The URLs for the latest versions of any of the specifications discussed in this book are found in Appendix B.

What are some of the XML features that IE5 supports?

This is an abbreviated list of IE5-supported XML technologies:
- W3 Consortium's document type definition (DTD) standards
- XML-Data schema
- Embedded "data islands" in HTML documents
- Data persistence
- Use of CSS2 standards
- XSL standards
- Behavior technique
- XML Document Object Model (DOM)
- VML standards

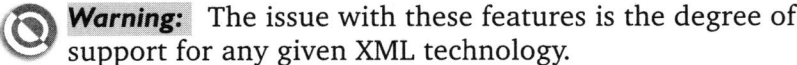 **Warning:** The issue with these features is the degree of support for any given XML technology.

What is meant by behaviors?

IE5 supports the CSS2 selector behavior. It permits you to separate script code from the HTML or XML elements.

What is an implementation of behaviors in IE5?

One of the implementations is the use of HTML Components (HTC). HTC permits you to define a custom component's interface using special XML elements. The element set includes:
- <COMPONENT> (the parent)
- <ATTACH>
- <METHOD>
- <EVENT>
- <PROPERTY>

 Note: Look for *HTC Reference* on http://msdn.microsoft. com for the latest details on this implementation.

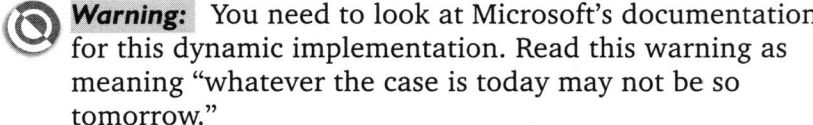 **Warning:** You need to look at Microsoft's documentation for this dynamic implementation. Read this warning as meaning "whatever the case is today may not be so tomorrow."

Warning: Microsoft recommends using an XML namespace for these elements. This is valuable because these elements have unique meanings within IE5. You could very easily have markup collisions with these elements with other XML documents.

How does CSS2 work with XML?

CSS2 works with XML in a similar manner as it does with HTML.

 Note: See Chapter 8 on XSL implementation tips in contrast to CSS2. Also, see Chapter 15 on XSLT.

How does IE5 handle the parsing of XML documents?

The script code running in IE5 accesses a loaded XML document and extracts or updates the content. This is possible because each XML element is available in a tree structure.

How does IE5 handle CSS2 and XSL?

With IE5, XSL uses CSS2-type properties and HTML elements to define output appearance.

What is an important XSL feature for handling XSL?

IE5 has a built-in default XSL stylesheet. An indication of this feature is when you load an XML document directly into the browser it displays line breaks, indents, and outline indicators (plus and minus signs).

What are some of the XSL functions that IE5 can handle?

At the highest level of functions, IE5 can handle:
- Template manipulation
- Pattern manipulation
- XML document transformations

What are XML-Data schema?

Microsoft, along with other vendors, has proposed a system that defines an XML document's structure different from the one using a DTD. XML-Data schema use the same syntax as the rest of the document. This technique allows for a single parser for the complete process. This means that the reading of an XML document and validating it are one process.

Does IE5 support XLink and XPointer?

Currently IE5 does not support XLink or XPointer.

What are the available XML schema elements?

There are eight special XML schema elements. These elements are recognized through a required default namespace. The elements are:

■ Schema
■ ElementType
■ element
■ AttributeType
■ attribute
■ description
■ datatype
■ group

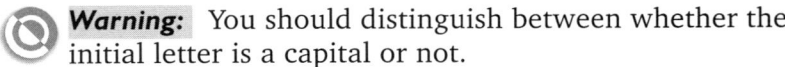 **Warning:** You should distinguish between whether the initial letter is a capital or not.

What is the syntax for the required namespace?

The current name space syntax for IE5 is as follows:

```
<Schema name="Schema1"
        xmlns="urn:schema-microsoft-com:xml-data"
        xmlns:prefix="urn:schema-microsoft-com:datatype">
```

 Note: Schema1 can be any name.

What is the function of the <Schema> element?

The Schema element as the base (root) element encloses the schema. It has three attributes:

- name   Defines the schema name
- xmnls   Specifies the default namespace
- xmnls:prefix   Specifies the namespace URI for the datatype element attributes

What is the function of the <ElementType> element?

The ElementType element defines the type of element used within the schema or the XML document. It has five attributes:

- content   Defines content type
- dt:type   Indicates the text's data type
- model   Defines whether the element can accept data not defined within the schema
- name   Indicates the unique string for the element within the schema
- order   Defines how sequences of the element can appear

What is the function of the <element> element?

The element element defines instances of the child element that can appear within the parent element. It has three attributes:

- type   Defines the name of the element type
- minOccurs   Defines whether the element is optional in instances of the parent
- maxOccurs   Defines the maximum amount of times that an element can appear in instances of the parent element

What is the function of the <AttributeType> element?

The AttributeType element defines the attribute type used within elements in the schema. It has six attributes:

- dt:type   Defines one of ten predefined specific data types
- dt:value   Defines a value set that forms an enumerated type
- default   Defines the attribute's default value

■ name   Defines the AttributeType element's unique string used within the schema

■ model   Defines whether the attribute can accept content that is not defined in the schema

■ required   Defines whether a value for the attribute is required

What is the function of the <attribute> element?

The attribute element is used within the ElementType element. It has two attributes:

■ default   Defines the default value of the attribute

■ required   Specifies whether a value for the attribute is required

What is the function of the <description> element?

The description element provides information about either an element or an attribute. It has no attributes.

What is the function of the <datatype> element?

The datatype element defines the type of data that an element or an attribute can contain. It has six attributes:

■ **dt:max**   States the maximum inclusive value that the element or attribute can accept.

■ **dt:maxExclusive**   States the maximum exclusive value that the element or attribute can accept.

■ **dt:maxlength**   States the maximum length of the element or the attribute.

■ **dt:min**   States the minimum inclusive value that the element or attribute can accept.

■ **dt:minExclusive**   States the minimum exclusive value that the element or attribute can accept.

■ **dt:type**   Specifies one of ten predefined specific data types.

What is the function of the <group> element?

The group element collects a series of <element> elements so they can be assigned a specific sequence in the schema. It has three attributes:

- minOccurs — Defines whether the group is optional in the document based on the schema.
- maxOccurs — Defines the maximum occurrences of a group in a document based on the schema.
- order — Defines sequences of the groups and element types contained with the group.

Is inheritance possible in XML-Data schema?

Yes. Inheritance is possible for elements.

Does Remote Data Service Control (RDS) work with XML documents?

No.

Does Tabular Data Control (TDC) work with XML documents?

No.

What is the <XML> element in IE?

The <XML> element in IE is used to create a data island in an HTML page. This is supported using the C++ Data Source Object (DSO). A data island is simply a section of an HTML page that is to be treated as XML.

 Warning: The <XML> element is an HTML element, and not an XML element. The essential syntax is <XML>content</XML>.

How do I create a data island?

The essential syntax for creating a data island is as follows using the CD-Library scenario from Chapter 5:

```
<XML ID="DSOCDList">
      <?xml version="1.0"?>
      <CD-Library>
        <CD>
            <!- - CD n content - ->
        </CD>
        <CD>
            <!- - CD n + 1 content - ->
        </CD>
      </CD-Library>
</XML>
```

How can I link an XML data file?

Instead of having a directly embedded file you can use the SRC attribute of the <XML> element. You would have the following "one-liner":
<XML ID=DSOCDList" SRC="CDLirary.xml"></XML>.

 Warning: You cannot use an empty-tag syntax.

Can I do data binding with a DSO?

In the broadest sense, there are four types of data bindings permissible:
■ Tabular
■ Current record
■ Event
■ Attribute

 Note: For information on this subject you should look for documentation on IE5 programming since this is a peripheral area to this book's focus.

Can I run XML data in the background of a Web page?

Yes. This function is done through custom scripting within a DSO.

What is the purpose of the XML Document Object Model (DOM)?

The purpose of the XML DOM is to permit the browser or any application to build an internal structured representation (model) of the XML data as it is loaded.

 Note: When you remove the adjective "XML," a DOM is a "standard" technique within its own right that can handle general data for a browser. XML DOM is a specific instance of the DOM instance.

Is there a W3C document on a standard DOM?

There is a W3C document on a standard DOM. However, the language of the document uses "interfaces" rather than "objects." The latest version of the document can be found at http://www.w3.org/TR/REC-DOM-Level-1. The current date of the specification is October 1, 1998.

 Note: Microsoft has announced full support of this recommendation. However, Microsoft has added additional features.

What are the basic differences between the handling of an HTML and an XML document using DOM?

An HTML document has an images collection and a forms collection. An XML document has nodes. This difference is caused by the major differences in document structure. HTML always has child objects (some may be empty). XML document structure is very flexible. There may be leaf nodes (nodes without children).

Why is the concept of recursion important to parsing an XML document?

The basic structure of an XML document is considered a tree within DOM. A programming technique to resolve a tree is recursion. Recursion means repeating a certain function until a condition is met. This means each instance of the function is nested until the looping is completed.

Terms and Definitions

When "Rule [n]" is referred to in this glossary, it is a reference to an XML production rule in XML Recommendation 1.0 (February 10, 1998). Appendix C lists the XML production rules. When a term or definition is not XML, then it will be noted by (XSL), (XLink), etc.

When a term is identified with (XSL) it is from Extensible Stylesheet Language (XSL) Version 1.0 W3C Working Draft (January 12, 2000). This version is found at http://www.w3.org/TR/2000/WD-xsl-20000112. The latest version is found at http://www.w3.org/TR/xsl.

When a term is identified with (XLink), it is from XML Linking Language (XLink) (December 20, 1999) found at http://www.w3.org/TR/1999/WD-xlink-19991220. The latest version is found at http://www.w3.org/TR/xlink.

When a term is identified with (XPointer), it is from XML Pointer Language (XPointer) (December 6, 1999) found at http://www.w3.org/TR/1999/WD-xptr-19991206. The latest version is found at http://www.w3.org/TR/xptr.

When a term is identified with (Namespaces), it is from Namespaces in XML (January 14, 1999) found at http://www.w3.org/TR/1999/REC-xml-names-19990114. The latest version is found at http://www.w3.org/TR/REC-xml-names.

When a term is identified with (SVG), it is from Scalable Vector Graphics (SVG) 1.0 Specification (December 3, 1999) found at http://www.w3.org/TR/1999/WD-SVG-19991203. The latest version is found at http://www.w3.org/TR/SVG.

When a term is identified with (VML), it is from Vector Markup Language (VML) (May 13, 1998) found at http://www.w3.org/TR/1998/NOTE-VML-19980513. The latest version is found at http://www.w3.org/TR/NOTE-VML.

When a term is identified with (XPath), it is from XML Path Language (XPath) 1.0 (October 8, 1999) found at http://www.w3.org/TR/1999/PR-xpath-19991008. The latest version is found at http//www.w3.org/TR/xpath.

When a term is identified with (XSLT), it is from XSL Transformations (XSLT) 1.0 (November 16, 1999) found at http://www.w3.org/TR/1999/REC-xslt-19991116. The latest version is found at http://www.w3.org/TR/xslt.

absolute location	(XPointer) It points to one or more elements or XML document locations without any reference to another source.
addressing	(XLink/XPointer) It is the method of finding two linked objects.
ancestor	(XPointer) This keyword identifies the nodes that contain a location source.
application	The software module on behalf of which an XML processor does its work.
arc	(VML) A predefined shape that draws an oval segment.
attribute	Governed by Rule [41]. Associates name-value pairs with elements.
attribute list	The specified or declared attributes within a tag.
attribute node	(XPath) Two available attribute nodes are xml:lang and xml:space. An attribute node has an expanded-name and a string-value.
attribute set	(XSLT) It is defined by using the xsl:attribute element. The name of an attribute set is defined by the xsl:attribute-set element.
attribute type	Governed by Rule [54]. Three kinds: a string type, a set of tokenized types, and enumerated types.
attribute uniqueness	(Namespaces) An attribute is unique when no element (tag) has two attributes with the same name or no qualified name with the same prefix and local part has been bound to identical namespaces.
attribute-list declaration	Governed by Rule [52] – [53]. Specifies the name, data type, and default value (if any) of each attribute associated with a given element type.
axis	(XPath) An axis is defined by XPath production [6] AxisName. The 13 axes are primarily based on ancestry.
background	(VML) A top-level element that describes the fill of a page's background using vector graphic fills.

background	(VML) An element that can be used to customize a Web page.
base node	(XSLT) It is a node's URI that resolves attributes values that represent relative URIs to absolute URIs.
block-progression-direction	(XSL) In Western writing systems, the block-progression-direction is "top-to-bottom." The use of block with the specification tries to eliminate absolute indicators. The value of the writing-mode property is used.
CDATA section	Governed by Rules [18] – [21]. May occur anywhere character data may occur. It is used to escape blocks of text containing characters that would otherwise be recognized as markup. It begins with the string "<![CDATA[" and ends with the string "]]>".
character	Governed by Rule [2] and Rules [84] – [89]. An atomic unit of text as specified by ISO/IEC 10646. Legal characters are tab, carriage return, line feed, and the legal graphic characters of Unicode and ISO/IEC 10646.
character data	Governed by Rule [14]. It is any text that is not markup.
character reference	Governed by Rule [66]. A specific character in the ISO/IEC 10646 character set, for example, one not directly accessible from available input devices.
child	(XPointer) This keyword identifies the location source's direct child nodes.
children	Governed by Rules [47] - [50]. Elements without content.
class	Within XML, a class is a document type. Within the publishing world, examples are manuals, novels, and letters.
clipping	(SVG) It is the functionality or path that permits the "inside" of an outline to show, while the "outside" does not show.
clipping path	(SVG) It restricts the region for applying paint.
color	(XSL) It is a set of values used to identify a particular color from a color space. Currently, only RGB colors are supported.
comment	Governed by Rule [15]. Marked off by <-- -->. May appear anywhere in a document outside other markup. It may appear within the document type declaration at places allowed by the grammar.

compatibility	A feature of XML included solely to ensure that XML remains compatible with SGML.
conditional section	Governed by Rules [61] – [65]. Portion of the document type declaration external subset which is included in, or excluded from, the logical structure of the DTD based on the keyword which governs it.
conditionality	(XSL) See space-specifier. It is a Boolean value, which controls whether a space-specifier has effect at the beginning or end of a reference-area; for a conditional space-specifier, this value is true.
constraint	A rule for an XML processor for determining declaration errors. A constraint can be either one of well-formedness or validity.
content	Governed by Rule [43]. It usually is the text between an element's start-tag and end-tag. It can also be character data, entity references, CDATA sections, processing instructions, and comments.
content model	Describes what might occur with instances of a given element type. It is found in the DTD.
content of elements	Governed by Rule [43]. The text between the start-tag and end-tag is called the element's content.
coordinate system	(SVG) It determines how coordinates and attributes are mapped onto the canvas, the location where SVG graphical objects are drawn.
core function library	(XPath) It the library that must be included with any XPath implementation. The types of functions that must be included are those that support the expression objects.
curve	(VML) A predefined shape that draws a cubic bézier curve.
declaration	A formal statement for production. Rules that declare include document types, element types, attribute-lists, entity, text, and notations.
default declaration	Governed by Rule [60]. Declares how an XML processor should react if a declared attribute is absent in a document.

defaultAttName	(Namespaces) Governed by production rule [NS 3] and also uses a restricted XML name. The default name namespace is the namespace name in the attribute value. The default value, however, can be empty.
delimited text	Text surrounded by a delimiter that is a special character that states the limits of a string. Common delimiters are single and double quotation marks.
descendant	(XPointer) This keyword identifies nodes within a location source's content.
directly derived traits	(XSL) The computed value of a property of the same name on the generating formatting object.
document	Not defined in the XML Recommendation. Since XML is a subset of SGML one might use the definition in ISO 8879. A document can be "a collection of information that is processed as a unit." Unit can be modified by "logically." A document can be located in more than one physical location or unit.
document element	See root element.
document entity	Governed by Rule [1]. Serves as the starting point for the XML processor and may contain the whole document.
document type	A document class with a common set of properties. See class.
document type declaration	Defines constraints on the logical structure and to support the use of predefined storage units; must appear before the first element in the document.
document type definition	Represented by DTD. It contains the grammar for a class of documents found in the XML document type declaration that contains or points to markup declarations.
EBNF	Extended Backus-Naur Form of notation. The notation to form the production rules that uses as its basic form the right-handed form of symbol ::= expression. This reads that a symbol consists of an expression. The expression can have multiple parts.
element	Governed by Rule [39]. Content of a document delimited by start-tags and end-tags, or, for empty elements, by an empty-element tag. A logical unit within an XML document.

element tree	(XLink) It is a hierarchical representation of the specified XML elements and attributes.
element tree	(XPointer) It is a relevant or hierarchical structure that is an abstraction that shows the "genealogy" of the XML elements, attributes, and any other markup constructs.
element type declaration	Governed by Rule [45]. Constrains the element's content.
empty-element tag	Governed by Rule [44]. A logical structure delimiter. May be used for any element that has no content.
encoding declaration	Governed by Rule [78]. Parsed entities stored in an encoding other than UTF-8 or UTF-16 must begin with a text declaration containing an encoding declaration. It is part of the XML declaration.
end-tag	Governed by Rule [42]. It is the end of every non-empty XML element. It echoes the element's type as given in the start-tag.
entity	Any data that can be treated as a "virtual" storage unit.
entity declaration	Governed by Rules [70] – [74]. The Name identifies the entity in an entity reference or, in the case of an unparsed entity, in the value of an ENTITY or ENTITIES attribute.
entity reference	Governed by Rule [67]. The content of a named entity. It signifies that a copy of the entity is to be included at this point.
entity value	Governed by Rule [9]. It is the literal text within an internal entity declaration.
enumerated attributes type	Governed by Rule [57]. There are two kinds of enumerated types: notation and enumeration.
error	A violation of the constraints of the XML specification. The results are undefined. A conforming processor may detect and report an error and may recover from it.
expression objects	(XPath) The basic types of expression objects are Boolean, node-set (can be unordered), numeric (floating-point), and string (UCS characters).
Extended Backus-Naur Form	See EBNF.
extended link	(XLink) It can connect any number of resources, rather than a single optional one local resource and one remote resource.

extended link group element	(XLink) It is a special extended link that can store a list of links to other documents that together constitute an interlinked group. Each document is identified by means of an extended link document element, a special locator element.
Extensible Markup Language	Usually noted as XML. Describes a class of data objects called XML documents and partially describes the behavior of computer programs which process them. XML is an application profile or restricted form of SGML, the Standard Generalized Markup Language [ISO 8879]. By construction, XML documents conform to SGML documents.
Extensible Stylesheet Language	(XSL) XSL is a language for expressing stylesheets. It consists of a language for transforming XML documents and an XML vocabulary for specifying formatting semantics.
external entity	Governed by Rule [75]. Any entity that is not an internal entity.
external subset	Governed by Rule [30]. It consists of a series of complete markup declarations of the types allowed by the non-terminal symbol markupdecl, interspersed with white space or parameter-entity references.
fatal error	A well-formedness constraint error which a conforming XML processor must detect and report to the application. Once a fatal error is detected, however, the processor must not continue normal processing (that is, it must not continue to pass character data and information about the document's logical structure to the application in the normal way).
fill	(VML) An element that defines a fill within a shape other than a solid color.
filling	(SVG) Painting an object's interior.
fo:	(XSL) The prefix used for referring to elements in an XSL namespace.
following	(XPointer) This keyword identifies the nodes that appear after a location source.
formatting	(XSL) The process of turning the result of an XSL transformation into a tangible form for the reader or listener.

325

formatting objects	(XSL) They are elements in the formatting-object tree, whose names are from the XSL namespace. A formatting object belongs to a class of formatting objects identified by its element name. Some formatting objects are block-level and others are inline-level. There are three kinds of formatting objects: (1) those that generate areas, (2) those that return areas, but do not generate them, and (3) those that are used in the generation of areas.
formulas	(VML) An element that varies a shape's path.
fsibling	(XPointer) This keyword identifies the sibling (same parent) nodes that appear after a location source: ftp://ftp.isi.edu/in-notes/iana/assignments/character-sets.
general entities	Entities for use within the document content.
generic identifier	The name assigned to an element type. The "name" of a tag <GI> </GI>.
glyph-area	(XSL) An inline-area that has no child areas, and has a single glyph image as content.
gradients	(SVG) Gradients, whether linear or radial, consist of continuously smooth color transitions across a vector.
grammar (XML)	The rules for creating markup that are defined by a document type definition (DTD) and the parsing constraints of the XML Recommendation.
group	(VML) A top-level element that describes a set of shapes as a unit, that is, it defines a collection of shapes so that they can be transformed as one.
handles	(VML) An element that defines user interface elements that can vary the adjustable values of a shape.
IANA	(Internet Assigned Numbers Authority) The organization responsible for the Official Names for Character Sets, ed. Keld Simonsen et al.
IETF RFC 1766	(Internet Engineering Task Force). RFC 1766: Tags for the Identification of Languages, ed. H. Alvestrand. 1995.
image	(VML) A predefined shape that draws a bitmap retrieved from an external source.
imagedata	(VML) An element that defines a picture to be rendered on top of a shape.

indirectly derived traits	(XSL) They are the results of a computation involving the computed values of one or more properties on the generating formatting object.
inheritance	(XSL) The property takes the same computed value as the property for the formatting object's parent object.
inline link	(XLink) Concretely, an inline link is where the linking element's content serves as a participating resource. Abstractly, an inline link is when the link serves as one of its own resources.
inline-progression-direction	(XSL) In Western writing systems, the inline-progression direction is "left-to-right." The use of inline with the specification tries to eliminate absolute indicators. The value of the writing-mode property is used.
internal entity	An entity whose value is given in its entity declaration in the DTD. An internal entity is a parsed entity.
interoperability	A non-binding recommendation to increase the chances that XML documents can be processed by the existing installed base of SGML processors which predate the Web SGML Adaptations Annex to ISO 8879.
ISO	Refers to the International Organization for Standardization (English) or Organization Internationale de Normalization (French). It is not an acronym.
ISO 639	(International Organization for Standardization). ISO 639:1988 (E). Code for the representation of names of languages. [Geneva]: International Organization for Standardization, 1988.
ISO 3166	(International Organization for Standardization). ISO 3166-1:1997 (E). Codes for the representation of names of countries and their subdivisions — Part 1: Country codes [Geneva]: International Organization for Standardization, 1997.
ISO/IEC 10646	(International Organization for Standardization). ISO/IEC 10646-1993 (E). Information technology — Universal Multiple-Octet Coded Character Set (UCS) — Part 1: Architecture and Basic Multilingual Plane. [Geneva]: International Organization for Standardization, 1993 (plus amendments AM 1 through AM 7).

key	(XSLT) It handles an implicit cross-reference structure within a document. An explicit cross-reference structure uses the XML ID, IDREF, and IDREFS attribute types. A key requires a node, name, and a value.
keywords	(XSL) Special tokens in the grammar that provide access to calculated values or other property values.
language identification	Governed by Rules [33] – [38]. Identifies the natural or formal language in which the content is written. The language identifiers, as defined by IETF RFC 1766, are "Tags for the Identification of Languages"
letter	Consists of an alphabetic or syllabic base character possibly followed by one or more combining characters, or of an ideographic character.
line	(VML) A predefined shape that specifies a line.
line-area	(XSL) A block-area whose children are all inline-areas.
link	(XLink) A link is an explicit relationship between or among data objects or data object portions.
link	(XPointer) It is an explicit relationship between or among data objects or portions of data objects.
link behavior	(XLink) It focuses on what happens when the link is traversed, such as opening, closing, or scrolling windows or panes; displaying the data from various resources in various ways; testing, authenticating, or logging user and context information; or executing various programs.
link element	(XLink) There are two types of linking elements. First, there is a simple link, which is usually inline and always one-directional. Second, there is an extended link that may be either inline or out-of-line and must be used for such link types as multidirectional links and links originating from read-only resources.
link formatting	(XLink) It focuses on the appearance or treatment of the link prior to any user action, such as choice of font, color, icons, and other devices to show that a link is present.
linking	(XLink/XPointer) The method of establishing a relationship between two linked objects.
linking element	(XLink/XPointer)) An element that describes a link's characteristics.

literal	Any quoted string not containing the quotation mark used as a delimiter for that string. Literals are used for specifying the content of internal entities (EntityValue, Rule [9]), the values of attributes (AttValue, Rule [10]), and external identifiers (SystemLiteral, Rule [11]).
local coordinate space	(VML) The function permits you to define the specific space on the canvas for a shape or a group, that is, it defines a visible vector graphic element.
local resource	(XLink) A local resource as an inline linking element's content.
location path	(XPath) It is an expression that selects a node-set relative to the context node. The location path is the most important construct in XPath.
location term	(XPointer) It is the basic unit for addressing information. A combination of location terms results in a precise location specification. The location term, of course, is the XPointer.
locator	(XLink) It is the part of a link that identifies a resource.
locator	(XLink) It is a URI (Uniform Resource Identifier). The URI specifications used to develop the XLink specification are found in Request for Comments (RFCs) 1738 and 1808 (ftp://ftp.nic.ddn.mil/rfc/rfcNNNN.txt).
locator	(XPointer) It is the link's part, usually a Uniform Resource Identifier (URI), which identifies a resource.
locator string	(XLink) It identifies a participating resource.
locator value	(XLink) A value of a locator must contain either a URI or a fragment identifier in order to locate an XML document or a part of the document.
logical structure	The document structure that is declarations, elements, comments, character references, and processing instructions, all of which are indicated in the document by explicit markup.
markup	The tags that describe the document's storage layout and logical structure: start-tags, end-tags, empty-element tags, entity references, character references, comments, CDATA section delimiters, document type declarations, and processing instructions.

markup declaration	Either an element type declaration, an attribute-list declaration, an entity declaration, or a notation declaration.
masking	(SVG) When used with compositing, permits a semi-transparent mask for compositing foreground objects into the current background.
match (of strings or names)	Two strings or names being compared must be identical. Characters with multiple possible representations in ISO/IEC 10646 match only if they have the same representation in both strings.
mixed content	Governed by Rule [51]. Mixed content is when elements of an element type may contain character data, optionally interspersed with child elements.
mode	(XSLT) It permits multiple processing of an element. Each result is different.
multidirectional link	(XLink) It is a link whose traversal can be initiated from any of its participating resources.
name	Governed by Rules [5] – [8]. A token beginning with a letter or one of a few punctuation characters, and continuing with letters, digits, hyphens, underscores, colons, or full stops, together known as name characters.
named template	(XSLT) Any template that can be invoked by name.
namespace declaration	(Namespaces) Applies to an element in all of its instances until overridden by another namespace declaration. A single element can have multiple namespaces declared as attributes.
namespace	(namespace) A set of unique names. The colon (:) may be used to resolve the issue when a document uses two DTDs that both use an element type or entity with the same name. For example, the namespaces would be DTDname1:samename and DTDname2:samename.
namespaces	(Namespaces) They associate certain names within XML documents using Uniform Resource Identifiers (URIs). An XML namespace is a collection of names and should not be considered in the same sense as a non-XML namespace, which is a name set. In addition, for URIs to be identical they must be character-for-character the same exactly. Simply stated, a namespace is an XML

namespaces (cont.)	convention that uses processing instructions (PIs) to assign unique names in a document to URIs.
NCName	(Namespaces) Governed by production rule [NS 4]. Shows that an NCName found in production rule [2] can begin either with a letter or an underscore (_) followed by zero or more occurrences of a NCNameChar.
nesting	A property of well-formed documents, that is, the logical instances are contained correctly with each other.
Nmtoken	Stands for name token. Any mixture of name characters.
node test	(XPath) It is a test that is true if the declared axis has its appropriate principle node type.
non-validating parser	A parser that checks the well-formedness constraints.
notation declaration	Governed by Rule [82]. Identifies by name the format of unparsed entities, the format of elements that bear a notation attribute, or the application to which a processing instruction is addressed. For example, the format could be a BMP image.
NSAttName	(Namespaces) Governed by production rule [NS 1]. Means that the namespace name identifies the namespace as a URI reference, the attribute's value.
numeric	(XSL) A numeric represents all the types of numbers in an XSL expression. Some of these numbers are absolute values. Others are relative to some other set of values. All of these values use a floating-point number to represent the number-part of their definition.
origin absolute location	(XPointer) It points to a place within the same document.
out-of-line link	(XLink) It is a link that does not serve as one of the link's participating resources. They are generally required for supporting multidirectional link traversal and for reading read-only resources.
out-of-line simple link	(XLink) It is "one-ended" and associates discrete semantic properties with locations.
oval	(VML) A predefined shape that draws an oval as defined by the CSS2 content width and height.
parameter	(XSLT) It is a default value of a binding.
parameter entities	Entities for use within the DTD.
parsed data	Data that has to be parsed that is made up of characters, either character or markup.

parsed entity	Contains text, a sequence of characters, which may represent markup or character data. Invoked by name using entity references.
parser	It is a processor that analyzes notated text and determines if a notation is correct in accordance with defined grammar. An XML parser analyzes markup and content and uses well-formedness constraints and perhaps validity constraints.
participating resource	(XLink) It is a resource that belongs to a link.
path	(SVG) It is a current point that can be changed and then an object outline (open or closed) can be defined.
path	(VML) An element that uses a string containing a rich collection of pen movement commands that define the path that makes up a shape.
path transformation	(VML) It means that VML generates locations, related information for vector paths, and related objects.
pattern	(XSLT) It is matched against elements in the input tree.
pattern	(SVG) A predefined graphic object used to fill or stroke an object.
physical structure	The document structure that is in units or entities. A document begins in a "root" or document entity.
polyline	(VML) A predefined shape that dpecifies a shape of connected line segments.
precedence	(XSL) See space-specifier. It has a value, which is either an integer or the special token force.
preceding	(XPointer) This keyword identifies the nodes that appear before a location source.
predefined shapes	(VML) There are eight predefined shapes. They have the same properties as the <shape> element, except the type attribute is not permitted.
predicate	(XPath) It acts a node-set filter.
PrefixedAttName	(Namespaces) Governed by production rule [NS 2]. Reflects the use of an XML restricted name.
processing instruction	Represented by PI. It is governed by Rule [16]. It allows documents to contain instructions for applications.

processor	A software module that reads XML documents and provides access to their content and structure. It reads XML data and the information and provides the results to an application.
production Rule	See Appendix C for a listing of XML production rules. Uses the EBNF notation of symbol ::= expression.
prolog	The part of the XML document (Rule [1]) that includes the XML declaration and DTD. It precedes the actual document element.
psibling	(XPointer) This keyword identifies the sibling (same parent) nodes that appear before a location source.
qualified name	(Namespaces) Declared when an XML document is in conformance to the Namespaces in the XML specification. A name (a construct corresponding to the non-terminal Name XML production [5]) may be declared as a qualified name.
rect	(VML) A predefined shape that draws a simple rectangle.
refinement	(XSL) This is a computational process, which finalizes the specification of properties, based on the attribute values in the XML result tree. This process involves property value propagation, evaluation, conversion, and construction. This complex process may involve look-ahead, back-tracking, or control-splicing with other processes in the formatter.
relative location	(XPointer) It points to one or more elements or XML document locations with a reference to another source, a location source.
remote resource	(XLink) Any participating resource of a link is that pointed to with a locator.
rendering model	(SVG) This is a developing area within the working draft. However, there is the expectation that while individual processors may handle rendering differently, the results should be the same.
replacement text	A parsed entity's contents and this text are considered an integral part of the document.
reserved names	Any name beginning with the string "xml" or any string that would match (('X'|'x') ('M'|'m') ('L'|'l')).

resource	(XLink) Concretely, it is any reachable use of a locator in some linking element. Abstractly, it is any addressable service or unit of information that participates in a link.
resource	(XPointer) Concretely, it is anything that can be reached by a locator. Abstractly, it is an informational address unit such as a file, an image, or a document.
root element	It is the element that contains all the other elements. The root element is specified in the document type declaration. It is the point where the parser begins processing.
roundrect	(VML) A predefined shape that draws a rectangle with rounded corners.
Scalable Vector Graphics	(SVG) See SVG.
shadow	(VML) An element that defines the shadow effect for a shape.
shape	(VML) A top-level element that describes a shape.
shapetype	(VML) A top-level element that describes a shape so it can be referenced at a later point in a document.
simple links	(XLink) They can approximate the functionality of a basic HTML <A> element. A simple link has one locator, and thus combines the functions of a linking element and a locator into a single element.
space-specifier	(XSL) It is a compound datatype consisting of a minimum, optimum, and maximum, conditionality, and precedence.
standalone document declaration	Governed by Rule [32]. May appear as a component of the XML declaration, and signals whether or not there are such declarations which appear external to the document entity.
start-tag	Governed by Rule [40]. It is the beginning of every non-empty XML element.
string	A sequence of characters usually delimited by single or double quotation marks.
stroke	(VML) An element that specifies a color and weight for a shape's outline.
stroking	(SVG) Painting an object's outline.
style sheet	It is an instruction set that specifies how each structural object within an XML document is to be formatted.

stylesheet	(XSLT) It contains a set of template rules. A template rule contains a pattern and a template.
subresource	(XLink) A portion of a resource that is pointed to as the precise link destination.
subresource	(XPointer) The precise resource portion that points to a specific link destination.
SVG	(SVG) It describes two-dimensional graphics in XML. SVG permits three graphic object types: vector graphics, images, and text.
tag	It is a type of markup that is delimited by a less-than symbol or right-handed bracket and the greater-than symbol or left-handed bracket. Usually refers to the start-tag and end-tag of an element.
template	(XSLT) It is used to create part of the output tree.
template rule	(XSLT) It has a pattern that applies to the input trees and a template that produces output trees when the pattern is matched. An xsl:template element is a template rule.
text	It consists of intermingled character data and markup.
text declaration	Governed by Rule [77]. External parsed entities may each begin with a text declaration. The text declaration must be provided literally, not by reference to a parsed entity. No text declaration may appear at any position other than the beginning of an external parsed entity.
text node	(XPath) It is a grouping of character data. A group may only consist of one character. An example of a text node is a CDATA section.
textbox	(VML) An element that defines text that is to appear inside a shape.
textpath	(VML) An element that defines a vector path based on the supplied text data, font, and font styles.
textual object	It is a well-formed XML document if it matches the production labeled document, meets all the XML specification's well-formedness constraints, and each of the referenced parsed entities is well formed.
token	It is a document indivisible unit type. Examples as used in markup are DOCTYPE, ELEMENT, and ATTLIST.
top-level element	(XSLT) Any element that is a child of an xsl:stylesheet element.

transformation	(SVG) The method by which one modifies the location of an SVG drawing transformation. Transformations include rotation, scaling, skewing, and translation
traversal	(XLink) It is the action of using a link, that is, accessing a resource. It can be either user initiated or under program control.
tree	(XSLT) A data structure that begins with a node called a root and then has a series of connecting nodes. This tree is similar to a genealogical chart with ancestors and descendants. Nodes without children, descendants, are called leaves.
Unicode	The Unicode Consortium. The Unicode Standard, Version 2.0. Reading, Mass.: Addison-Wesley Developers Press, 1996.
units	(SVG) They are the coordinates and lengths in SVG. Units correspond closely to those defined by CSS2.
unparsed entities	They are invoked by name, given in the value of ENTITY or ENTITIES attributes.
valid document	An XML document that follows all the rules specified by its document type declaration.
validating parser	A parser that checks for the constraints as defined in the XML specification.
validity constraint	A rule that applies to all valid XML documents. Violations of validity constraints are errors; they must, at user option, be reported by validating XML processors.
variable	(XSLT) It is a name that may be bound to a value.
Vector Markup Language	(VML) See VML.
VML	(VML) It is an early XML application development. It interacts with both XML and HTML 4.0.
well-formed document	An XML document that conforms to the XML Recommendation but does not necessarily adhere to the validity constraints.
well-formedness constraint	A rule, which applies to all well-formed XML documents. Violations of well-formedness constraints are fatal errors.
white space	Governed by Rule [3]. Consists of one or more space characters (#x20), carriage returns (#xD), line feeds (#xA), or tabs (#x9).

XLink Language	(XLink) It is a hyperlinking functionality that allows you to establish links in your XML documents and have them recognized as such.
XLinks	(XLink) They are used to extend an XML document's internal logical and physical structure into the area of bi-directional object links.
XML Path Language	(XPath) See XPath.
XML Pointer Language	(XPointer) Used to extend an XML document's internal logical and physical structure by providing a specific reference to elements, character strings, and other XML instances.
XML tree	(XSLT) It consists of elements and their content. However, XSL extends the notion of nodes so there are seven node types.
XPath	(XPath) It handles addressing to internal XML document parts. Second. XPath provides the capabilities for string, number, and Boolean manipulations.
XSL Namespace	The XSL namespace has the URI http://www.w3.org/1999/XSL/Format.
XSL stylesheet	(XSL) It specifies the presentation of a class of XML documents by describing how an instance of the class is transformed into an XML document that uses the formatting vocabulary.
XSL Transformations	(XLST) See XSLT. The XSL transformations are of the nature to do transformations for documents that adhere to the XSL specification rather than of a general XML nature.
XSLT	(XSLT) Converts an input tree into an output tree. Both trees are normally XML documents. The practical application is to move data from one XML document to another without worrying about presentation, that is, the rendering of a human-readable display.

Important URLs

New XML sites are being created every day. The key three are the big two (World Wide Web Consortium and XML FAQ) and Robin Cover's site, listed under individual Web sites.

Primary Web Sites

World Wide Web Consortium (W3C) is where the latest as well as the earlier versions of the XML Recommendations, or de facto standards, are located. This is the technical source for all XML type specifications: http://www.w3.org/.

This book uses the following W3C specifications:

- Extensible Markup Language (XML) 1.0 W3C Recommendation (February 10, 1998) found at http://www.w3.org/TR/1998/REC-xml-19980210. The latest version is found at http://www.w3.org/TR/REC-xml.
- Extensible Stylesheet Language (XSL) Version 1.0 W3C Working Draft (January 12, 2000) found at http://www.w3.org/TR/2000/WD-xsl-20000112. The latest version is found at http://www.w3.org/TR/xsl.
- XML Linking Language (XLink) W3C Working Draft (December 20, 1999) found at http://www.w3.org/TR/1999/WD-xlink-19991220. The latest version is found at http://www.w3.org/TR/xlink.
- XML Pointer Language (XPointer) W3C Working Draft (December 6, 1999) found at http://www.w3.org/TR/1999/WD-xptr-19991206. The latest version is found at http://www.w3.org/TR/xptr.
- Namespaces in XML World Wide Web Consortium (January 14, 1999) found at http://www.w3.org/TR/1999/REC-xml-names-19990114. The latest version is found at http://www.w3.org/TR/REC-xml-names.
- Scalable Vector Graphics (SVG) 1.0 SpecificationW3C Working Draft (December 3, 1999) found at http://www.w3.org/TR/1999/WD-SVG-19991203. The latest version is found at http://www.w3.org/TR/SVG.
- Vector Markup Language (VML) World Wide Web Consortium Note(May 13, 1998) found at http://www.w3.org/TR/1998/NOTE-VML-

19980513. The latest version is found at http://www.w3.org/TR/NOTE-VML.

- XML Path Language (XPath) Version 1.0 W3C Proposed Recommendation (October 8, 1999) found at http://www.w3.org/TR/1999/PR-xpath-19991018. The latest version is found at http//www.w3.org/TR/xpath.

- XSL Transformations (XSLT) Version 1.0 W3C Recommendation (November 16, 1999) found at http://www.w3.org/TR/1999/REC-xslt-19991116. The latest version is found at http://www.w3.org/TR/xslt.

- The Recommendation uses the Extended Backus-Naur Form (EBNF) notation for the XML formal grammar. To find out more information on EBNF, go to http://braid.rad.jhu.edu/til/AboutBNF.html.

- The XML FAQ (Frequently Asked Questions) site is maintained by the W3C's XML Working Group. This is a quick way to get at some of the fundamental issues or concerns with XML: http://www.ucc.ie/xml/.

Web Sites of Organizations and Companies

See ArborText's site to find out about the ADEPT XML editor and its other tools. ArborText is a pioneer in this area for SGML and XML: http://www.arbortext.com.

One of the areas that XML is being used is push technology. For more details on this development area, see DataChannel's site: http://www.datachannel.com.

Some librarians and computer specialists have undertaken a project, Dublin Core, to devise a searchable language oriented towards documents: http://purl.oclc.org/dc.

To get more information about XML conferences, courses, and publications in general, the Graphics Communication Association's site is the place to go: http://www.gca.org.

Microsoft has its own MSXML and parser. To find out the latest on Microsoft's view of XML, see its page: http://msdn.microsoft.com/xml/.

 Note: Microsoft does frequently revise its pages; if this URL does not work, just use the top page. Microsoft has many types of pages on XML.

To learn more about virtual database (VDB) technology and how XML is involved, see Junglee's site: http://www.junglee.com/tech/index.html.

SoftQuad has developed XMetal and HoTMetal. These tools support XML: http://www.sq.com.

The Unicode Consortium's site has details on character sets, the Unicode Standard (Unicode 2.1): http://charts.unicode.org/.

Yahoo has collected a set of XML development links: http://dir.yahoo.com/ Computers_and_Internet/Information_and_Documentation/Data_Format/XML.

Web Sites of Individuals

Tim Bray is a founding father of XML. He is one of the co-authors of the XML Recommendation 1.0. He is also a programmer. He developed Lark, a Java-based XML processor, to validate the XML design requirements: http://www.textuality.com/Lark/.

James Clark is dedicated to the development of SGML and XML tools. Most of his work is free: http://www.jclark.com/.

Robin Cover, an expert on SGML and XML, maintains the most extensive resource site on these two areas by an individual. Besides having source materials, the site has many links: http://www.oasis-open.org.

Because XML is a subset of SGML there may be reasons for understanding this markup language better. Look at Dianne Kennedy's SGML Resource Center: http:// www.mcs.net/~dken/xml.htm.

URLs by Chapter

- Chapters 1 and 2 —

  The latest version of the XML specification is found at
  http://www.w3.org/TR/REC-XML.

- Chapter 5 —

  A proposal has been put forth to the W3C entitled *XML-QL: A Query Language for XML* (August 19, 1998). This proposal is found at http://www.w3.org/TR/NOTE-xml-ql.

  For details on CML, see the site of Venus Internet of London, England: http://www.venus.co/uk/.

  For details on MathML, see the MathML Information Center at http://www.webeq.com/mathml.

- Chapter 6 —

  See either of these sites for the ISO 639 and IANA codes:
  http://www.ics.uci.edu/pub/ietf/http/related/iso639.txt
  ftp://ftp.isi.edu/in-notes/iana/assignments/character-sets

- Chapter 7 —

  By doing a search on CDF at http:///msdn.microsoft.com, you can find various examples of this XML implementation.

  Jumbo is distributed with classes for displaying the basic CML elements and is found at http://www.xml-cml.org.

  The latest version of the MathML specification is found at http://www.w3.org/TR/REC-MathML.

  For a download of Amaya, a browser from the W3 Consortium that implements MathML, see http://www.w3.org/Amaya.

  For more information on GEDCOM, see http://www.tiac.net/users/pmcbride/gedcom/55gcint.htm#S1.

  webMethods made a Submission Request to W3C on September 22, 1997 (http://www.w3c.org/Submission/1997/15/). webMethods is a provider of XML-based business-to-business (B2B) integration solutions and holds copyright to the WIDL Specification.

  This URL has links to the WIDL Specifications, the WIDL Specification DTD, the WIDL Mappings, and the WIDL Mapping DTD: http://www.transactnet.com/products/toolkit/userguide/refman/widl/overview.html

- Chapter 8 —

  The latest version of the XSL specification is found at the URL: http://www.w3.org/TR/xsl

  For the latest information on CSS2, see http://www.w3.org/TR/REC-CSS2.

  For the latest information on Document Style Semantics and Specification Language, see http://www.jclark.com/dsssl.

  The XSL formatting-objects namespace has the placeholder (imaginary) URI http://www.w3.org/TR/WD-xsl/FO.

- Chapter 9 —

  This chapter covers, in detail, the XML Linking Language (XLink) W3C Working Draft (December 20, 1999). This version is found at: http://www.w3.org/TR/1999/WD-xlink-19991220.

  The latest version is found at http://www.w3.org/TR/xlink.

  The URI specifications used to develop the XLink specification are found in Request for Comments (RFCs) 1738 and 1808 (ftp://ftp.nic.ddn.mil/rfc/rfcNNNN.txt).

- Chapter 10 —

  This chapter covers the XML Pointer Language (XPointer) W3C Working Draft (December 5, 1999). This version is found at: http://www.w3.org/TR/1999/WD-xptr-19991206.

  The latest version is found at http://www.w3.org/TR/xptr.

- Chapter 11 —

  This chapter covers the Namespaces in XML Working Draft (January 14, 1999). The URL is http://www.w3.org/TR/1999/REC-xml-names-19990114. The latest version of this specification is found at http://www.w3.org/TR/REC-xml-names.

  The prefix xml is by definition bound to the namespace name http://www.w3.org/XML/1998/namespace.

- Chapter 12 —

  The basis for the tips in this chapter is the Scalable Vector Graphics (SVG) 1.0 Specification (December 3, 1999) found at http://www.w3.org/TR/1999/WD-SVG-19991203. The latest version is found at http://www.w3.org/TR/SVG.

- Chapter 13 —

  The version of the initial draft specification used for the tips in the chapter is Vector Markup Language (VML) (May 13, 1998) found at http://www.w3.org/TR/1998/NOTE-VML-19980513. The latest version is found at http://www.w3.org/TR/NOTE-VML.

- Chapter 14 —

  The XML Path Language (XPath) Version 1.0 W3C Proposed Recommendation (October 8, 1999) is found at http://www.w3.org/TR/1999/PR-xpath-19991018. The latest version is found at http//www.w3.org/TR/xpath.

- Chapter 15 —

  XSL Transformations (XSLT) Version 1.0 W3C Recommendation (November 16, 1999) is found at http://www.w3.org/TR/1999/REC-xslt-19991116. The latest version is found at http://www.w3.org/TR/xslt.

  The XSLT namespace URI is http://www.w3.org/1999/XSL/Transform.

- Chapter 16 —

  You might look at "XML Software Guide: XML Parsers" at http://wdvl.com/Software/XML/parsers.html.

- Chapter 17 —

  For links and more detailed descriptions of most of these initiatives, see http://www.oasis-open.org/cover/xmlIntro.html/xml#applications.

- Chapter 18 —

  To get the latest information on IE try Microsoft's Web site at http://www.microsoft.com/windows.ie.

  The latest on XML specifications can be found at http://www.w3.org.

  The latest version of a standard Data Object Model (DOM) can be found at http://www.w3.org/TR/REC-DOM-Level-1.

Appendix C

XML Production Rules

 Note: These rules are from Extensible Markup Language 1.0 W3C Recommendation February 10, 1998.

[1] document ::= prolog element Misc*

[2] Char ::= #x9 | #xA | #xD | [#x20-#xD7FF] |
    [#xE000-#xFFFD] | [#x10000-#x10FFFF]/* any Unicode
    character, excluding the surrogate blocks, FFFE, and
    FFFF. */

[3] S ::= (#x20 | #x9 | #xD | #xA)+

[4] NameChar ::= Letter | Digit | '.' | '-' | '_' | ':' |
    CombiningChar | Extender
    [5] Name ::= (Letter | '_' | ':') (NameChar)*
    [6] Names ::= Name (S Name)*
    [7] Nmtoken ::= (NameChar)+
    [8] Nmtokens ::= Nmtoken (S Nmtoken)*

[9] EntityValue ::= '"' ([^%&"] | PEReference |
    Reference)* '"'
    | "'" ([^%&'] | PEReference | Reference)* "'"
    [10] AttValue ::= '"' ([^<&"] | Reference)* '"'
    | "'" ([^<&'] | Reference)* "'"
    [11] SystemLiteral ::= ('"' [^"]* '"') | ("'" [^']* "'")
    [12] PubidLiteral ::= '"' PubidChar* '"' | "'" (PubidChar
    - "'")* "'"
    [13] PubidChar ::= #x20 | #xD | #xA | [a-zA-Z0-9] |
    [-'()+,./:=?;!*#@$_%]

[14] CharData ::= [^<&]* - ([^<&]* ']]>' [^<&]*)

[15] Comment ::= '<!--' ((Char - '-') | ('-' (Char -
    '-')))* '-->'

[16] PI ::= '<?' PITarget (S (Char* - (Char* '?>'
Char*)))? '?>'
[17] PITarget ::= Name - (('X' | 'x') ('M' | 'm') ('L' |
'l'))

[18] CDSect ::= CDStart CData CDEnd
[19] CDStart ::= '<![CDATA['
[20] CData ::= (Char* - (Char* ']]>' Char*))
[21] CDEnd ::= ']]>'

[22] prolog ::= XMLDecl? Misc* (doctypedecl Misc*)?
[23] XMLDecl ::= '<?xml' VersionInfo EncodingDecl?
SDDecl? S? '?>'
[24] VersionInfo ::= S 'version' Eq (' VersionNum ' | "
VersionNum ")
[25] Eq ::= S? '=' S?
[26] VersionNum ::= ([a-zA-Z0-9_.:] | '-')+
[27] Misc ::= Comment | PI | S

Warning: Production rule [24] implies that one can
state version=1.0. This is incorrect, it has to be either
version='1.0' or version="1.0". The quotation marks are
literals. Rule [24] should read VersionInfo ::= S 'version' Eq
(""'VersionNum'"" | "'" VersionNum "'").

[28] doctypedecl ::= '<!DOCTYPE' S Name (S ExternalID)?
S? ('[' (markupdecl | PEReference | S)* ']' S?)? '>'[
VC: Root Element Type]
[29] markupdecl ::= elementdecl | AttlistDecl |
EntityDecl | NotationDecl | PI | Comment [VC: Proper
Declaration/PE Nesting]
[WFC: PEs in Internal Subset]

[30] extSubset ::= TextDecl? extSubsetDecl
[31] extSubsetDecl ::= (markupdecl | conditionalSect |
PEReference | S)*

[32] SDDecl ::= S 'standalone' Eq ((""' ('yes' | 'no')
""') | ("'" ('yes' | 'no') "'")) [VC: Standalone
Document Declaration]

[33] LanguageID ::= Langcode ('-' Subcode)*
[34] Langcode ::= ISO639Code | IanaCode | UserCode
[35] ISO639Code ::= ([a-z] | [A-Z]) ([a-z] | [A-Z])
[36] IanaCode ::= ('i' | 'I') '-' ([a-z] | [A-Z])+
[37] UserCode ::= ('x' | 'X') '-' ([a-z] | [A-Z])+

[38] Subcode ::= ([a-z] | [A-Z])+

[39] element ::= EmptyElemTag
     | STag content ETag[WFC: Element Type Match]
     [VC: Element Valid]

[40] STag ::= '<' Name (S Attribute)* S? '>'[WFC: Unique
     Att Spec]
     [41] Attribute ::= Name Eq AttValue[VC: Attribute Value
     Type]
     [WFC: No External Entity References]
     [WFC: No < in Attribute Values]

[42] ETag ::= '</' Name S? '>'

[43] content ::= (element | CharData | Reference | CDSect
     | PI | Comment)*

[44] EmptyElemTag ::= '<' Name (S Attribute)* S? '/>'[
     WFC: Unique Att Spec]

[45] elementdecl ::= '<!ELEMENT' S Name S contentspec S?
     '>'[VC: Unique Element Type Declaration]
     [46] contentspec ::= 'EMPTY' | 'ANY' | Mixed | children

[47] children ::= (choice | seq) ('?' | '*' | '+')?
     [48] cp ::= (Name | choice | seq) ('?' | '*' | '+')?
     [49] choice ::= '(' S? cp (S? '|' S? cp)* S? ')'[VC:
     Proper Group/PE Nesting]
     [50] seq ::= '(' S? cp (S? ',' S? cp)* S? ')'[VC:
     Proper Group/PE Nesting]

[51] Mixed ::= '(' S? '#PCDATA' (S? '|' S? Name)* S? ')*'

     | '(' S? '#PCDATA' S? ')' [VC: Proper Group/PE Nesting
     ]
     [VC: No Duplicate Types]

[52] AttlistDecl ::= '<!ATTLIST' S Name AttDef* S? '>'
     [53] AttDef ::= S Name S AttType S DefaultDecl

[54] AttType ::= StringType | TokenizedType |
     EnumeratedType
     [55] StringType ::= 'CDATA'
     [56] TokenizedType ::= 'ID'[VC: ID]
     [VC: One ID per Element Type]
     [VC: ID Attribute Default]

| 'IDREF'[VC: IDREF]
| 'IDREFS'[VC: IDREF]
| 'ENTITY'[VC: Entity Name]
| 'ENTITIES'[VC: Entity Name]
| 'NMTOKEN'[VC: Name Token]
| 'NMTOKENS'[VC: Name Token]

[57] EnumeratedType ::= NotationType | Enumeration
    [58] NotationType ::= 'NOTATION' S '(' S? Name (S? '|' S?
    Name)* S? ')' [VC: Notation Attributes]
    [59] Enumeration ::= '(' S? Nmtoken (S? '|' S? Nmtoken)*
    S? ')'[VC: Enumeration]

[60] DefaultDecl ::= '#REQUIRED' | '#IMPLIED'
    | (('#FIXED' S)? AttValue)[VC: Required Attribute]
    [VC: Attribute Default Legal]
    [WFC: No < in Attribute Values]
    [VC: Fixed Attribute Default]

[61] conditionalSect ::= includeSect | ignoreSect
    [62] includeSect ::= '<![' S? 'INCLUDE' S? '['
    extSubsetDecl ']]>'
    [63] ignoreSect ::= '<![' S? 'IGNORE' S? '['
    ignoreSectContents* ']]>'
    [64] ignoreSectContents ::= Ignore ('<!['
    ignoreSectContents ']]>' Ignore)*
    [65] Ignore ::= Char* - (Char* ('<![' | ']]>') Char*)

[66] CharRef ::= '&#' [0-9]+ ';'
    | '&#x' [0-9a-fA-F]+ ';'[WFC: Legal Character]

[67] Reference ::= EntityRef | CharRef
    [68] EntityRef ::= '&' Name ';'[WFC: Entity Declared]
    [VC: Entity Declared]
    [WFC: Parsed Entity]
    [WFC: No Recursion]
    [69] PEReference ::= '%' Name ';'[VC: Entity Declared]
    [WFC: No Recursion]
    [WFC: In DTD]

[70] EntityDecl ::= GEDecl | PEDecl
    [71] GEDecl ::= '<!ENTITY' S Name S EntityDef S? '>'
    [72] PEDecl ::= '<!ENTITY' S '%' S Name S PEDef S? '>'
    [73] EntityDef ::= EntityValue | (ExternalID NDataDecl?)
    [74] PEDef ::= EntityValue | ExternalID

[75] ExternalID ::= 'SYSTEM' S SystemLiteral
    | 'PUBLIC' S PubidLiteral S SystemLiteral
    [76] NDataDecl ::= S 'NDATA' S Name[VC: Notation
    Declared]

[77] TextDecl ::= '<?xml' VersionInfo? EncodingDecl S?
    '?>'

[78] extParsedEnt ::= TextDecl? content
    [79] extPE ::= TextDecl? extSubsetDecl

[80] EncodingDecl ::= S 'encoding' Eq ('"' EncName '"' |
    "'" EncName "'")
    [81] EncName ::= [A-Za-z] ([A-Za-z0-9._] | '-')*/*
    Encoding name contains only Latin characters */

[82] NotationDecl ::= '<!NOTATION' S Name S (ExternalID |
    PublicID) S? '>'
    [83] PublicID ::= 'PUBLIC' S PubidLiteral

[84] Letter ::= BaseChar | Ideographic
    [85] BaseChar ::= [#x0041-#x005A] | [#x0061-#x007A] |
    [#x00C0-#x00D6] | [#x00D8-#x00F6] | [#x00F8-#x00FF] |
    [#x0100-#x0131] | [#x0134-#x013E] | [#x0141-#x0148] |
    [#x014A-#x017E] | [#x0180-#x01C3] | [#x01CD-#x01F0] |
    [#x01F4-#x01F5] | [#x01FA-#x0217] | [#x0250-#x02A8] |
    [#x02BB-#x02C1] | #x0386 | [#x0388-#x038A] | #x038C |
    [#x038E-#x03A1] | [#x03A3-#x03CE] | [#x03D0-#x03D6] |
    #x03DA | #x03DC | #x03DE | #x03E0 | [#x03E2-#x03F3] |
    [#x0401-#x040C] | [#x040E-#x044F] | [#x0451-#x045C] |
    [#x045E-#x0481] | [#x0490-#x04C4] | [#x04C7-#x04C8] |
    [#x04CB-#x04CC] | [#x04D0-#x04EB] | [#x04EE-#x04F5] |
    [#x04F8-#x04F9] | [#x0531-#x0556] | #x0559 |
    [#x0561-#x0586] | [#x05D0-#x05EA] | [#x05F0-#x05F2] |
    [#x0621-#x063A] | [#x0641-#x064A] | [#x0671-#x06B7] |
    [#x06BA-#x06BE] | [#x06C0-#x06CE] | [#x06D0-#x06D3] |
    #x06D5 | [#x06E5-#x06E6] | [#x0905-#x0939] | #x093D |
    [#x0958-#x0961] | [#x0985-#x098C] | [#x098F-#x0990] |
    [#x0993-#x09A8] | [#x09AA-#x09B0] | #x09B2 |
    [#x09B6-#x09B9] | [#x09DC-#x09DD] | [#x09DF-#x09E1] |
    [#x09F0-#x09F1] | [#x0A05-#x0A0A] | [#x0A0F-#x0A10] |
    [#x0A13-#x0A28] | [#x0A2A-#x0A30] | [#x0A32-#x0A33] |
    [#x0A35-#x0A36] | [#x0A38-#x0A39] | [#x0A59-#x0A5C] |
    #x0A5E | [#x0A72-#x0A74] | [#x0A85-#x0A8B] | #x0A8D |
    [#x0A8F-#x0A91] | [#x0A93-#x0AA8] | [#x0AAA-#x0AB0] |
    [#x0AB2-#x0AB3] | [#x0AB5-#x0AB9] | #x0ABD | #x0AE0 |
    [#x0B05-#x0B0C] | [#x0B0F-#x0B10] | [#x0B13-#x0B28] |

[#x0B2A-#x0B30] | [#x0B32-#x0B33] | [#x0B36-#x0B39] |
#x0B3D | [#x0B5C-#x0B5D] | [#x0B5F-#x0B61] |
[#x0B85-#x0B8A] | [#x0B8E-#x0B90] | [#x0B92-#x0B95] |
[#x0B99-#x0B9A] | #x0B9C | [#x0B9E-#x0B9F] |
[#x0BA3-#x0BA4] | [#x0BA8-#x0BAA] | [#x0BAE-#x0BB5] |
[#x0BB7-#x0BB9] | [#x0C05-#x0C0C] | [#x0C0E-#x0C10] |
[#x0C12-#x0C28] | [#x0C2A-#x0C33] | [#x0C35-#x0C39] |
[#x0C60-#x0C61] | [#x0C85-#x0C8C] | [#x0C8E-#x0C90] |
[#x0C92-#x0CA8] | [#x0CAA-#x0CB3] | [#x0CB5-#x0CB9] |
#x0CDE | [#x0CE0-#x0CE1] | [#x0D05-#x0D0C] |
[#x0D0E-#x0D10] | [#x0D12-#x0D28] | [#x0D2A-#x0D39] |
[#x0D60-#x0D61] | [#x0E01-#x0E2E] | #x0E30 |
[#x0E32-#x0E33] | [#x0E40-#x0E45] | [#x0E81-#x0E82] |
#x0E84 | [#x0E87-#x0E88] | #x0E8A | #x0E8D |
[#x0E94-#x0E97] | [#x0E99-#x0E9F] | [#x0EA1-#x0EA3] |
#x0EA5 | #x0EA7 | [#x0EAA-#x0EAB] | [#x0EAD-#x0EAE] |
#x0EB0 | [#x0EB2-#x0EB3] | #x0EBD | [#x0EC0-#x0EC4] |
[#x0F40-#x0F47] | [#x0F49-#x0F69] | [#x10A0-#x10C5] |
[#x10D0-#x10F6] | #x1100 | [#x1102-#x1103] |
[#x1105-#x1107] | #x1109 | [#x110B-#x110C] |
[#x110E-#x1112] | #x113C | #x113E | #x1140 | #x114C |
#x114E | #x1150 | [#x1154-#x1155] | #x1159 |
[#x115F-#x1161] | #x1163 | #x1165 | #x1167 | #x1169 |
[#x116D-#x116E] | [#x1172-#x1173] | #x1175 | #x119E |
#x11A8 | #x11AB | [#x11AE-#x11AF] | [#x11B7-#x11B8] |
#x11BA | [#x11BC-#x11C2] | #x11EB | #x11F0 | #x11F9 |
[#x1E00-#x1E9B] | [#x1EA0-#x1EF9] | [#x1F00-#x1F15] |
[#x1F18-#x1F1D] | [#x1F20-#x1F45] | [#x1F48-#x1F4D] |
[#x1F50-#x1F57] | #x1F59 | #x1F5B | #x1F5D |
[#x1F5F-#x1F7D] | [#x1F80-#x1FB4] | [#x1FB6-#x1FBC] |
#x1FBE | [#x1FC2-#x1FC4] | [#x1FC6-#x1FCC] |
[#x1FD0-#x1FD3] | [#x1FD6-#x1FDB] | [#x1FE0-#x1FEC] |
[#x1FF2-#x1FF4] | [#x1FF6-#x1FFC] | #x2126 |
[#x212A-#x212B] | #x212E | [#x2180-#x2182] |
[#x3041-#x3094] | [#x30A1-#x30FA] | [#x3105-#x312C] |
[#xAC00-#xD7A3]
[86] Ideographic ::= [#x4E00-#x9FA5] | #x3007 |
[#x3021-#x3029]
[87] CombiningChar ::= [#x0300-#x0345] | [#x0360-#x0361]
| [#x0483-#x0486] | [#x0591-#x05A1] | [#x05A3-#x05B9] |
[#x05BB-#x05BD] | #x05BF | [#x05C1-#x05C2] | #x05C4 |
[#x064B-#x0652] | #x0670 | [#x06D6-#x06DC] |
[#x06DD-#x06DF] | [#x06E0-#x06E4] | [#x06E7-#x06E8] |
[#x06EA-#x06ED] | [#x0901-#x0903] | #x093C |
[#x093E-#x094C] | #x094D | [#x0951-#x0954] |
[#x0962-#x0963] | [#x0981-#x0983] | #x09BC | #x09BE |
#x09BF | [#x09C0-#x09C4] | [#x09C7-#x09C8] |

[#x09CB-#x09CD] | #x09D7 | [#x09E2-#x09E3] | #x0A02 |
#x0A3C | #x0A3E | #x0A3F | [#x0A40-#x0A42] |
[#x0A47-#x0A48] | [#x0A4B-#x0A4D] | [#x0A70-#x0A71] |
[#x0A81-#x0A83] | #x0ABC | [#x0ABE-#x0AC5] |
[#x0AC7-#x0AC9] | [#x0ACB-#x0ACD] | [#x0B01-#x0B03] |
#x0B3C | [#x0B3E-#x0B43] | [#x0B47-#x0B48] |
[#x0B4B-#x0B4D] | [#x0B56-#x0B57] | [#x0B82-#x0B83] |
[#x0BBE-#x0BC2] | [#x0BC6-#x0BC8] | [#x0BCA-#x0BCD] |
#x0BD7 | [#x0C01-#x0C03] | [#x0C3E-#x0C44] |
[#x0C46-#x0C48] | [#x0C4A-#x0C4D] | [#x0C55-#x0C56] |
[#x0C82-#x0C83] | [#x0CBE-#x0CC4] | [#x0CC6-#x0CC8] |
[#x0CCA-#x0CCD] | [#x0CD5-#x0CD6] | [#x0D02-#x0D03] |
[#x0D3E-#x0D43] | [#x0D46-#x0D48] | [#x0D4A-#x0D4D] |
#x0D57 | #x0E31 | [#x0E34-#x0E3A] | [#x0E47-#x0E4E] |
#x0EB1 | [#x0EB4-#x0EB9] | [#x0EBB-#x0EBC] |
[#x0EC8-#x0ECD] | [#x0F18-#x0F19] | #x0F35 | #x0F37 |
#x0F39 | #x0F3E | #x0F3F | [#x0F71-#x0F84] |
[#x0F86-#x0F8B] | [#x0F90-#x0F95] | #x0F97 |
[#x0F99-#x0FAD] | [#x0FB1-#x0FB7] | #x0FB9 |
[#x20D0-#x20DC] | #x20E1 | [#x302A-#x302F] | #x3099 |
#x309A
[88] Digit ::= [#x0030-#x0039] | [#x0660-#x0669] |
[#x06F0-#x06F9] | [#x0966-#x096F] | [#x09E6-#x09EF] |
[#x0A66-#x0A6F] | [#x0AE6-#x0AEF] | [#x0B66-#x0B6F] |
[#x0BE7-#x0BEF] | [#x0C66-#x0C6F] | [#x0CE6-#x0CEF] |
[#x0D66-#x0D6F] | [#x0E50-#x0E59] | [#x0ED0-#x0ED9] |
[#x0F20-#x0F29]
[89] Extender ::= #x00B7 | #x02D0 | #x02D1 | #x0387 |
#x0640 | #x0E46 | #x0EC6 | #x3005 | [#x3031-#x3035] |
[#x309D-#x309E] | [#x30FC-#x30FE]

Appendix D

Differences Between SGML and XML

This appendix is in kind of a brainstorming format. It is a set of unordered thoughts on the differences between SGML and XML. There is a minimum amount of commentary. Some of the differences between SGML and XML include:

- SGML has evolved into a general standard with a high degree of complexity.
- All XML documents are valid SGML documents, but not all SGML documents are valid XML documents.
- Many SGML documents are for large sets of documents, such as those used in the aerospace industry, without having the goal of being displayed over the Internet, but rather in a localized situation.
- XML is a subset of SGML.
- SGML permits the omission of start- and end-tags, while XML does not.
- SGML permits conditional sections within document content, while XML does not.

 Note: The XML specification designates certain sections as "for compatibility" and "for interoperability" to give some insurance of the compatibility and interoperability of XML and SGML. In addition, see Appendix C of the XML specification for XML restrictions in terms of full SGML.

One of the design goals of the XML specification is "XML shall be compatible with SGML." This goal is important for the opportunity to use SGML with XML. The goal has required the ISO 8879 on SGML to be revised.

XML simplifies SGML in a number of ways. This technical simplification includes:

- Empty-tag syntax is specific
- Marked sections can only be CDATA sections

- No AND (&) content model groups
- No attribute types
- No inclusions and exclusions
- No LINK, SUBDOC, CONCUR, RCDATA, #CURRENT, and #CONREF
- No name groups
- No SGML declaration requirement
- No tag minimization
- Restricted mixed content model
- Simplification of comments
- Simplification of entities

An essential description of SGML includes:

- SGML is an international standard (ISO 8879).
- SGML describes languages that represent documents.
- SGML elements may have attributes.
- SGML entities are used for storing SGML documents.
- SGML has a three-part document structure, that is, SGML declaration, DTD, and a document instance.
- SGML is defined within a document type definition (DTD).
- The DTD describes element types and their possible relationships.
- The DTD design establishes the names of element types and their attributes.

Differences Between HTML and XML

There are many ways to present the differences between HTML and XML. Perhaps the simplest method is compare two very simple memos, one in HTML and the other in XML. You can also consider some important technical differences that go beyond the markup differences, such as HTML works within the concept of the page, while XML works within the concept of the document.

A simple HTML memo snippet:

```
<!- - HTML Snippet - ->
<h1>Memo</h1>
<p>Date : January 22, 2000
<p>From : George
<p>To : Ray
<p>Subject : Happy Birthday
<p>May you have many more in good health.
```

Now compare this XML document:

```
<!- - XML Snippet - ->
<memo>
<date month="1" day= "22" year="2000"/>
<from>George</from>
<to>Ray</to>
<subject>Happy Birthday</subject>
<text>May you have many more in good health.</text>
</memo>
```

These two snippets give the essential differences between HTML and XML. The differences include:

- XML is easier for a computer to process.
- The XML describes the document's content.
- XML markup has sets of start- and end-tags or an empty-tag indicator (/>).
- XML tag (markup) is user defined.

The other differences that may not be clearly seen from this example include:

- XML liberates you from a fix-tag set.
- XML is extensible, while HTML is not.
- XML is a framework for a markup language, while HTML is an example.
- XML tags can be used for a specific instance of content rather than trying to use an HTML tag for a variety of different instances of content.
- XML preserves data or text (information).
- Some of the HTML tags include presentation functionality. You have to extend XML with XSL to have content presentation.
- HMTL has a hypertext-linking functionality as implemented by its <A> element. XML had to be extended by XLink and XPointer.
- XSL uses flow objects that are specific to HTML output.
- HTML permits mangled markup for the sake of appearance.
- HTML may become a subset vocabulary of XML, while XML will not become a subset of HTML.

Index

I don't have time for learning curves.

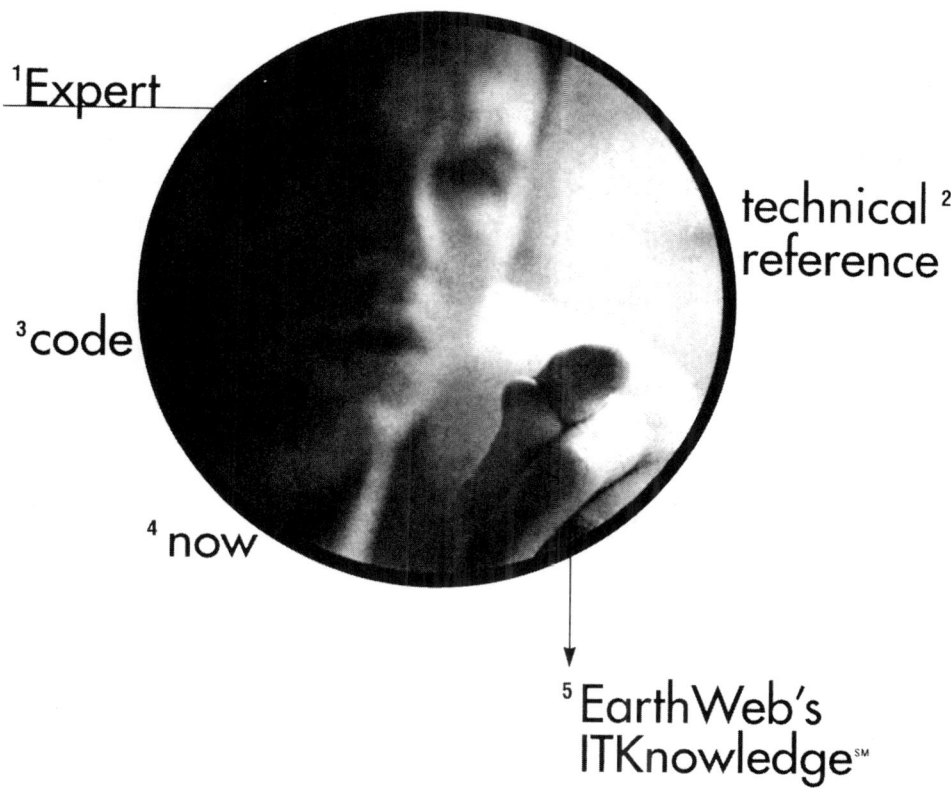

¹Expert

technical ²
reference

³code

⁴ now

⁵ EarthWeb's
ITKnowledge℠

They rely on you to be the ❶ expert on tough development challenges. There's no time for learning curves, so you go online for ❷ technical references from the experts who wrote the books. Find answers fast simply by clicking on our search engine. Access hundreds of online books, tutorials and even source ❸ code samples ❹ now. Go to ❺ EarthWeb's ITKnowledge, get immediate answers, and get down to it.

Get your FREE ITKnowledge trial subscription today at itkgo.com.
Use code number 026.

EARTHWEB
Go further *faster*

About the CD

Through a special arrangement between Wordware Publishing and Extensibility, a 10-use trial version of Turbo XML is included on the companion CD-ROM. Turbo XML is the most comprehensive suite of XML solutions available and it will be an integral part of your XML initiatives.

The Turbo XML suite consists of XML Authority for developing, managing, and processing XML schemas for e-business; XML Instance, a schema-driven XML business document editor; and XML Console, which enables the centralized conversion, validation, and documentation management of XML schemas and instance documents within a workgroup. Each product has its own executable file for installation.

To get started, simply run the executable files located on the CD. Each solution in Turbo XML contains a helpful QuickTour designed to make you familiar with the software in less than 15 minutes.

To purchase licensing for Turbo XML, please visit Extensibility's Web site at www.extensibility.com. If you have questions or if you require assistance during your use of Turbo XML, please contact Extensibility directly at 919-969-6500 or send an e-mail to support@extensibility.com.

Warning: Opening the CD package makes this book nonreturnable.